More praise from across the JobBank series:

"Help on the job hunt ... Anyone who is job-hunting in the New York area can find a lot of useful ideas in a new paperback called *The Metropolitan New York JobBank*...."

-Angela Taylor, *New York Times*

"A timely book for Chicago job hunters follows books from the same publisher that were well received in New York and Boston ... [*The Chicago JobBank* is] a fine tool for job hunters...."

-Clarence Peterson, *Chicago Tribune*

"Because our listing is seen by people across the nation, it generates lots for resumes for us. We encourage unsolicited resumes. We'll always be listed [in *The Chicago JobBank*] as long as I'm in this career."

-Tom Fitzpatrick, Director of Human Resources
Merchandise Mart Properties, Inc.

"Job hunting is never fun, but this book can ease the ordeal ...[*The Los Angeles JobBank*] will help allay fears, build confidence, and avoid wheel-spinning."

-Robert W. Ross, *Los Angeles Times*

"*The Seattle JobBank* is an essential resource for job hunters."

-Gil Lopez, Staffing Team Manager
Battelle Pacific Northwest Laboratories

"*The Phoenix JobBank* is a first-class publication. The information provided is useful and current."

-Lyndon Denton
Director of Human Resources and Materials Management
Apache Nitrogen Products, Inc.

"*The Florida JobBank* is an invaluable job-search reference tool. It provides the most up-to-date information and contact names available for companies in Florida. I should know – it worked for me!"

-Rhonda Cody, Human Resources Consultant
Aetna Life and Casualty

"I read through the 'Basics of Job Winning' and 'Resumes' sections [in *The Dallas-Fort Worth JobBank*] and found them to be very informative, with some positive tips for the job searcher. I believe the strategies outlined will bring success to any determined candidate."

-Camilla Norder, Professional Recruiter
Presbyterian Hospital of Dallas

"Through *The Dallas-Fort Worth JobBank,* we've been able to attract high-quality candidates for several positions."

-Rob Bertino, Southern States Sales Manager
CompuServe

What makes the JobBank series the nation's premier line of employment guides?

With vital employment information on thousands of employers across the nation, the JobBank series is the most comprehensive and authoritative set of career directories available today.

Each book in the series provides information on **dozens of different industries** in a given city or area, with the primary employer listings providing contact information, telephone and fax numbers, e-mail addresses, Websites, a summary of the firm's business, internships, and in many cases descriptions of the firm's typical professional job categories.

All of the reference information in the JobBank series is as up-to-date and accurate as possible. Every year, the entire database is thoroughly researched and verified by mail and by telephone. Adams Media Corporation publishes **more local employment guides more often** than any other publisher of career directories.

The JobBank series offers **20 regional titles**, from Boston to San Francisco. All of the information is organized geographically, because most people look for jobs in specific areas of the country.

A condensed, but thorough, review of the entire job search process is presented in the chapter **The Basics of Job Winning**, a feature that has received many compliments from career counselors. In addition, each JobBank directory includes a section on **resumes and cover letters** the *New York Times* has acclaimed as "excellent."

The JobBank series gives job hunters the most comprehensive, timely, and accurate career information, organized and indexed to facilitate your job search. An entire career reference library, JobBank books are designed to help you find optimal employment in any market.

Top career publications from Adams Media

14th Edition

THE Colorado JobBank

adams
media

Published by Adams Media, an F+W Publications Company
57 Littlefield Street, Avon, MA 02322 U.S.A.
www.adamsmedia.com

ISBN: 1-59869-058-2
ISSN: 1072-5962
Manufactured in the United States of America.

Product or brand names used in this book are proprietary property of the applicable firm, subject to trademark protection, and registered with government offices. Any use of these names does not convey endorsement by or other affiliation with the name holder.

Because addresses and telephone numbers of smaller companies change rapidly, we recommend you call each company and verify the information before mailing to the employers listed in this book. Mass mailings are not recommended.

While the publisher has made every reasonable effort to obtain and verify accurate information, occasional errors are possible due to the magnitude of the data. Should you discover an error, or if a company is missing, please write the editors at the above address so that we may update future editions.

"This publication is designed to provide accurate and authoritative information with regard to the subject matter covered. It is sold with the understanding that the publisher is not engaged in rendering legal, accounting, or other professional advice. If legal advice or other expert assistance is required, the services of a competent professional person should be sought."
--From a *Declaration of Principles* jointly adopted by a Committee of the American Bar Association and a Committee of Publishers and Associations

This book is available on standing order and at quantity discounts for bulk purchases.
For information, call 800/872-5627 (in Massachusetts, 508/427-7100)
or e-mail: jobbank@adamsmedia.com

TABLE OF CONTENTS

- Industrial Vehicles and Moving Equipment
- Motor Vehicles and Equipment
- Travel Trailers and Campers

Banking, Savings and Loans, and Other Depository Institutions/69

- Banks
- Bank Holding Companies and Associations
- Lending Firms/Financial Services Institutions

Biotechnology, Pharmaceuticals, and Scientific R&D/72

- Clinical Labs
- Lab Equipment Manufacturers
- Pharmaceutical Manufacturers and Distributors

Business Services and Non-Scientific Research/76

- Adjustment and Collection Services
- Cleaning, Maintenance, and Pest Control Services
- Credit Reporting Services
- Detective, Guard, and Armored Car Services/Security Systems Services
- Miscellaneous Equipment Rental and Leasing
- Secretarial and Court Reporting Services

Charities and Social Services/80

- Social and Human Service Agencies
- Job Training and Vocational Rehabilitation Services
- Nonprofit Organizations

Chemicals, Rubber, and Plastics/83

- Adhesives, Detergents, Inks, Paints, Soaps, Varnishes
- Agricultural Chemicals and Fertilizers
- Carbon and Graphite Products
- Chemical Engineering Firms
- Industrial Gases

Communications: Telecommunications and Broadcasting/84

- Cable/Pay Television Services
- Communications Equipment
- Radio and Television Broadcasting Stations
- Telephone, Telegraph, and Other Message Communications

Computer Hardware, Software, and Services/88

- Computer Components and Hardware Manufacturers
- Consultants and Computer Training Companies
- Internet and Online Service Providers
- Networking and Systems Services
- Repair Services/Rental and Leasing
- Resellers, Wholesalers, and Distributors
- Software Developers/Programming Services

Educational Services/100

- Business/Secretarial/Data Processing Schools
- Colleges/Universities/Professional Schools
- Community Colleges/Technical Schools/Vocational Schools
- Elementary and Secondary Schools
- Preschool and Child Daycare Services

Electronic/Industrial Electrical Equipment and Components/104

- Electronic Machines and Systems
- Semiconductor Manufacturers

Environmental and Waste Management Services/109

- Environmental Engineering Firms
- Sanitary Services

Fabricated Metal Products and Primary Metals/112

- Aluminum and Copper Foundries
- Die-Castings

- Iron and Steel Foundries/Steel Works, Blast Furnaces, and Rolling Mills

Financial Services/115
- Consumer Financing and Credit Agencies
- Investment Specialists
- Mortgage Bankers and Loan Brokers
- Security and Commodity Brokers, Dealers, and Exchanges

Food and Beverages/Agriculture/117
- Crop Services and Farm Supplies
- Dairy Farms
- Food Manufacturers/Processors and Agricultural Producers
- Tobacco Products

Government/122
- Courts
- Executive, Legislative, and General Government
- Public Agencies (Firefighters, Military, Police)
- United States Postal Service

Health Care Services, Equipment, and Products/126
- Dental Labs and Equipment
- Home Health Care Agencies
- Hospitals and Medical Centers
- Medical Equipment Manufacturers and Wholesalers
- Offices and Clinics of Health Practitioners
- Residential Treatment Centers/Nursing Homes
- Veterinary Services

Hotels and Restaurants/136
Insurance/141
Legal Services/144
Manufacturing: Miscellaneous Consumer/145
- Art Supplies
- Batteries
- Cosmetics and Related Products
- Household Appliances and Audio/Video Equipment
- Jewelry, Silverware, and Plated Ware
- Miscellaneous Household Furniture and Fixtures
- Musical Instruments
- Tools
- Toys and Sporting Goods

Manufacturing: Miscellaneous Industrial/147
- Ball and Roller Bearings
- Commercial Furniture and Fixtures
- Fans, Blowers, and Purification Equipment
- Industrial Machinery and Equipment
- Motors and Generators/Compressors and Engine Parts
- Vending Machines

Mining, Gas, Petroleum, Energy Related/152
- Anthracite, Coal, and Ore Mining
- Mining Machinery and Equipment
- Oil and Gas Field Services
- Petroleum and Natural Gas

Paper and Wood Products/156
- Forest and Wood Products and Services
- Lumber and Wood Wholesale
- Millwork, Plywood, and Structural Members
- Paper and Wood Mills

Printing and Publishing/158
- Book, Newspaper, and Periodical Publishers

SECTION FOUR: INDUSTRY ASSOCIATIONS

Associations by Industry/177

SECTION FIVE: INDEX

Index of Primary Employers/233

INTRODUCTION

HOW TO USE THIS BOOK

Right now, you hold in your hands one of the most effective job-hunting tools available anywhere. In *The Colorado JobBank*, you will find valuable information to help you launch or continue a rewarding career. But before you open to the book's employer listings and start calling about current job openings, take a few minutes to learn how best to use the resources presented in *The Colorado JobBank*.

The Colorado JobBank will help you to stand out from other jobseekers. While many people looking for a new job rely solely on newspaper help-wanted ads, this book offers you a much more effective job-search method -- direct contact. The direct contact method has been proven twice as effective as scanning the help-wanted ads. Instead of waiting for employers to come looking for you, you'll be far more effective going to them. While many of your competitors will use trial and error methods in trying to set up interviews, you'll learn not only how to get interviews, but what to expect once you've got them.

In the next few pages, we'll take you through each section of the book so you'll be prepared to get a jump-start on your competition.

Basics of Job Winning

Preparation. Strategy. Time management. These are three of the most important elements of a successful job search. *Basics of Job Winning* helps you address these and all the other elements needed to find the right job.

One of your first priorities should be to define your personal career objectives. What qualities make a job desirable to you? Creativity? High pay? Prestige? Use *Basics of Job Winning* to weigh these questions. Then use the rest of the chapter to design a strategy to find a job that matches your criteria.

In *Basics of Job Winning,* you'll learn which job-hunting techniques work, and which don't. We've reviewed the pros and cons of mass mailings, help-wanted ads, and direct contact. We'll show you how to develop and approach contacts in your field; how to research a prospective employer; and how to use that information to get an interview and the job.

Also included in *Basics of Job Winning*: interview dress code and etiquette, the "do's and don'ts" of interviewing, sample interview questions, and more. We also deal with some of the unique problems faced by those jobseekers who are currently employed, those who have lost a job, and college students conducting their first job search.

Resumes and Cover Letters

The approach you take to writing your resume and cover letter can often mean the difference between getting an interview and never being noticed. In this section, we discuss different formats, as well as what to put on (and what to leave off) your resume. We review the benefits and drawbacks of professional resume writers, and the importance of a follow-up letter. Also included in this section are sample resumes and cover letters which you can use as models.

The Employer Listings

Employers are listed alphabetically by industry. When a company does business under a person's name, like "John Smith & Co.," the company is usually listed by the surname's spelling (in this case "S"). Exceptions occur when a company's name is widely recognized, like "JCPenney" or "Howard Johnson Motor Lodge." In those cases, the company's first name is the key ("J" and "H" respectively).

The Colorado JobBank covers a very wide range of industries. Each company profile is assigned to one of the industry chapters listed below.

Accounting and Management Consulting
Advertising, Marketing, and Public
   Relations
Aerospace
Apparel, Fashion, and Textiles
Architecture, Construction, and Engineering
Arts, Entertainment, Sports, and Recreation
Automotive
Banking/Savings and Loans
Biotechnology, Pharmaceuticals, and
   Scientific R&D
Business Services and Non-Scientific
   Research
Charities and Social Services
Chemicals/Rubber and Plastics
Communications: Telecommunications and
   Broadcasting
Computer Hardware, Software, and
   Services
Educational Services
Electronic/Industrial Electrical Equipment
   and Components

Environmental and Waste Management
   Services
Fabricated/Primary Metals and Products
Financial Services
Food and Beverages/Agriculture
Government
Health Care: Services, Equipment, and
   Products
Hotels and Restaurants
Insurance
Legal Services
Manufacturing: Miscellaneous Consumer
Manufacturing: Miscellaneous Industrial
Mining/Gas/Petroleum/Energy Related
Paper and Wood Products
Printing and Publishing
Real Estate
Retail
Stone, Clay, Glass, and Concrete Products
Transportation/Travel
Utilities: Electric/Gas/Water
Miscellaneous Wholesaling

Many of the company listings offer detailed company profiles. In addition to company names, addresses, and phone numbers, these listings also include contact names or hiring departments, and descriptions of each company's products and/or services. Many of these listings also feature a variety of additional information including:

Positions advertised - A list of open positions the company was advertising at the time our research was conducted. Note: Keep in mind that *The Colorado JobBank* is a directory of major employers in the area, not a directory of openings currently available. Positions listed in this book that were advertised at the time research was conducted may no longer be open. Many of the companies listed will be hiring, others will not. However, since most professional job openings are filled without the placement of help-wanted ads, contacting the employers in this book directly is still a more effective method than browsing the Sunday papers.

Special programs - Does the company offer training programs, internships, or apprenticeships? These programs can be important to first time jobseekers and college students looking for practical work experience. Many employer profiles will include information on these programs.

Parent company - If an employer is a subsidiary of a larger company, the name of that parent company will often be listed here. Use this information to supplement your company research before contacting the employer.

Number of employees - The number of workers a company employs.

Company listings may also include information on other U.S. locations and any stock exchanges the firm may be listed on.

A note on all employer listings that appear in *The Colorado JobBank*: This book is intended as a starting point. It is not intended to replace any effort that you, the jobseeker, should devote to your job hunt. Keep in mind that while a great deal of effort has been put into collecting and verifying the company profiles provided in this book, addresses and contact names change regularly. Inevitably, some contact names listed herein have changed even before you read this. We recommend you contact a company before mailing your resume to ensure nothing has changed.

Industry Associations

This section includes a select list of professional and trade associations organized by industry. Many of these associations can provide employment advice and job-search help, offer magazines that cover the industry, and provide additional information or directories that may supplement the employer listings in this book.

Index of Primary Employers

The Colorado JobBank index is listed alphabetically by company name.

THE JOB SEARCH

THE BASICS OF JOB WINNING: A CONDENSED REVIEW

This chapter is divided into four sections. The first section explains the fundamentals that every jobseeker should know, especially first-time jobseekers. The next three sections deal with special situations faced by specific types of jobseekers: those who are currently employed, those who have lost a job, and college students.

THE BASICS:
Things Everyone Needs to Know

Career Planning

The first step to finding your ideal job is to clearly define your objectives. This is better known as career planning (or life planning if you wish to emphasize the importance of combining the two). Career planning has become a field of study in and of itself.

If you are thinking of choosing or switching careers, we particularly emphasize two things. First, choose a career where you will enjoy most of the day-to-day tasks. This sounds obvious, but most of us have at some point found the idea of a glamour industry or prestigious job title attractive without thinking of the key consideration: Would we enjoy performing the *everyday* tasks the position entails?

The second key consideration is that you are not merely choosing a career, but also a lifestyle. Career counselors indicate that one of the most common problems people encounter in jobseeking is that they fail to consider how well-suited they are for a particular position or career. For example, some people, attracted to management consulting by good salaries, early responsibility, and high-level corporate exposure, do not adapt well to the long hours, heavy travel demands, and constant pressure to produce. Be sure to ask yourself how you might adapt to the day-to-day duties and working environment that a specific position entails. Then ask yourself how you might adapt to the demands of that career or industry as a whole.

Choosing Your Strategy

Assuming that you've established your career objectives, the next step of the job search is to develop a strategy. If you don't take the time to develop a plan, you may find yourself going in circles after several weeks of randomly searching for opportunities that always seem just beyond your reach.

The most common jobseeking techniques are:

- following up on help-wanted advertisements (in the newspaper or online)
- using employment services
- relying on personal contacts
- contacting employers directly (the Direct Contact method)

Each of these approaches can lead to better jobs. However, the Direct Contact method boasts twice the success rate of the others. So unless you have specific reasons to employ other strategies, Direct Contact should form the foundation of your job search.

If you choose to use other methods as well, try to expend at least half your energy on Direct Contact. Millions of other jobseekers have already proven that Direct Contact has been twice as effective in obtaining employment, so why not follow in their footsteps?

Setting Your Schedule

Okay, so now that you've targeted a strategy it's time to work out the details of your job search. The most important detail is setting up a schedule. Of course, since job searches aren't something most people do regularly, it may be hard to estimate how long each step will take. Nonetheless, it is important to have a plan so that you can monitor your progress.

When outlining your job search schedule, have a realistic time frame in mind. If you will be job-searching full-time, your search could take at least two months or more. If you can only devote part-time effort, it will probably take at least four months.

You probably know a few people who seem to spend their whole lives searching for a better job in their spare time. Don't be one of them. If you are presently working and don't feel like devoting a lot of energy to jobseeking right now, then wait. Focus on enjoying your present position, performing your best on the job, and storing up energy for when you are really ready to begin your job search.

> **The first step in beginning your job search is to clearly define your objectives.**

Those of you who are currently unemployed should remember that *job-hunting is tough work, both physically and emotionally*. It is also intellectually demanding work that requires you to be at your best. So don't tire yourself out by working on your job campaign around the clock. At the same time, be sure to discipline yourself. The most logical way to manage your time while looking for a job is to keep your regular working hours.

If you are searching full-time and have decided to choose several different strategies, we recommend that you divide up each week, designating some time for each method. By trying several approaches at once, you can evaluate how promising each seems and alter your schedule accordingly. Keep in mind that the *majority of openings are filled without being advertised*. Remember also that positions advertised on the Internet are just as likely to already be filled as those found in the newspaper!

If you are searching part-time and decide to try several different contact methods, we recommend that you try them sequentially. You simply won't have enough time to put a meaningful amount of effort into more than one method at once. Estimate the length of your job search, and then allocate so many weeks or months for each contact method, beginning with Direct Contact. The purpose of setting this schedule is not to rush you to your goal but to help you periodically evaluate your progress.

The Direct Contact Method

Once you have scheduled your time, you are ready to begin your search in earnest. Beginning with the Direct Contact method, the first step is to develop a checklist for categorizing the types of firms for which you'd like to work. You might categorize firms by product line, size, customer type (such as industrial or consumer), growth prospects, or geographical location. Keep in mind, the shorter the list the easier it will be to locate a company that is right for you.

Next you will want to use this *JobBank* book to assemble your list of potential employers. Choose firms where *you* are most likely to be able to find a job. Try matching your skills with those that a specific job demands. Consider where your skills might be in demand, the degree of competition for employment, and the employment outlook at each company.

Separate your prospect list into three groups. The first 25 percent will be your primary target group, the next 25 percent will be your secondary group, and the remaining names will be your reserve group.

After you form your prospect list, begin working on your resume. Refer to the Resumes and Cover Letters section following this chapter for more information.

Once your resume is complete, begin researching your first batch of prospective employers. You will want to determine whether you would be happy working at the firms you are researching and to get a better idea of what their employment needs might be. You also need to obtain enough information to sound highly informed about the company during phone conversations and in mail correspondence. But don't go all out on your research yet! You probably won't be able to arrange interviews with some of these firms, so save your big research effort until you start to arrange interviews. Nevertheless, you should plan to spend several hours researching each firm. Do your research in batches to save time and energy. Start with this book, and find out what you can about each of the firms in your primary target group. For answers to specific questions, contact any pertinent professional associations that may be able to help you learn more about an employer. Read industry publications looking for articles on the firm. (Addresses of associations and names of important publications are listed after each section of employer listings in this book.) Then look up the company on the Internet or try additional resources at your local library. Keep organized, and maintain a folder on each firm.

> **The more you know about a company, the more likely you are to catch an interviewer's eye. (You'll also face fewer surprises once you get the job!)**

Information to look for includes: company size; president, CEO, or owner's name; when the company was established; what each division does; and benefits that are important to you. An abundance of company information can now be found electronically, through the World Wide Web or commercial online services. Researching companies online is a convenient means of obtaining information quickly and easily. If you have access to the Internet, you can search from your home at any time of day.

You may search a particular company's Website for current information that may be otherwise unavailable in print. In fact, many companies that maintain a site update their information daily. In addition, you may also search articles written about the company online. Today, most of the nation's largest newspapers, magazines, trade publications, and regional business periodicals have online versions of their publications. To find additional resources, use a search engine like Yahoo! or Alta Vista and type in the keyword "companies" or "employers."

If you discover something that really disturbs you about the firm (they are about to close their only local office), or if you discover that your chances of getting a job there are practically nil (they have just instituted a hiring freeze), then cross them off your prospect list. If possible, supplement your research efforts by contacting individuals who know the firm well. Ideally you should make an informal contact with someone at that particular firm, but often a direct competitor or a major customer will be able to supply you with just as much information. At the very least, try to obtain whatever printed information the company has available -- not just annual reports, but product brochures, company profiles, or catalogs. This information is often available on the Internet.

Getting the Interview

Now it is time to make Direct Contact with the goal of arranging interviews. If you have read any books on job-searching, you may have noticed that most of these books tell you to avoid the human resources office like the plague. It is said that the human resources office never hires people; they screen candidates. Unfortunately, this is often the case. If you can identify the appropriate manager with the authority to hire you, you should try to contact that person directly.

The obvious means of initiating Direct Contact are:

* Mail (postal or electronic)
* Phone calls

Mail contact is a good choice if you have not been in the job market for a while. You can take your time to prepare a letter, say exactly what you want, and of course include your resume. Remember that employers receive many resumes every day. Don't be surprised if you do not get a response to your inquiry, *and don't spend weeks waiting for responses that may never come.* If you do send a letter, follow it up (or precede it) with a phone call. This will increase your impact, and because of the initial research you did, will underscore both your familiarity with and your interest in the firm. Bear in mind that your goal is to make your name a familiar one with prospective employers, so that when a position becomes available, your resume will be one of the first the hiring manager seeks out.

DEVELOPING YOUR CONTACTS: NETWORKING

Some career counselors feel that the best route to a better job is through somebody you already know or through somebody to whom you can be introduced. These counselors recommend that you build your contact base beyond your current acquaintances by asking each one to introduce you, or refer you, to additional people in your field of interest.

The theory goes like this: You might start with 15 personal contacts, each of whom introduces you to three additional people, for a total of 45 additional contacts. Then each of these people introduces you to three additional people, which adds 135 additional contacts. Theoretically, you will soon know every person in the industry.

Of course, developing your personal contacts does not work quite as smoothly as the theory suggests because some people will not be able to introduce you to anyone. The further you stray from your initial contact base, the weaker your references may be. So, if you do try developing your own contacts, try to begin with as many people that you know personally as you can. Dig into your personal phone book and your holiday greeting card list and locate old classmates from school. Be particularly sure to approach people who perform your personal business such as your lawyer, accountant, banker, doctor, stockbroker, and insurance agent. These people develop a very broad contact base due to the nature of their professions.

If you send a fax, always follow with a hard copy of your resume and cover letter in the mail. Often, through no fault of your own, a fax will come through illegibly and employers do not often have time to let candidates know.

Another alternative is to make a "cover call." Your cover call should be just like your cover letter: concise. Your first statement should interest the employer in you. Then try to subtly mention your familiarity with the firm. Don't be overbearing; keep your introduction to three sentences or less. Be pleasant, self-confident, and relaxed. This will greatly increase the chances of the person at the other end of the line developing the conversation. But don't press. If you are asked to follow up with "something in the mail," this signals the conversation's natural end. Don't try to prolong the conversation once it has ended, and don't ask what they want to receive in the mail. Always send your resume and a highly personalized follow-up letter, reminding the addressee of the phone conversation. *Always* include a cover letter if you are asked to send a resume, and treat your resume and cover letter as a total package. Gear your letter toward the specific position you are applying for and prove why you would be a "good match" for the position.

> **Always include a cover letter if you are asked to send a resume.**

Unless you are in telephone sales, making smooth and relaxed cover calls will probably not come easily. Practice them on your own, and then with your friends or relatives.

DON'T BOTHER WITH MASS MAILINGS OR BARRAGES OF PHONE CALLS

Direct Contact does not mean burying every firm within a hundred miles with mail and phone calls. Mass mailings rarely work in the job hunt. This also applies to those letters that are personalized -- but dehumanized -- on an automatic typewriter or computer. Don't waste your time or money on such a project; you will fool no one but yourself.

The worst part of sending out mass mailings, or making unplanned phone calls to companies you have not researched, is that you are likely to be remembered as someone with little genuine interest in the firm, who lacks sincerity -- somebody that nobody wants to hire.

If you obtain an interview as a result of a telephone conversation, be sure to send a thank-you note reiterating the points you made during the conversation. You will appear more professional and increase your impact. However, unless specifically requested, don't mail your resume once an interview has been arranged. Take it with you to the interview instead.

You should never show up to seek a professional position without an appointment. Even if you are somehow lucky enough to obtain an interview, you will appear so unprofessional that you will not be seriously considered.

HELP WANTED ADVERTISEMENTS

Only a small fraction of professional job openings are advertised. Yet the majority of jobseekers -- and quite a few people not in the job market -- spend a lot of time studying the help wanted ads. As a result, the competition for advertised openings is often very severe.

A moderate-sized employer told us about their experience advertising in the help wanted section of a major Sunday newspaper:

It was a disaster. We had over 500 responses from this relatively small ad in just one week. We have only two phone lines in this office and one was totally knocked out. We'll never advertise for professional help again.

If you insist on following up on help wanted ads, then research a firm before you reply to an ad. Preliminary research might help to separate you from all of the other professionals responding to that ad, many of whom will have only a passing interest in the opportunity. It will also give you insight about a particular firm, to help you determine if it is potentially a good match. That said, your chances of obtaining a job through the want ads are still much smaller than they are with the Direct Contact method.

Preparing for the Interview

As each interview is arranged, begin your in-depth research. You should arrive at an interview knowing the company upside-down and inside-out. You need to know the company's products, types of customers, subsidiaries, parent company, principal locations, rank in the industry, sales and profit trends, type of ownership, size, current plans, and much more. By this time you have probably narrowed your job search to one industry. Even if you haven't, you should still be familiar with common industry terms, the trends in the firm's industry, the firm's principal competitors and their relative performance, and the direction in which the industry leaders are headed.

Dig into every resource you can! Surf the Internet. Read the company literature, the trade press, the business press, and if the company is public, call your stockbroker (if you have one) and ask for additional information. If possible, speak to someone at the firm before the

> **You should arrive at an interview knowing the company upside-down and inside-out.**

interview, or if not, speak to someone at a competing firm. The more time you spend, the better. Even if you feel extremely pressed for time, you should set aside several hours for pre-interview research.

If you have been out of the job market for some time, don't be surprised if you find yourself tense during your first few interviews. It will probably happen every time you re-enter the market, not just when you seek your first job after getting out of school.

Tension is natural during an interview, but knowing you have done a thorough research job should put you more at ease. Make a list of questions that you think might be asked in each interview. Think out your answers carefully and practice them with a friend. Tape record your responses to the problem questions. (*See also in this chapter: Informational Interviews.*) If you feel particularly unsure of your interviewing skills, arrange your first interviews at firms you are not as interested in. (But remember it is common courtesy to seem enthusiastic about the possibility of working for any firm at which you interview.) Practice again on your own after these first few interviews. Go over the difficult questions that you were asked.

Take some time to really think about how you will convey your work history. Present "bad experiences" as "learning experiences." Instead of saying "I hated my position as a salesperson because I had to bother people on the phone," say "I realized that cold-calling was not my strong suit. Though I love working with people, I decided my talents would be best used in a more face-to-face atmosphere." Always find some sort of lesson from previous jobs, as they all have one.

Interview Attire

How important is the proper dress for a job interview? Buying a complete wardrobe, donning new shoes, and having your hair styled every morning are not enough to guarantee you a career position as an investment banker. But on the other hand, if you can't find a clean, conservative suit or won't take the time to wash your hair, then you are just wasting your time by interviewing at all.

Personal grooming is as important as finding appropriate clothes for a job interview. Careful grooming indicates both a sense of thoroughness and self-confidence. This is not the time to make a statement -- take out the extra earrings and avoid any garish hair colors not found in nature. Women should not wear excessive makeup, and both men and women should refrain from wearing any perfume or cologne (it only takes a small spritz to leave an allergic interviewer with a fit of sneezing and a bad impression of your meeting). Men should be freshly shaven, even if the interview is late in the day, and men with long hair should have it pulled back and neat.

Men applying for any professional position should wear a suit, preferably in a conservative color such as navy or charcoal gray. It is easy to get away with wearing the same dark suit to consecutive interviews at the same company; just be sure to wear a different shirt and tie for each interview.

Women should also wear a business suit. Professionalism still dictates a suit with a skirt, rather than slacks, as proper interview garb for women. This is usually true even at companies where pants are acceptable attire for female employees. As much as you may disagree with this guideline, the more prudent time to fight this standard is after you land the job.

The final selection of candidates for a job opening won't be determined by dress, of course. However, inappropriate dress can quickly eliminate a first-round candidate. So while you shouldn't spend a fortune on a new wardrobe, you should be sure that your clothes are appropriate. The key is to dress at least as or slightly more formally and conservatively than the position would suggest.

What to Bring

Be complete. Everyone needs a watch, a pen, and a notepad. Finally, a briefcase or a leather-bound folder (containing extra, *unfolded*, copies of your resume) will help complete the look of professionalism.

Sometimes the interviewer will be running behind schedule. Don't be upset, be sympathetic. There is often pressure to interview a lot of candidates and to quickly fill a demanding position. So be sure to come to your interview with good reading material to keep yourself occupied and relaxed.

The Interview

The very beginning of the interview is the most important part because it determines the tone for the rest of it. Those first few moments are especially crucial. Do you smile when you meet? Do you establish enough eye contact, but not too much? Do you walk into the office with a self-assured and confident stride? Do you shake hands firmly? Do you make small talk easily without being garrulous? It is human nature to judge people by that first impression, so make sure it is a good one. But most of all, try to be yourself.

BE PREPARED:
Some Common Interview Questions

Tell me about yourself.

Why did you leave your last job?

What excites you in your current job?

Where would you like to be in five years?

How much overtime are you willing to work?

What would your previous/present employer tell me about you?

Tell me about a difficult situation that you
faced at your previous/present job.

What are your greatest strengths?

What are your weaknesses?

Describe a work situation where you took initiative
and went beyond your normal responsibilities.

Why should we hire you?

Often the interviewer will begin, after the small talk, by telling you about the company, the division, the department, or perhaps, the position. Because of your detailed research, the information about the company should be repetitive for you, and the interviewer would probably like nothing better than to avoid this regurgitation of the company biography. So if you can do so tactfully, indicate to the interviewer that you are very familiar with the firm. If he or she seems intent on providing you with background information, despite your hints, then acquiesce.

But be sure to remain attentive. If you can manage to generate a brief discussion of the company or the industry at this point, without being forceful, great. It will help to further build rapport, underscore your interest, and increase your impact.

> **The interviewer's job is to find a reason to turn you down; your job is to not provide that reason.**
>
> -John L. LaFevre, author, *How You Really Get Hired*
>
> Reprinted from the 1989/90 *CPC Annual,* with permission of the National Association of Colleges and Employers (formerly College Placement Council, Inc.), copyright holder.

Soon (if it didn't begin that way) the interviewer will begin the questions, many of which you will have already practiced. This period of the interview usually falls into one of two categories (or somewhere in between): either a structured interview, where the interviewer has a prescribed set of questions to ask; or an unstructured interview, where the interviewer will ask only leading questions to get you to talk about yourself, your experiences, and your goals. Try to sense as quickly as possible in which direction the interviewer wishes to proceed. This will make the interviewer feel more relaxed and in control of the situation.

Remember to keep attuned to the interviewer and make the length of your answers appropriate to the situation. If you are really unsure as to how detailed a response the interviewer is seeking, then ask.

As the interview progresses, the interviewer will probably mention some of the most important responsibilities of the position. If applicable, draw parallels between your experience and the demands of the position as detailed by the interviewer. Describe your past experience in the same manner that you do on your resume: emphasizing results and achievements and not merely describing activities. But don't exaggerate. Be on the level about your abilities.

The first interview is often the toughest, where many candidates are screened out. If you are interviewing for a very competitive position, you will have to make an impression that will last. Focus on a few of your greatest strengths that are relevant to the position. Develop these points carefully, state them again in different words, and then try to summarize them briefly at the end of the interview.

Often the interviewer will pause toward the end and ask if you have any questions. Particularly in a structured interview, this might be the one chance to really show your knowledge of and interest in the firm. Have a list prepared of specific questions that are of real interest to you. Let your questions subtly show your research and your knowledge of the firm's activities. It is wise to have an extensive list of questions, as several of them may be answered during the interview.

Do not turn your opportunity to ask questions into an interrogation. Avoid reading directly from your list of questions, and ask questions that you are fairly certain the interviewer can answer (remember how you feel when you cannot answer a question during an interview).

Even if you are unable to determine the salary range beforehand, do not ask about it during the first interview. You can always ask later. Above all, don't ask about fringe benefits until you have been offered a position. (Then be sure to get all the details.)

Try not to be negative about anything during the interview, particularly any past employer or any previous job. Be cheerful. Everyone likes to work with someone who seems to be happy. Even if you detest your current/former job or manager, do not make disparaging comments. The interviewer may construe this as a sign of a potential attitude problem and not consider you a strong candidate.

Don't let a tough question throw you off base. If you don't know the answer to a question, simply say so -- do not apologize. Just smile. Nobody can answer every question -- particularly some of the questions that are asked in job interviews.

Before your first interview, you may be able to determine how many rounds of interviews there usually are for positions at your level. (Of course it may differ quite a bit even within the different levels of one firm.) Usually you can count on attending at least two or three interviews, although some firms are known to give a minimum of six interviews for all professional positions. While you should be more relaxed as you return for subsequent interviews, the pressure will be on. The more prepared you are, the better.

Depending on what information you are able to obtain, you might want to vary your strategy quite a bit from interview to interview. For instance, if the first interview is a screening interview, then be sure a few of your strengths really stand out. On the other hand, if later interviews are primarily with people who are in a position to veto your hiring, but not to push it forward, then you should primarily focus on building rapport as opposed to reiterating and developing your key strengths.

If it looks as though your skills and background do not match the position the interviewer was hoping to fill, ask him or her if there is another division or subsidiary that perhaps could profit from your talents.

After the Interview

Write a follow-up letter immediately after the interview, while it is still fresh in the interviewer's mind (see the sample follow-up letter format found in the Resumes and Cover Letters chapter). Not only is this a thank-you, but it also gives you the chance to provide the interviewer with any details you may have forgotten (as long as they can be tactfully added in). If you haven't heard back from the interviewer within a week of sending your thank-you letter, call to stress your continued interest in the firm and the position. If you lost any points during the interview for any reason, this letter can help you regain footing. Be polite and make sure to stress your continued interest and competency to fill the position. Just don't forget to proofread it thoroughly. If you are unsure of the spelling of the interviewer's name, call the receptionist and ask.

THE BALANCING ACT:
Looking for a New Job While Currently Employed

For those of you who are still employed, job-searching will be particularly tiring because it must be done in addition to your normal work responsibilities. So don't overwork yourself to the point where you show up to interviews looking exhausted or start to slip behind at your current job. On the other hand, don't be tempted to quit your present job! The long hours are worth it. Searching for a job while you have one puts you in a position of strength.

Making Contact

If you must be at your office during the business day, then you have additional problems to deal with. How can you work interviews into the business day? And if you work in an open office, how can you even call to set up interviews? Obviously, you should keep up the effort and the appearances on your present job. So maximize your use of the lunch hour, early mornings, and late afternoons for calling. If you keep trying, you'll be surprised how often you will be able to reach the executive you are trying to contact during your out-of-office hours. You can catch people as early as 8 a.m. and as late as 6 p.m. on frequent occasions.

Scheduling Interviews

Your inability to interview at any time other than lunch just might work to your advantage. If you can, try to set up as many interviews as possible for your lunch hour. This will go a long way to creating a relaxed atmosphere. But be sure the interviews don't stray too far from the agenda on hand.

Lunchtime interviews are much easier to obtain if you have substantial career experience. People with less experience will often find no alternative to taking time off for interviews. If you have to take time off, you have to take time off. But try to do this as little as possible. Try to take the whole day off in order to avoid being blatantly obvious about your job search, and try to schedule two to three interviews for the same day. (It is very difficult to maintain an optimum level of energy at more than three interviews in one day.) Explain to the interviewer why you might have to juggle your interview schedule; he/she should honor the respect you're showing your current employer by minimizing your days off and will probably appreciate the fact that another prospective employer is interested in you.

> **Try calling as early as 8 a.m. and as late as 6 p.m. You'll be surprised how often you will be able to reach the executive you want during these times of the day.**

References

What do you tell an interviewer who asks for references from your current employer? Just say that while you are happy to have your former employers contacted, you are trying to keep your job search confidential and would rather that your current employer not be contacted until you have been given a firm offer.

IF YOU'RE FIRED OR LAID OFF:
Picking Yourself Up and Dusting Yourself Off

If you've been fired or laid off, you are not the first and will not be the last to go through this traumatic experience. In today's changing economy, thousands of professionals lose their jobs every year. Even if you were terminated with just cause, do not lose heart. Remember, being fired is not a reflection on you as a person. It is usually a reflection of your company's staffing needs and its perception of your recent job performance and attitude. And if you were not performing up to par or enjoying your work, then you will probably be better off at another company anyway.

> ## Be prepared for the question "Why were you fired?" during job interviews.

A thorough job search could take months, so be sure to negotiate a reasonable severance package, if possible, and determine to what benefits, such as health insurance, you are still legally entitled. Also, register for unemployment compensation immediately. Don't be surprised to find other professionals collecting unemployment compensation -- it is for everyone who has lost their job.

Don't start your job search with a flurry of unplanned activity. Start by choosing a strategy and working out a plan. Now is not the time for major changes in your life. If possible, remain in the same career and in the same geographical location, at least until you have been working again for a while. On the other hand, if the only industry for which you are trained is leaving, or is severely depressed in your area, then you should give prompt consideration to moving or switching careers.

Avoid mentioning you were fired when arranging interviews, but be prepared for the question "Why were you fired?" during an interview. If you were laid off as a result of downsizing, briefly explain, being sure to reinforce that your job loss was not due to performance. If you were in fact fired, be honest, but try to detail the reason as favorably as possible and portray what you have learned from your mistakes. If you are confident one of your past managers will give you a good reference, tell the interviewer to contact that person. Do not to speak negatively of your past employer and try not to sound particularly worried about your status of being temporarily unemployed.

Finally, don't spend too much time reflecting on why you were let go or how you might have avoided it. Think positively, look to the future, and be sure to follow a careful plan during your job search.

THE COLLEGE STUDENT:
Conducting Your First Job Search

While you will be able to apply many of the basics covered earlier in this chapter to your job search, there are some situations unique to the college student's job search.

> ### THE GPA QUESTION
>
> You are interviewing for the job of your dreams. Everything is going well: You've established a good rapport, the interviewer seems impressed with your qualifications, and you're almost positive the job is yours. Then you're asked about your GPA, which is pitifully low. Do you tell the truth and watch your dream job fly out the window?
>
> *Never* lie about your GPA (they may request your transcript, and no company will hire a liar). You can, however, explain if there is a reason you don't feel your grades reflect your abilities, and mention any other impressive statistics. For example, if you have a high GPA in your major, or in the last few semesters (as opposed to your cumulative college career), you can use that fact to your advantage.

Perhaps the biggest problem college students face is lack of experience. Many schools have internship programs designed to give students exposure to the field of their choice, as well as the opportunity to make valuable contacts. Check out your school's career services department to see what internships are available. If your school does not have a formal internship program, or if there are no available internships that appeal to you, try contacting local businesses and offering your services. Often, businesses will be more than willing to have an extra pair of hands (especially if those hands are unpaid!) for a day or two each week. Or try contacting school alumni to see if you can "shadow" them for a few days, and see what their daily duties are like.

Informational Interviews

Although many jobseekers do not do this, it can be extremely helpful to arrange an informational interview with a college alumnus or someone else who works in your desired industry. You interview them about their job, their company, and their industry with questions you have prepared in advance. This can be done over the phone but is usually done in person. This will provide you with a contact in the industry who may give you more valuable information -- or perhaps even a job opportunity -- in the future. Always follow up with a thank you letter that includes your contact information.

The goal is to try to begin building experience and establishing contacts as early as possible in your college career.

What do you do if, for whatever reason, you weren't able to get experience directly related to your desired career? First, look at your previous jobs and see if there's anything you can highlight. Did you supervise or train other employees? Did you reorganize the accounting system, or boost productivity in some way? Accomplishments like these demonstrate leadership, responsibility, and innovation -- qualities that most companies look for in employees. And don't forget volunteer activities and school clubs, which can also showcase these traits.

On-Campus Recruiting

Companies will often send recruiters to interview on-site at various colleges. This gives students a chance to interview with companies that may not have interviewed them otherwise. This is particularly true if a company schedules "open" interviews, in which the only screening process is who is first in line at the sign-ups. Of course, since many more applicants gain interviews in this format, this also means that many more people are rejected. The on-campus interview is generally a screening interview, to see if it is worth the company's time to invite you in for a second interview. So do everything possible to make yourself stand out from the crowd.

The first step, of course, is to check out any and all information your school's career center has on the company. If the information seems out of date, check out the company on the Internet or call the company's headquarters and ask for any printed information.

Many companies will host an informational meeting for interviewees, often the evening before interviews are scheduled to take place. DO NOT MISS THIS MEETING. The recruiter will almost certainly ask if you attended. Make an effort to stay after the meeting and talk with the company's representatives. Not only does this give you an opportunity to find out more information about both the company and the position, it also makes you stand out in the recruiter's mind. If there's a particular company that you had your heart set on, but you weren't able to get an interview with them, attend the information session anyway. You may be able to persuade the recruiter to squeeze you into the schedule. (Or you may discover that the company really isn't the right fit for you after all.)

Try to check out the interview site beforehand. Some colleges may conduct "mock" interviews that take place in one of the standard interview rooms. Or you may be able to convince a career counselor (or even a custodian) to let you sneak a peek during off-hours. Either way, having an idea of the room's setup will help you to mentally prepare.

Arrive at least 15 minutes early to the interview. The recruiter may be ahead of schedule, and might meet you early. But don't be surprised if previous interviews have run over, resulting in your 30-minute slot being reduced to 20 minutes (or less). Don't complain or appear anxious; just use the time you do have as efficiently as possible to showcase the reasons *you* are the ideal candidate. Staying calm and composed in these situations will work to your advantage.

LAST WORDS

A parting word of advice. Again and again during your job search you will face rejection. You will be rejected when you apply for interviews. You will be rejected after interviews. For every job offer you finally receive, you probably will have been rejected many times. Don't let rejections slow you down. Keep reminding yourself that the sooner you go out, start your job search, and get those rejections flowing in, the closer you will be to obtaining the job you want.

RESUMES AND COVER LETTERS

When filling a position, an employer will often have 100-plus applicants, but time to interview only a handful of the most promising ones. As a result, he or she will reject most applicants after only briefly skimming their resumes.

Unless you have phoned and talked to the employer -- which you should do whenever you can -- you will be chosen or rejected for an interview entirely on the basis of your resume and cover letter. *Your cover letter must catch the employer's attention, and your resume must hold it.* (But remember -- a resume is no substitute for a job search campaign. *You* must seek a job. Your resume is only one tool, albeit a critical one.)

RESUME FORMAT:
Mechanics of a First Impression

The Basics

Employers dislike long resumes, so unless you have an unusually strong background with many years of experience and a diversity of outstanding achievements, keep your resume length to one page. If you must squeeze in more information than would otherwise fit, try using a smaller typeface or changing the margins. Watch also for "widows" at the end of paragraphs. You can often free up some space if you can shorten the information enough to get rid of those single words taking up an entire line. Another tactic that works with some word processing programs is to decrease the font size of your paragraph returns and changing the spacing between lines.

Print your resume on standard 8 1/2" x 11" paper. Since recruiters often get resumes in batches of hundreds, a smaller-sized resume may be lost in the pile. Oversized resumes are likely to get crumpled at the edges, and won't fit easily in their files.

First impressions matter, so make sure the recruiter's first impression of your resume is a good one. Never hand-write your resume (or cover letter)! Print your resume on quality paper that has weight and texture, in a conservative color such as white, ivory, or pale gray. Good resume paper is easy to find at many stores that sell stationery or office products. It is even available at some drug stores. Use *matching* paper and envelopes for both your resume and cover letter. One hiring manager at a major magazine throws out all resumes that arrive on paper that differs in color from the envelope!

Do not buy paper with images of clouds and rainbows in the background or anything that looks like casual stationery that you would send to your favorite aunt. Do not spray perfume or cologne on your resume. Do not include your picture with your resume unless you have a specific and appropriate reason to do so.

Another tip: Do a test print of your resume (and cover letter), to make sure the watermark is on the same side as the text so that you can read it. Also make sure it is right-side up. As trivial as this may sound, some recruiters check for this! One recruiter at a law firm in New Hampshire sheepishly admitted this is the first thing he checks. *"I open each envelope and check the watermarks on the resume and cover letter. Those candidates that have it wrong go into a different pile."*

Getting it on Paper

Modern photocomposition typesetting gives you the clearest, sharpest image, a wide variety of type styles, and effects such as italics, bold-facing, and book-like justified margins. It is also too expensive for many jobseekers. The quality of today's laser printers means that a computer-generated resume can look just as impressive as one that has been professionally typeset.

A computer with a word processing or desktop publishing program is the most common way to generate your resume. This allows you the flexibility to make changes almost instantly and to store different drafts on disk. Word processing and desktop publishing programs also offer many different fonts to choose from, each taking up different amounts of space. (It is generally best to stay between 9-point and 12-point font size.) Many other options are also available, such as bold-facing or italicizing for emphasis and the ability to change and manipulate spacing. It is generally recommended to leave the right-hand margin unjustified as this keeps the spacing between the text even and therefore easier to read. It is not wrong to justify both margins of text, but if possible try it both ways before you decide.

For a resume on paper, the end result will be largely determined by the quality of the printer you use. Laser printers will generally provide the best quality. Do not use a dot matrix printer.

Many companies now use scanning equipment to screen the resumes they receive, and certain paper, fonts, and other features are more compatible with this technology. White paper is preferable, as well as a standard font such as Courier or Helvetica. You should use at least a 10-point font, and avoid bolding, italics, underlining, borders, boxes, or graphics.

Household typewriters and office typewriters with nylon or other cloth ribbons are *not* good enough for typing your resume. If you don't have access to a quality word processing program, hire a professional with the resources to prepare your resume for you. Keep in mind that businesses such as Kinko's (open 24 hours) provide access to computers with quality printers.

Don't make your copies on an office photocopier. Only the human resources office may see the resume you mail. Everyone else may see only a copy of it, and copies of copies quickly become unreadable. Furthermore, sending photocopies of your resume or cover letter is completely unprofessional. Either print out each copy individually, or take your resume to a professional copy shop, which will generally offer professionally maintained, extra-high-quality photocopiers and charge fairly reasonable prices. You want your resume to represent you with the look of polished quality.

Proof with Care

Whether you typed it or paid to have it produced professionally, mistakes on resumes are not only embarrassing, but will usually remove you from consideration (particularly if something obvious such as your name is misspelled). No matter how much you paid someone else to type, write, or typeset your resume, *you* lose if there is a mistake. So proofread it as carefully as possible. Get a friend to help you. Read your draft aloud as your friend checks the proof copy. Then have your friend read aloud while you check. Next, read it letter by letter to check spelling and punctuation.

If you are having it typed or typeset by a resume service or a printer, and you don't have time to proof it, pay for it and take it home. Proof it there and bring it back later to get it corrected and printed.

If you wrote your resume with a word processing program, use the built-in spell checker to double-check for spelling errors. Keep in mind that a spell checker will not find errors such as "to" for "two" or "wok" for "work." Many spell check programs do not recognize missing or misused punctuation, nor are they set to check the spelling of capitalized words. It's important that you still proofread your resume to check for grammatical mistakes and other problems, even after it has been spellchecked. If you find mistakes, do not make edits in pen or pencil or use white-out to fix them on the final copy!

Electronic Resumes

As companies rely increasingly on emerging technologies to find qualified candidates for job openings, you may opt to create an electronic resume in order to remain competitive in today's job market. Why is this important? Companies today sometimes request that resumes be submitted by e-mail, and many hiring managers regularly check online resume databases for candidates to fill unadvertised job openings. Other companies enlist the services of electronic employment database services, which charge jobseekers a nominal fee to have their resumes posted to the database to be viewed by potential employers. Still other companies use their own automated applicant tracking systems, in which case your resume is fed through a scanner that sends the image to a computer that "reads" your resume, looking for keywords, and files it accordingly in its database.

Whether you're posting your resume online, e-mailing it directly to an employer, sending it to an electronic employment database, or sending it to a company you suspect uses an automated applicant tracking system, you must create some form of electronic resume to take advantage of the technology. Don't panic! An electronic resume is simply a modified version of your conventional resume. An electronic resume is one that is sparsely formatted, but filled with keywords and important facts.

In order to post your resume to the Internet -- either to an online resume database or through direct e-mail to an employer -- you will need to change the way your resume is formatted. Instead of a Word, WordPerfect, or other word processing document, save your resume as a plain text, DOS, or ASCII file. These three terms are basically interchangeable, and describe text at its simplest, most basic level, without the formatting such as boldface or italics that most jobseekers use to make their resumes look more interesting. If you use e-mail, you'll notice that all of your messages are written and received in this format. First, you should remove all formatting from your resume including boldface, italics, underlining, bullets, differing font sizes, and graphics. Then, convert and save your resume as a plain text file. Most word processing programs have a "save as" feature that allows you to save files in different formats. Here, you should choose "text only" or "plain text."

Another option is to create a resume in HTML (hypertext markup language), the text formatting language used to publish information on the World Wide Web. However, the real usefulness of HTML resumes is still being explored. Most of the major online databases do not accept HTML resumes, and the vast majority of companies only accept plain text resumes through their e-mail.

Finally, if you simply wish to send your resume to an electronic employment database or a company that uses an automated applicant tracking system, there is no need to convert your resume to a plain text file. The only change you need to make is to organize the information in your resume by keywords. Employers are likely to do keyword searches for information, such as degree held or knowledge of particular types of software. Therefore, using the right keywords or key phrases in your resume is critical to its ultimate success. Keywords are usually nouns or short phrases that the computer searches for which refer to experience, training, skills, and abilities. For example, let's say an employer searches an employment database for a sales representative with the following criteria:

BS/BA
exceeded quota
cold calls
high energy
willing to travel

Even if you have the right qualifications, neglecting to use these keywords would result in the computer passing over your resume. Although there is no way to know for sure which keywords employers are most likely to search for, you can make educated guesses by checking the help-wanted ads or online job postings for your type of job. You should also arrange keywords in a keyword summary, a paragraph listing your qualifications that immediately follows your name and address (see sample letter in this chapter). In addition, choose a nondecorative font with clear, distinct characters, such as Helvetica or Times. It is more difficult for a scanner to accurately pick up the more unusual fonts. Boldface and all capital letters are best used only for major section headings, such as "Experience" and "Education." It is also best to avoid using italics or underlining, since this can cause the letters to bleed into one another.

Types of Resumes

The most common resume formats are the functional resume, the chronological resume, and the combination resume. (Examples can be found at the end of this chapter.) A functional resume focuses on skills and de-emphasizes job titles, employers, etc. A functional resume is best if you have been out of the work force for a long time or are changing careers. It is also good if you want to highlight specific skills and strengths, especially if all of your work experience has been at one company. This format can also be a good choice if you are just out of school or have no experience in your desired field.

Choose a chronological format if you are currently working or were working recently, and if your most recent experiences relate to your desired field. Use reverse chronological order and include dates. To a recruiter your last job and your latest schooling are the most important, so put the last first and list the rest going back in time.

A combination resume is perhaps the most common. This resume simply combines elements of the functional and chronological resume formats. This is used by many jobseekers with a solid track record who find elements of both types useful.

Organization

Your name, phone number, e-mail address (if you have one), and a complete mailing address should be at the top of your resume. Try to make your name stand out by using a slightly larger font size or all capital letters. Be sure to spell out everything. Never abbreviate St. for Street or Rd. for Road. If you are a college student, you should also put your home address and phone number at the top. Change your message on your answering machine if necessary – RUSH blaring in the background or your sorority sisters screaming may not come across well to all recruiters. If you think you may be moving within six months then include a second address and phone number of a trusted friend or relative who can reach you no matter where you are.

Remember that employers will keep your resume on file and
may contact you months later if a position opens that fits your qualifications.
All too often, candidates are unreachable because they have moved and had not
previously provided enough contact options on their resume.

Next, list your experience, then your education. If you are a recent graduate, list your education first, unless your experience is more important than your education. (For example, if you have just graduated from a teaching school, have some business experience, and are applying for a job in business, you would list your business experience first.)

Keep everything easy to find. Put the dates of your employment and education on the left of the page. Put the names of the companies you worked for and the schools you attended a few spaces to the right of the dates. Put the city and state, or the city and country, where you studied or worked to the right of the page.

The important thing is simply to break up the text in some logical way that makes your resume visually attractive and easy to scan, so experiment to see which layout works best for your resume. However you set it up, *stay consistent.* Inconsistencies in fonts, spacing, or tenses will make your resume look sloppy. Also, be sure to use tabs to keep your information vertically lined up, rather than the less precise space bar.

RESUME CONTENT:
Say it with Style
Sell Yourself

You are selling your skills and accomplishments in your resume, so it is important to inventory yourself and know yourself. If you have achieved something, say so. Put it in the best possible light, but avoid subjective statements, such as "I am a hard worker" or "I get along well with my coworkers." Just stick to the facts.

While you shouldn't hold back or be modest, don't exaggerate your achievements to the point of misrepresentation. Be honest. Many companies will immediately drop an applicant from consideration (or fire a current employee) upon discovering inaccurate or untrue information on a resume or other application material.

Write down the important (and pertinent) things you have done, but do it in as few words as possible. Your resume will be scanned, not read, and short, concise phrases are much more effective than long-winded sentences. Avoid the use of "I" when emphasizing your accomplishments. Instead, use brief phrases beginning with action verbs.

While some technical terms will be unavoidable, you should try to avoid excessive "technicalese." Keep in mind that the first person to see your resume may be a human resources person who won't necessarily know all the jargon -- and how can they be impressed by something they don't understand?

Keep it Brief

Also, try to hold your paragraphs to six lines or less. If you have more than six lines of information about one job or school, put it in two or more paragraphs.

A short resume will be examined more carefully. Remember: Your resume usually has between eight and 45 seconds to catch an employer's eye. So make every second count.

Job Objective

A functional resume may require a job objective to give it focus. One or two sentences describing the job you are seeking can clarify in what capacity your skills will be best put to use. Be sure that your stated objective is in line with the position you're applying for.

Examples:

> An entry-level editorial assistant position in the publishing industry.
> A senior management position with a telecommunications firm.

Don't include a job objective on a chronological resume unless your previous work experiences are <u>completely</u> unrelated to the position for which you're applying. The presence of an overly specific job objective might eliminate you from consideration for other positions that a recruiter feels are a better match for your qualifications. But even if you don't put an objective on paper, having a career goal in mind as you write can help give your resume a solid sense of direction.

USE ACTION VERBS

How you write your resume is just as important as *what* you write. In describing previous work experiences, the strongest resumes use short phrases beginning with action verbs. Below are a few you may want to use. (This list is not all-inclusive.)

achieved	developed	integrated	purchased
administered	devised	interpreted	reduced
advised	directed	interviewed	regulated
arranged	distributed	launched	represented
assisted	established	managed	resolved
attained	evaluated	marketed	restored
budgeted	examined	mediated	restructured
built	executed	monitored	revised
calculated	expanded	negotiated	scheduled
collaborated	expedited	obtained	selected
collected	facilitated	operated	served
compiled	formulated	ordered	sold
completed	founded	organized	solved
computed	generated	participated	streamlined
conducted	headed	performed	studied
consolidated	identified	planned	supervised
constructed	implemented	prepared	supplied
consulted	improved	presented	supported
controlled	increased	processed	tested
coordinated	initiated	produced	trained
created	installed	proposed	updated
determined	instructed	published	wrote

Some jobseekers may choose to include both "Relevant Experience" and "Additional Experience" sections. This can be useful, as it allows the jobseeker to place more emphasis on certain experiences and to de-emphasize others.

Emphasize continued experience in a particular job area or continued interest in a particular industry. De-emphasize irrelevant positions. It is okay to include one opening line providing a general description of each company you've worked at. Delete positions that you held for less than four months (unless you are a very recent college grad or still in school). Stress your <u>results</u> and your achievements, elaborating on how you contributed in your previous jobs. Did you increase sales, reduce costs, improve a product, implement a new program? Were you promoted? Use specific numbers (i.e., quantities, percentages, dollar amounts) whenever possible.

Education

Keep it brief if you have more than two years of career experience. Elaborate more if you have less experience. If you are a recent college graduate, you may choose to include any high school activities that are directly relevant to your career. If you've been out of school for a while you don't need to list your education prior to college.

Mention degrees received and any honors or special awards. Note individual courses or projects you participated in that might be relevant for employers. For example, if you are an English major applying for a position as a business writer, be sure to mention any business or economics courses. Previous experience such as Editor-in-Chief of the school newspaper would be relevant as well.

If you are uploading your resume to an online job hunting site such as CareerCity.com, action verbs are still important, but the key words or key nouns that a computer would search for become more important. For example, if you're seeking an accounting position, key nouns that a computer would search for such as "Lotus 1-2-3" or "CPA" or "payroll" become very important.

Highlight Impressive Skills

Be sure to mention any computer skills you may have. You may wish to include a section entitled "Additional Skills" or "Computer Skills," in which you list any software programs you know. An additional skills section is also an ideal place to mention fluency in a foreign language.

Personal Data

This section is optional, but if you choose to include it, keep it brief. A one-word mention of hobbies such as fishing, chess, baseball, cooking, etc., can give the person who will interview you a good way to open up the conversation.

Team sports experience is looked at favorably. It doesn't hurt to include activities that are somewhat unusual (fencing, Akido, '70s music) or that somehow relate to the position or the company to which you're applying. For instance, it would be worth noting if you are a member of a professional organization in your industry of interest. Never include information about your age, alias, date of birth, health, physical characteristics, marital status, religious affiliation, or political/moral beliefs.

References

The most that is needed is the sentence "References available upon request" at the bottom of your resume. If you choose to leave it out, that's fine. This line is not really necessary. It is understood that references will most likely be asked for and provided by you later on in the interviewing process. Do not actually send references with your resume and cover letter unless specifically requested.

HIRING A RESUME WRITER:
Is it the Right Choice for You?

If you write reasonably well, it is to your advantage to write your own resume. Writing your resume forces you to review your experiences and figure out how to explain your accomplishments in clear, brief phrases. This will help you when you explain your work to interviewers. It is also easier to tailor your resume to each position you're applying for when you have put it together yourself.

If you write your resume, everything will be in your own words; it will sound like you. It will say what you want it to say. If you are a good writer, know yourself well, and have a good idea of which parts of your background employers are looking for, you should be able to write your own resume better than someone else. If you decide to write your resume yourself, have as many people as possible review and proofread it. Welcome objective opinions and other perspectives.

When to Get Help

If you have difficulty writing in "resume style" (which is quite unlike normal written language), if you are unsure which parts of your background to emphasize, or if you think your resume would make your case better if it did not follow one of the standard forms outlined either here or in a book on resumes, then you should consider having it professionally written.

Even some professional resume writers we know have had their resumes written with the help of fellow professionals. They sought the help of someone who could be objective about their background, as well as provide an experienced sounding board to help focus their thoughts.

If You Hire a Pro

The best way to choose a writer is by reputation: the recommendation of a friend, a personnel director, your school placement officer, or someone else knowledgeable in the field.

Important questions:
- "How long have you been writing resumes?"
- "If I'm not satisfied with what you write, will you go over it with me and change it?"
- "Do you charge by the hour or a flat rate?"

There is no sure relation between price and quality, except that you are unlikely to get a good writer for less than $50 for an uncomplicated resume and you shouldn't have to pay more than $300 unless your experience is very extensive or complicated. There will be additional charges for printing. Assume nothing no matter how much you pay. It is your career at stake if there are mistakes on your resume!

Few resume services will give you a firm price over the phone, simply because some resumes are too complicated and take too long to do for a predetermined price. Some services will quote you a price that applies to almost all of their customers. Once you decide to use a specific writer, you should insist on a firm price quote *before* engaging their services. Also, find out how expensive minor changes will be.

COVER LETTERS:
Quick, Clear, and Concise

Always mail a cover letter with your resume. In a cover letter you can show an interest in the company that you can't show in a resume. You can also point out one or two of your skills or accomplishments the company can put to good use.

Make it Personal

The more personal you can get, the better, so long as you keep it professional. If someone known to the person you are writing has recommended that you contact the company, get permission to include his/her name in the letter. If you can get the name of a person to send the letter to, address it directly to that person (after first calling the company to verify the spelling of the person's name, correct title, and mailing address). Be sure to put the person's name and title on both the letter and the envelope. This will ensure that your letter will get through to the proper person, even if a new person now occupies this position. It will not always be possible to get the name of a person. Always strive to get at least a title.

Be sure to mention something about why you have an interest in the company -- *so many candidates apply for jobs with no apparent knowledge of what the company does!* This conveys the message that they just want any job.

Type cover letters in full. Don't try the cheap and easy ways, like using a computer mail merge program or photocopying the body of your letter and typing in the inside address and salutation. You will give the impression that you are mailing to a host of companies and have no particular interest in any one.

Print your cover letter on the same color and same high-quality paper as your resume.

Cover letter basic format

<u>Paragraph 1:</u> State what the position is that you are seeking. It is not always necessary to state how you found out about the position -- often you will apply without knowing that a position is open.
<u>Paragraph 2:</u> Include what you know about the company and why you are interested in working there. Mention any prior contact with the company or someone known to the hiring person if relevant. Briefly state your qualifications and what you can offer. (Do not talk about what you cannot do).
<u>Paragraph 3:</u> Close with your phone number and where/when you can be reached. Make a request for an interview. State when you will follow up by phone (or mail or e-mail if the ad requests no phone calls). Do not wait long -- generally five working days. If you say you're going to follow up, then actually do it! This phone call can get your resume noticed when it might otherwise sit in a stack of 225 other resumes.

Cover letter do's and don'ts

- *Do* keep your cover letter brief and to the point.
- *Do* be sure it is error-free.
- *Do* accentuate what you can offer the company, not what you hope to gain.

- *Do* be sure your phone number and address is on your cover letter just in case it gets separated from your resume (this happens!).
- *Do* check the watermark by holding the paper up to a light -- be sure it is facing forward so it is readable -- on the same side as the text, and right-side up.
- *Do* sign your cover letter (or type your name if you are sending it electronically). Blue or black ink are both fine. Do not use red ink.
- *Don't* just repeat information verbatim from your resume.
- *Don't* overuse the personal pronoun "I."
- *Don't* send a generic cover letter -- show your personal knowledge of and interest in that particular company.

THANK YOU LETTERS:
Another Way to Stand Out

As mentioned earlier, *always* send a thank you letter after an interview (see the sample later in this section). So few candidates do this and it is yet another way for you to stand out. Be sure to mention something specific from the interview and restate your interest in the company and the position.

It is generally acceptable to handwrite your thank you letter on a generic thank you card (but *never* a postcard). Make sure handwritten notes are neat and legible. However, if you are in doubt, typing your letter is always the safe bet. If you met with several people it is fine to send them each an individual thank you letter. Call the company if you need to check on the correct spelling of their names.

Remember to:
- Keep it short.
- Proofread it carefully.
- Send it *promptly*.

FUNCTIONAL RESUME

C.J. RAVENCLAW
129 Pennsylvania Avenue
Washington DC 20500
202/555-6652
e-mail: ravenclaw@dcpress.net

Objective
A position as a graphic designer commensurate with my acquired skills and expertise.

Summary
Extensive experience in plate making, separations, color matching, background definition, printing, mechanicals, color corrections, and personnel supervision. A highly motivated manager and effective communicator. Proven ability to:

• **Create Commercial Graphics**	• **Control Quality**
• **Produce Embossed Drawings**	• **Resolve Printing Problems**
• **Color Separate**	• **Analyze Customer Satisfaction**

Qualifications
Printing:
Knowledgeable in black and white as well as color printing. Excellent judgment in determining acceptability of color reproduction through comparison with original. Proficient at producing four- or five-color corrections on all media, as well as restyling previously reproduced four-color artwork.

Customer Relations:
Routinely work closely with customers to ensure specifications are met. Capable of striking a balance between technical printing capabilities and need for customer satisfaction through entire production process.

Specialties:
Practiced at creating silk screen overlays for a multitude of processes including velo bind, GBC bind, and perfect bind. Creative design and timely preparation of posters, flyers, and personalized stationery.

Personnel Supervision:
Skillful at fostering atmosphere that encourages highly talented artists to balance high-level creativity with maximum production. Consistently beat production deadlines. Instruct new employees, apprentices, and students in both artistry and technical operations.

Experience
Graphic Arts Professor, Ohio State University, Columbus OH (1998-2002).
Manager, Design Graphics, Washington DC (2003-present).

Education
Massachusetts Conservatory of Art, Ph.D. 1996
University of Massachusetts, B.A. 1994

CHRONOLOGICAL RESUME

HARRY SEABORN
557 Shoreline Drive
Seattle, WA 98404
(206) 555-6584
e-mail: hseaborn@centco.com

EXPERIENCE

THE CENTER COMPANY   Seattle, WA
Systems Programmer   2002-present
  • Develop and maintain customer accounting and order tracking
  database using a Visual Basic front end and SQL server.
  • Plan and implement migration of company wide transition from
  mainframe-based dumb terminals to a true client server environment
  using Windows NT Workstation and Server.
  • Oversee general local and wide area network administration
  including the development of a variety of intranet modules to
  improve internal company communication and planning across
  divisions.

INFO TECH, INC.   Seattle, WA
Technical Manager   1996-2002
  • Designed and managed the implementation of a network providing
  the legal community with a direct line to Supreme Court cases
  across the Internet using SQL Server and a variety of Internet tools.
  • Developed a system to make the entire library catalog available on
  line using PERL scripts and SQL.
  • Used Visual Basic and Microsoft Access to create a registration
  system for university registrar.

EDUCATION

SALEM STATE UNIVERSITY   Salem, OR
       M.S. in Computer Science.   1999
       B.S. in Computer Science.   1997

COMPUTER SKILLS

  • Programming Languages: Visual Basic, Java, C++, SQL, PERL
  • Software: SQL Server, Internet Information Server, Oracle
  • Operating Systems: Windows NT, UNIX, Linux

FUNCTIONAL RESUME

Donna Hermione Moss
703 Wizard's Way
Chicago, IL 60601
(312) 555-8841
e-mail: donna@cowfire.com

OBJECTIVE:
To contribute over five years of experience in promotion, communications, and administration to an entry-level position in advertising.

SUMMARY OF QUALIFICATIONS:
- Performed advertising duties for small business.
- Experience in business writing and communications skills.
- General knowledge of office management.
- Demonstrated ability to work well with others, in both supervisory and support staff roles.
- Type 75 words per minute.

SELECTED ACHIEVEMENTS AND RESULTS:
Promotion:
Composing, editing, and proofreading correspondence and public relations materials for own catering service. Large-scale mailings.

Communication:
Instruction; curriculum and lesson planning; student evaluation; parent-teacher conferences; development of educational materials. Training and supervising clerks.

Computer Skills:
Proficient in MS Word, Lotus 1-2-3, Excel, and Filemaker Pro.

Administration:
Record-keeping and file maintenance. Data processing and computer operations, accounts receivable, accounts payable, inventory control, and customer relations. Scheduling, office management, and telephone reception.

PROFESSIONAL HISTORY:
Teacher; Self-Employed (owner of catering service); Floor Manager; Administrative Assistant; Accounting Clerk.

EDUCATION:
Beloit College, Beloit, WI, BA in Education, 1997

CHRONOLOGICAL RESUME

PERCY ZIEGLER
16 Josiah Court
Marlborough CT 06447
203/555-9641 (h)
203/555-8176, x14 (w)

EDUCATION Keene State College, Keene NH
Bachelor of Arts in Elementary Education, 2003
- Graduated *magna cum laude*
- English minor
- Kappa Delta Pi member, inducted 2001

EXPERIENCE Elmer T. Thienes Elementary School, Marlborough CT
September 2003- *Part-time Kindergarten Teacher*
Present
- Instruct kindergartners in reading, spelling, language   arts, and
  music.
- Participate in the selection of textbooks and learning aids.
- Organize and supervise class field trips and coordinate in-class
  presentations.

Summers Keene YMCA, Youth Division, Keene NH
2000-2002 *Child-care Counselor*
- Oversaw summer program for low-income youth.
- Budgeted and coordinated special events and field trips,
  working with Program Director to initiate variations in the
  program.
- Served as Youth Advocate in cooperation with social worker to
  address the social needs and problems of participants.

Spring 2002 Wheelock Elementary School, Keene NH
Student Teacher
- Taught third-grade class in all elementary subjects.
- Designed and implemented a two-week unit on Native
  Americans.
- Assisted in revision of third-grade curriculum.

Fall 2001 Child Development Center, Keene NH
Daycare Worker
- Supervised preschool children on the playground and during art
  activities.
- Created a "Wishbone Corner," where children could quietly
  look at books or take a voluntary "time-out."

ADDITIONAL INTERESTS
Martial arts, Pokemon, politics, reading, skiing, writing.

ELECTRONIC RESUME

GRIFFIN DORE
69 Dursley Drive
Cambridge, MA 02138
(617) 555-5555

KEYWORD SUMMARY

Senior financial manager with over ten years experience in Accounting and Systems Management, Budgeting, Forecasting, Cost Containment, Financial Reporting, and International Accounting. MBA in Management. Proficient in Lotus, Excel, Solomon, and Windows.

EXPERIENCE

COLWELL CORPORATION, Wellesley, MA
Director of Accounting and Budgets, 1995 to present
     Direct staff of twenty in General Ledger, Accounts Payable, Accounts Receivable, and International Accounting.
     Facilitate month-end closing process with parent company and auditors.
     Implemented team-oriented cross-training program within accounting group, resulting in timely month-end closings and increased productivity of key accounting staff.
     Developed and implemented a strategy for Sales and Use Tax Compliance in all fifty states.
     Prepare monthly financial statements and analyses.

FRANKLIN AND DELANEY COMPANY, Melrose, MA
Senior Accountant, 1993-1996
     Managed Accounts Payable, General Ledger, transaction processing, and financial reporting. Supervised staff of five.

Staff Accountant, 1991-1993
     Managed Accounts Payable, including vouchering, cash disbursements, and bank reconciliation.
     Wrote and issued policies.
     Maintained supporting schedules used during year-end audits.
     Trained new employees.

EDUCATION

MBA in Management, Northeastern University, Boston, MA, 1995
BS in Accounting, Boston College, Boston, MA, 1991

ASSOCIATIONS

National Association of Accountants

GENERAL MODEL
FOR A COVER LETTER

Your mailing address
Date

Contact's name
Contact's title
Company
Company's mailing address

Dear Mr./Ms. _____:

Immediately explain why your background makes you the best candidate for the position that you are applying for. Describe what prompted you to write (want ad, article you read about the company, networking contact, etc.). Keep the first paragraph short and hard-hitting.

Detail what you could contribute to this company. Show how your qualifications will benefit this firm. Describe your interest in the corporation. Subtly emphasizing your knowledge about this firm and your familiarity with the industry will set you apart from other candidates. Remember to keep this letter short; few recruiters will read a cover letter longer than half a page.

If possible, your closing paragraph should request specific action on the part of the reader. Include your phone number and the hours when you can be reached. Mention that if you do not hear from the reader by a specific date, you will follow up with a phone call. Lastly, thank the reader for their time, consideration, etc.

Sincerely,

(signature)

Your full name (typed)

Enclosure (use this if there are other materials, such as your resume,
          that are included in the same envelope)

SAMPLE COVER LETTER

16 Josiah Court
Marlborough CT 06447
January 16, 2006

Ms. Leona Malfoy
Assistant Principal
Laningham Elementary School
43 Mayflower Drive
Keene NH 03431

Dear Ms. Malfoy:

Toby Potter recently informed me of a possible opening for a third grade teacher at Laningham Elementary School. With my experience instructing third-graders, both in schools and in summer programs, I feel I would be an ideal candidate for the position. Please accept this letter and the enclosed resume as my application.

Laningham's educational philosophy that every child can learn and succeed interests me, since it mirrors my own. My current position at Elmer T. Thienes Elementary has reinforced this philosophy, heightening my awareness of the different styles and paces of learning and increasing my sensitivity toward special needs children. Furthermore, as a direct result of my student teaching experience at Wheelock Elementary School, I am comfortable, confident, and knowledgeable working with third-graders.

I look forward to discussing the position and my qualifications for it in more detail. I can be reached at 203/555-9641 evenings or 203/555-8176, x14 weekdays. If I do not hear from you before Tuesday of next week, I will call to see if we can schedule a time to meet. Thank you for your time and consideration.

Sincerely,

Percy Ziegler

Percy Ziegler

Enclosure

GENERAL MODEL FOR A
THANK YOU/FOLLOW-UP LETTER

Your mailing address
Date

Contact's name
Contact's title
Company
Company's mailing address

Dear Mr./Ms._____:

Remind the interviewer of the reason (i.e., a specific opening, an informational interview, etc.) you were interviewed, as well as the date. Thank him/her for the interview, and try to personalize your thanks by mentioning some specific aspect of the interview.

Confirm your interest in the organization (and in the opening, if you were interviewing for a particular position). Use specifics to re-emphasize that you have researched the firm in detail and have considered how you would fit into the company and the position. This is a good time to say anything you wish you had said in the initial meeting. Be sure to keep this letter brief; a half page is plenty.

If appropriate, close with a suggestion for further action, such as a desire to have an additional interview, if possible. Mention your phone number and the hours you can be reached. Alternatively, you may prefer to mention that you will follow up with a phone call in several days. Once again, thank the person for meeting with you, and state that you would be happy to provide any additional information about your qualifications.

Sincerely,

(signature)

Your full name (typed)

PRIMARY EMPLOYERS

ACCOUNTING & MANAGEMENT CONSULTING

You can expect to find the following types of companies in this section:
Consulting and Research Firms • Industrial Accounting Firms • Management Services • Public Accounting Firms • Tax Preparation Companies

BBC RESEARCH & CONSULTING
3773 Cherry Creek North Drive, Suite 850, Denver CO 80209-3827. 303/321-2547. **Fax:** 303/399-0448. **Contact:** Human Resources. **E-mail address:** bbc@bbcresearch.com. **World Wide Web address:** http://www.bbcresearch.com. **Description:** An economic research and management consulting firm. **Corporate headquarters location:** This location. **Listed on:** Privately held. **Number of employees at this location:** 30.

BOOZ ALLEN HAMILTON
121 South Tejon Street, Suite 900, Colorado Springs CO 80903. 719/387-2000. **Fax:** 719/387-2020. **Contact:** Human Resources. **World Wide Web address:** http://www.boozallen.com. **Description:** A global strategy and technology consulting firm with major areas of expertise in strategy, organization, operations, systems, and technology. **Positions advertised include:** AF Science and Technology Business Development Lead; GIS Engineer; Proposal Analyst and Writer; Proposal Manager. **Corporate headquarters location:** McLean VA. **Number of employees worldwide:** 17,000.

CLIFTON GUNDERSON LLP
370 Interlocken Boulevard, Suite 500, Broomfield CO 80021. 303/466-8822. **Fax:** 303/466-9797. **Contact:** Personnel Director. **World Wide Web address:** http://www.cliftoncpa.com. **Description:** A certified public accounting and consulting firm. **Positions advertised include:** Sr. Audit Associate; Marketing Assistant; Sr. Tax Associate.

DELOITTE & TOUCHE LLP
555 17th Street, Suite 3600, Denver CO 80202-3942. 303/292-5400. **Contact:** Heather Cameron, Personnel Director. **World Wide Web address:** http://www.us.deloitte.com. **Description:** An international firm of certified public accountants providing professional accounting, auditing, tax, and management consulting services to widely diversified clients. The company has a specialized program consisting of national industry groups and functional groups that cross industry lines. Groups are involved in various disciplines including accounting, auditing, taxation management advisory services, small and growing businesses, mergers and acquisitions, and computer applications. **Positions advertised include:** Sr. Networking Manager; Sr. Auditor; Business Process and IT Risk and Control Consultant. **Special programs:** Internships. **Other U.S. locations:** Nationwide.

GRANT THORNTON LLP
707 17th Street, Suite 3200, Denver CO 80202. 303/813-4000. **Contact:** Managing Partner. **World Wide Web address:** http://www.grantthornton.com. **Description:** An international certified public accounting organization offering consulting and accounting services, as well as strategic and tactical planning assistance to a diverse clientele. **Positions advertised include:** Audit Manager; Tax Manager. **Corporate headquarters location:** Chicago IL. **Other U.S. locations:** Nationwide.

PRICEWATERHOUSECOOPERS
1670 Broadway Avenue, Suite 1000, Denver CO 80202. 720/931-7000. **Contact:** Recruiting. **World Wide Web address:** http://www.pwcglobal.com. **Description:** One of the largest certified public accounting firms in the world. PricewaterhouseCoopers provides public accounting, business advisory, management consulting, and taxation services. **Positions advertised include:** Sr. Tax Associate; Manager, ICAS Implementation; Audit Manager. **Corporate headquarters location:** New York NY. **Other U.S. locations:** Nationwide. **International locations:** Worldwide.

ADVERTISING, MARKETING, AND PUBLIC RELATIONS

You can expect to find the following types of companies in this section:
Advertising Agencies • Direct Mail Marketers • Market Research Firms • Public Relations Firms

---

AMERICOMM DIRECT MARKETING
4760 Oakland Street, Suite 175, Denver CO 80239. 303/371-4400. **Toll-free phone:** 877/737-5478. **Contact:** Human Resources Department. **World Wide Web address:** http://www.americomm.net. **Description:** A direct mail processing company.

BERNARD HODES GROUP
2399 Blake Street, Suite 160, Denver CO 80205. 720/904-0461. **Fax:** 720/904-0490. **Contact:** Human Resources. **World Wide Web address:** http://www.hodes.com. **Description:** An advertising agency specializing in recruitment and employee communications. **Corporate headquarters location:** New York NY. **International locations:** Worldwide. **Parent company:** Omnicom.

MILES ADVERTISING, INC.
1936 Market Street, Denver CO 80202. 303/293-9191. **Toll-free phone:** 800/342-8978. **Contact:** Human Resources. **Description:** A full-service advertising agency specializing in residential real estate. Founded in 1986. **NOTE:** Entry-level positions are offered. **Special programs:** Internships. **Corporate headquarters location:** This location. **Listed on:** Privately held. **CEO:** David R. Miles. **Annual sales/revenues:** $11 - $20 million. **Number of employees at this location:** 20.

AEROSPACE

You can expect to find the following types of companies in this section:
Aerospace Products and Services • Aircraft Equipment and Parts

AMI AIRCRAFT SEATING SYSTEMS
1275 North Newport Road, Colorado Springs CO 80916. 719/380-0020. **Fax:** 719/380-0040. **Contact:** Human Resources. **World Wide Web address:** http://www.goodrich.com. **Description:** Manufactures cockpit and cabin attendant seating, ejection seats, and service centers. **Positions advertised include:** Buyer/Planner; Machinist; Product Engineer; Design Engineer; Maintenance Technician; QC Inspector; Configuration and Document Control. **Parent company:** Goodrich Corporation.

BALL AEROSPACE & TECHNOLOGIES CORP.
P.O. Box 1062, Boulder CO 80301. 303/939-4000. **Physical address:** 1600 Commerce Street, Boulder CO 80301. **Fax:** 303/939-6104. **Contact:** Human Resources. **E-mail address:** info@ball.com. **World Wide Web address:** http://www.ballaerospace.com. **Description:** Ball Aerospace & Technologies Corp. provides imaging, communications, and information systems, products, software, and services to government and commercial aerospace customers. Founded in 1956. **NOTE:** Search and apply for positions online. **Positions advertised include:** Sr. Business Analyst; Business Analyst Manager; Engineering Manager; Project Engineer; Production Engineer; Manufacturing Engineer; Technical Specialist; Principal Engineer; Advanced Systems Manager. **Listed on:** New York Stock Exchange. **Stock exchange symbol:** BLL. **Number of employees at this location:** 2,500.

BOEING INTEGRATED DEFENSE SYSTEMS (IDS)
3800 Lewiston Street, Aurora CO 80011-1549. 303/307-3300. **Contact:** Human Resources. **World Wide Web address:** http://www.boeing.com. **Description:** Boeing Integrated Defense Systems combines weapons and aircraft capabilities, intelligence and surveillance systems, communications architectures and extensive large-scale integration expertise across its seven business units. **NOTE:** Search and apply for positions online. **Positions advertised include:** Software Engineer; Integrated Scheduler; Systems Administrator; Engineer; Network Architecture Engineer. **Other area locations:** Colorado Springs CO.

GOODRICH AEROSPACE
50 William White Boulevard, Pueblo CO 81001. 719/948-3500. **Contact:** Human Resources. **World Wide Web address:** http://www.goodrich.com. **Description:** A supplier of aerospace components, systems, and services. **Positions advertised include:** Human Resources Manager. **Corporate headquarters location:**

Charlotte NC. **Parent company:** Goodrich Corporation. **Listed on:** New York Stock Exchange. **Stock exchange symbol:** GR. **Number of employees worldwide:** 18,000.

HAMILTON SUNDSTRAND
2800 Sundstrand Way, Grand Junction CO 81506. 970/242-2600. **Contact:** Human Resources. **World Wide Web address:** http://www.hamiltonsundstrandcorp.com. **Description:** A manufacturing facility specializing in precision machining of aerospace components. Overall, Hamilton Sundstrand manufactures a wide range of aircraft components, systems, and subsystems. **Positions advertised include:** Cerro Operator; Engineering Manufacturing; Engineering Manager; Buyer. **Corporate headquarters location:** Windsor Locks CT. **Parent company:** United Technologies Corporation.

LOCKHEED MARTIN SPACE SYSTEMS
P.O. Box 179, Mail Stop DC1311, Littleton CO 80201. 303/977-3000. **Physical address:** 12257 South Wadsworth Boulevard, Littleton CO 80125. **Fax:** 303/971-3324. **Recorded jobline:** 303/977-2720. **Contact:** Human Resources. **World Wide Web address:** http://www.lockheedmartin.com. **Description:** This location is part of the Space Group segment of Lockheed Martin Corporation. The Space Group is engaged in the design, development, engineering, and production of civil and military space launch vehicles, satellites, spacecraft, space-based information and communications systems, and the Space Shuttle External Tank and associated electronics and instrumentation. **Positions advertised include:** Principle Business Development Analyst; Contracts Administrator; Cost Analyst; Documentation Engineer; Electrical Engineer; Electro-Optical Engineer. Financial Analyst. **Corporate headquarters location:** Bethesda MD. **Parent company:** Lockheed Martin Corporation. **Listed on:** New York Stock Exchange. **Stock exchange symbol:** LMT. **Number of employees at this location:** 6,000. **Number of employees nationwide:** 93,000.

NORTHROP GRUMMAN MISSION SYSTEMS
985 Space Center Drive, Suite 350, Colorado Springs CO 80915. 719/596-0700. **Contact:** Human Resources. **World Wide Web address:** http://www.ms.northropgrumman.com. **Description:** Focused on solutions that contribute to the welfare of the global community, the organization's technology spans three business areas: missile systems, command, control and intelligence, and technical and management services. **NOTE:** Search and apply for positions online. **Positions advertised include:** Test Engineer; Systems Engineer; ESD Network Engineer; Manager, Distributed Systems; engineering Center Manager; Program Control Analyst. **Corporate headquarters location:** Reston VA. **Number of employees worldwide:** 18,000.

RT LOGIC
1042 Elkton Drive, Colorado Springs CO 80907. 719/598-2801. **Contact:** Human Resources. **E-mail address:** jobs@rtlogic.com. **World Wide**

Web address: http://www.rtlogic.com. **Description:** RT Logic is a provider of products for ground-based space applications, primarily for satellite and launch range operations. **Positions advertised include:** Embedded software Engineer; Firmware Engineer; Satellite Communications Engineer; Sr. Systems Engineer/Project Manager; System Test Engineer; QA Manager. **Other area locations:** Englewood CO. **Parent company:** Integral Systems.

RAYTHEON

16800 East Centretech Parkway, Aurora CO 80011. 303/344-6000. **Contact:** Human Resources. **World Wide Web address:** http://www.raytheon.com. **Description:** The company develops and deploys information and data management systems that command and control satellites, manage space-based assets and facilitate global communication. The Aurora business site's customers include NASA and other U.S. federal agencies, satellite manufacturers, and international commercial communications satellite operators. **NOTE:** Search and apply for positions online. **Positions advertised include:** Director, Business Development; Industrial Security Specialist; Sr. IT Specialist; LAN/WAN Technologist; Proposal Analysis Manager; Property Administrator; Sr. Industrial Security Specialist; Sr. Principal Systems Engineer; Sr. Proposal Analyst; Sr. Manager-Program Management. **Corporate headquarters location:** Waltham MA. **Number of employees at this location:** 2,600. **Number of employees worldwide:** 78,000.

STANLEY AVIATION CORPORATION

2501 Dallas Street, Aurora CO 80010. 303/340-5200. **Fax:** 303/340-5254. **Contact:** Human Resources. **E-mail address:** hr@stanleyaviation.com. **World Wide Web address:** http://www.stanleyaviation.com. **Description:** Manufactures structural sheet metal and metal tube fabrications for the aircraft industry, couplings used in aircraft and missiles, structural ground support equipment for airlines, and large metal containers. **Corporate headquarters location:** This location. **Parent company:** Flight Refueling Ltd. **Listed on:** Privately held. **Number of employees at this location:** 180.

APPAREL, FASHION, AND TEXTILES

**You can expect to find the following types of companies
in this section:**
Broadwoven Fabric Mills • Knitting Mills • Yarn and Thread Mills •
Curtains and Draperies • Footwear • Nonwoven Fabrics • Textile Goods
and Finishing

FIBERLOK INC.
P.O. Box 1727, Fort Collins CO 80524. 970/221-1200. **Physical address:** 811 Stockton Avenue, Fort Collins CO 80824. **Contact:** Human Resources. **World Wide Web address:** http://www.fiberlok.com. **E-mail address:** info@fiberlok.com. **World Wide Web address:** http://stores.yahoo.com/fiberlok. **Description:** Manufactures heat seal transfers and sew on patches. **Positions advertised include:** Sales Manager; Marketing Manager; Marketing Services.

ROPER APPAREL AND FOOTWEAR
14707 East Second Avenue, 3rd Floor, Aurora CO 80011. 303/893-2320. **Fax:** 303/571-2248. **Contact:** Human Resources. **E-mail address:** jobs@roperusa.com. **World Wide Web address:** http://www.eroper.com. **Description:** Manufactures Western apparel. **Positions advertised include:** Apparel Designer. **Corporate headquarters location:** This location.

WESCO FABRICS INC.
4001 Forest Street, P.O. Box 16604, Denver CO 80216. 303/388-4101. **Contact:** Human Resources. **World Wide Web address:** http://www.wescofabrics.com. **Description:** Wholesales drapery fabrics and distributes window coverings and bedspreads on a wholesale trade basis. Wesco Fabrics also manufactures bedspreads. Founded in 1946. **Corporate headquarters location:** This location. **Chairman:** Richard Gentry.

ARCHITECTURE, CONSTRUCTION, AND ENGINEERING

You can expect to find the following types of companies in this section:
Architectural and Engineering Services • Civil and Mechanical Engineering Firms • Construction Products, Manufacturers, and Wholesalers • General Contractors/Specialized Trade Contractors

AIR PURIFICATION COMPANY
1860 West 64th Lane, Denver CO 80221. 303/428-2800. **Contact:** Bruce Wilde, President and Owner. **World Wide Web address:** http://www.airpurificationcompany.com. **Description:** A wholesaler of air conditioning, heating, and ventilation equipment.

ARINC RESEARCH CORPORATION
1925 Aerotech Drive, Suite 212, Colorado Springs CO 80916-4219. 719/574-9001. **Contact:** Human Resources. **World Wide Web address:** http://www.arinc.com. **Description:** An engineering and management consulting firm providing technical studies, analysis, and evaluations of aircraft, ship systems, communications, and information systems. **Positions advertised include:** Staff Principal Engineer; DAS Administrative Engineer; Test & Evaluation Engineer; Sr. Communications Network Engineer. **Corporate headquarters:** Annapolis MD. **Other U.S. locations:** Nationwide. **International locations:** Worldwide. **CEO:** James L. Pierce.

BLACK & VEATCH
30 Pikes Peak, Suite 200, Colorado Springs CO 80903. 719/667-7010. **Fax:** 719/667-7009. **Contact:** Human Resources Department. **World Wide Web address:** http://www.bv.com. **Description:** An environmental/civil engineering and construction firm serving utilities, commerce, industry, and government agencies in more than 40 countries throughout the world. Black & Veatch provides a broad range of study, design, construction management, and turnkey capabilities to clients in the water and wastewater fields. The firm is one of the leading authorities on drinking water treatment through the use of activated carbon, ozone, and other state-of-the-art processes. Black & Veatch is also engaged in wastewater treatment work including reclamation and reuse projects and the beneficial use of wastewater residuals. Other services are provided for solid waste recycling and disposal, transportation, and storm water management. In the energy field, Black & Veatch is a leader in providing engineering procurement and construction for electric power plants. The firm's areas of expertise include coal-fueled plants, simple and combined-cycle combustion turbines, waste-to-energy facilities, hydroelectric plants, and cogeneration facilities. Black & Veatch's capabilities also include nuclear power projects, advanced technology, air quality control, performance monitoring, plant life management, and facilities modification. In addition, Black & Veatch provides transmission

and distribution services. Black & Veatch offers a variety of management and financial services including institutional strengthening, privatization, strategic financial planning, and information management. **Positions advertised include:** Engineering Technician; Engineer; Business Development Director; Civil Engineer; Electrical Engineer. **Corporate headquarters location:** Kansas City MO.

BOYLE ENGINEERING CORPORATION
215 Union Boulevard, Suite 500, Lakewood CO 80228. 303/987-3443. **Fax:** 303/987-3908. **Contact:** Human Resources Department. **World Wide Web address:** http://www.boyleengineering.com. **Description:** Provides professional engineering services to create better infrastructure for public and private clients in the United States and abroad. Services range from project planning and feasibility studies to design and construction phases. The company is engaged in water treatment and distribution; wastewater collection, treatment, and reuse; streets, highways, and bridges construction; light and heavy rail; drainage and flood control; and land planning. **Positions advertised include:** Civil Engineer. **Corporate headquarters location:** Newport Beach CA.

CH2M HILL
6161 South Syracuse Way, Suite 200, Greenwood Village CO 80111. 303/706-0990. **Fax:** 303/706-1861. **Contact:** Human Resources. **World Wide Web address:** http://www.ch2mhill.com. **Description:** Provides mechanical, structural, and environmental engineering services through its operating divisions. **NOTE:** Interested jobseekers should fax resumes to 781/663-3733. **Corporate headquarters location:** Englewood CO. **Other area locations:** Colorado Springs CO; Golden CO. **International locations:** Worldwide. **Subsidiaries include:** CH2M Hill Engineering; Industrial Design Corporation; Operating Management International.

CARTER & BURGESS
707 17th Street, Suite 2300, Denver CO 80202-5131. 303/820-5240. **Fax:** 303/820-2402. **Contact:** Human Resources. **E-mail address:** denverinfo@c-b.com. **World Wide Web address:** http://www.c-b.com. **Description:** An architectural, engineering, and construction management firm with 32 offices in 19 states. **Positions advertised include:** CADD Technician; Design Project Manager; Civil Engineer; Civil Project Engineer; Electrical Engineer; GIS Database Solutions Project Manager; Landscape Architect; Proposal Coordinator; Sr. Marketing Coordinator; Water Resource Engineer. **Number of employees nationwide:** 2,700.

CENTEX HOMES
9250 East Costilla Avenue, Suite 200, Greenwood Village CO 80112. 303/792-9810. **Contact:** Personnel. **World Wide Web address:** http://www.centexhomes.com. **Description:** Builds and sells residential homes nationwide. **Corporate headquarters location:** Dallas TX. **Parent company:** Centex Corporation provides home building, mortgage banking, contracting, and construction products and services. **Listed on:** New York Stock Exchange. **Stock exchange symbol:** CTX.

CREATIVE TOUCH INTERIORS

3251 Lewiston Street, Unit #10, Aurora CO 80011. 303/363-3687. **Contact:** Human Resources. **World Wide Web address:** http://www.ctihome.com. **Description:** Engaged in the installation and refinishing of hardwood floors. The company is also engaged in the installation of carpet, vinyl, ceramic tile, and related floor coverings. Founded in 1959. **Positions advertised include:** Scheduler; Production Assistant; Customer Service Representative; Field Supervisor; Warehouse Driver; Corian Fabricators; Flooring Trainee.

HENSEL PHELPS CONSTRUCTION COMPANY

420 Sixth Avenue, Greeley CO 80632. 970/352-6565. **Fax:** 970/352-9311. **Contact:** Ron Norby, Vice President. **E-mail address:** careers@henselphelps.com. **World Wide Web address:** http://www.henselphelps.com. **Description:** A commercial construction company. **Number of employees nationwide:** 2,600.

ISEC, INC.

P.O. Box 6849, Englewood CO 80155. 303/790-1444. **Physical address:** 33 Inverness Drive East, Englewood CO 80112. **Contact:** Human Resources. **World Wide Web address:** http://www.isecinc.com. **Description:** Provides contract engineering services. **Corporate headquarters location:** this location. **Number of employees nationwide:** 1,000.

JACOBS ENGINEERING GROUP, INC.
JACOBS FACILITIES, INC.

1527 Cole Boulevard, Golden CO 80401. 303/462-7000. **Fax:** 303/462-7001. **Contact:** Human Resources. **E-mail address:** info@jacobs.com. **World Wide Web address:** http://www.jacobs.com. **Description:** An engineering and construction company that provides engineering, procurement, construction, and maintenance services to clients and industries. These industries include chemicals and polymers, federal programs, pulp and paper, semiconductor, petroleum refining, facilities and transportation, food and consumer products, pharmaceuticals and biotechnologies, and basic resources. Through Jacobs College and other site-specific programs, the company trains more than 5,000 employees per year in project and money management, health and safety, and numerous other performance enhancing topics. **Positions advertised include:** Project Controls Specialist. **Corporate headquarters location:** Pasadena CA. **Listed on:** New York Stock Exchange. **Stock exchange symbol:** JEC.

KIEWIT WESTERN COMPANY

7926 South Platte Canyon Road, Littleton CO 80128-5978. 303/979-9330. **Contact:** Mark Campbell, District Business Manager. **World Wide Web address:** http://www.kiewit.com. **Description:** A general contracting company. **Corporate headquarters location:** Omaha NE. **Parent company:** The Kiewit Companies. **Number of employees at this location:** 115.

MERRICK & COMPANY
2450 South Peoria Street, Aurora CO 80014. 303/751-0741. **Fax:** 303/751-2581. **Contact:** Human Resources. **E-mail address:** info@merrick.com. **World Wide Web address:** http://www.merrick.com. **Description:** A full-service engineering and architectural firm. Merrick & Company specializes in advanced technology, civil infrastructure, government, heavy industrial, and land development services. **Positions advertised include:** Piping Designer. **Corporate headquarters location:** This location. **Other U.S. locations:** Atlanta GA; Albuquerque NM; Los Alamos NM. **Listed on:** Privately held. **Number of employees nationwide:** 320.

NEXUS CORPORATION
10983 Leroy Drive, Northglenn CO 80233. 303/457-9199. **Fax:** 303/457-2801. **Contact:** Human Resources. **World Wide Web address:** http://www.nexuscorp.com. **Description:** Manufactures prefabricated, metal greenhouses.

NOLTE
8000 South Chester Street, Suite 200, Centennial CO 80112. 303/220-6400. **Fax:** 303/220-9001. **Contact:** Human Resources. **Email address:** denver_info@nolte.com. **World Wide Web address:** http://www.nolte.com. **Description:** Nolte is a full-service civil engineering firm with offices in the Western United States and Mexico. Areas of specialty include: flood control and drainage; land planning and development; structural engineering; surveying and mapping; traffic and transportation; water supply, distribution and treatment; wastewater engineering and water recycling; construction and program management. **Positions advertised include:** Sr. Office CM Engineer; Sr. Field CM Engineer; Jr. Surveyor; Sr. Office Surveyor; Sr. Engineer; Engineering Manager. **Number of employees nationwide:** 400.

GERALD H. PHIPPS, INC.
1530 West 13th Avenue, Denver CO 80204-2400. 303/571-5377. **Fax:** 303/629-7467. **Contact:** Human Resources. **E-mail address:** HRInquiries@ghpd.com. **World Wide Web address:** http://www.geraldhphipps.com. **Description:** A general contractor/construction manager for commercial buildings. Gerald H. Phipps, Inc. specializes in building medical complexes, high-tech buildings, universities, schools, offices that tenants finish, public facilities, biotechnology labs, and retail projects. Founded in 1952. **Positions advertised include:** Project Engineer; Superintendent, Concrete Division. **Corporate headquarters location:** This location. **Other area locations:** Colorado Springs CO. **Listed on:** Privately held. **Annual sales/revenues:** More than $100 million. **Number of employees at this location:** 250.

GEORGE T. SANDERS COMPANY
10201 West 49th Avenue, Wheat Ridge CO 80033. 303/423-9660. **Fax:** 303/420-8737. **Contact:** Human Resources. **E-mail address:** jobs@gtsanders.com. **World Wide Web address:**

http://www.gtsanders.com. **Description:** An independent wholesale distributor of plumbing and heating supplies. George T. Sanders Company operates seven locations in Colorado. **NOTE:** Entry-level positions and part-time jobs are offered. **Office hours:** Monday - Friday, 7:00 a.m. - 5:00 p.m. **Corporate headquarters location:** This location. **Listed on:** Privately held. **President:** Gary T. Sanders. **Purchasing Manager:** Kirk Anderson. **Annual sales/revenues:** $21 - $50 million.

SCIENCE APPLICATIONS INTERNATIONAL CORPORATION (SAIC)

405 Urban Street, Suite 400, Lakewood CO 80228. 303/969-6000. **Contact:** Human Resources. **World Wide Web address:** http://www.saic.com. **Description:** The largest employee-owned research and engineering firm in the U.S. Founded in 1969. **Positions advertised include:** Engineer; Sr. Water Resource Engineer Program Manager; NEPA Specialist; Environmental Analyst; Sr. Unix Systems Administrator; Network Analyst; Oracle Financial Database Administrator; Network Analyst. **Number of employees worldwide:** 43,000.

SPARTA, INC.

985 Space Center Drive, Suite 100, Colorado Springs CO 80915. 719/570-6998. **Fax:** 719/380-6495. **Contact:** Human Resources. **World Wide Web address:** http://www.sparta.com. **Description:** An employee-owned engineering and advanced technology company providing technical products and services to the defense, intelligence, and homeland security sectors of the federal government. **Positions advertised include:** Analyst; Communications/Systems Engineer; DoD Architect; DoD Architect Programmer; Senior Analyst; Space Systems Analyst; Sr. Configuration Management Analyst; Sr. Space Systems Analyst; Web Engineer; Web Portal Engineer. **Corporate headquarters location:** Lake Forest CA.

TERRACON

4172 Center Park Drive, Colorado Springs CO 80916. 719/597-2116. **Fax:** 719/597-2117. **Contact:** Human Resources. **Email address:** careers@terracon.com. **World Wide Web address:** http://www.terracon.com. **Description:** Terracon is an employee-owned provider of geotechnical, environmental, construction materials, and related services, with more than 70 offices in 25 states. Founded in 1965. **NOTE:** When applying, the position title, Req #, and office location must be specified. **Positions advertised include:** Project Structural Engineer; Construction Materials Technician. **Other area locations:** Denver CO; Fort Collins CO; Greeley CO; Pueblo CO. **Corporate headquarters location:** Lenexa KS.

TETRA TECH EM INC.

4940 Pearl East Circle, Suite 100, Boulder CO 80301. 303/441-7900. **Fax:** 303/447-5585. **World Wide Web address:** http://www.tetratech.com. **Description:** Provides specialized engineering management consulting and technical services in the areas of resource management, infrastructure, and communications. **Positions**

advertised include: Civil/Environmental Engineer; Engineering Intern; Human Health Risk Assessor. **Corporate headquarters location:** Pasadena CA. **Listed on:** NASDAQ. **Stock exchange symbol:** TTEK. **Number of employees worldwide:** 8,000.

TRANE COMPANY

101 William White Boulevard, Pueblo CO 81001. 719/585-3800. **Contact:** Human Resources. **World Wide Web address:** http://www.trane.com. **Description:** Develops, manufactures, and sells air-conditioning equipment. **Corporate headquarters location:** Piscataway NJ. **Parent company:** American Standard Companies, Inc. **Listed on:** New York Stock Exchange. **Stock exchange symbol:** ASD.

U.S. ENGINEERING COMPANY

729 Southeast 8th Street, Loveland CO 80537. 970/669-1666. **Fax:** 970/663-0685. **Contact:** Human Resources Department. **E-mail address:** jobs@usengineering.com. **World Wide Web address:** http://www.usengineering.com. **Description:** A contracting company that installs heating, air conditioning, piping, and sprinkler systems for businesses. **Positions advertised include:** Pre-Construction Engineer; Piping Detailer. **Corporate headquarters location:** Kansas City MO. **Listed on:** Privately held. **Annual sales/revenues:** More than $100 million. **Number of employees at this location:** 300. **Number of employees nationwide:** 600.

UNITED PIPELINE SYSTEMS, INC.

135 Turner Drive, Durango CO 81302. 970/259-0354. **Fax:** 970/259-0356. **Contact:** Project Manager. **World Wide Web address:** http://www.insituform.com. **Description:** Engaged in the restoration of pipes. **Parent company:** Insituform Technologies, Inc. uses various trenchless technologies for restoration, new construction, and improvements of pipeline systems including sewers, gas lines, industrial waste lines, water lines and oil field, mining, and industrial process pipelines. **Listed on:** NASDAQ. **Stock exchange symbol:** INSUA.

VANGUARD RESEARCH, INC.

770 Wooten Road, Colorado Springs CO 80915. 719/596-1174. **Contact:** General Manager. **E-mail address:** hr@vriusa.com. **World Wide Web address:** http://www.vriffx.com. **Description:** Provides engineering and technical support services. **Corporate headquarters location:** Arlington VA. **Other U.S. locations:** Bellevue NE. **President/CEO:** Mel Chaskin. **Facilities Manager:** Lee Morgan. **Number of employees at this location:** 30. **Number of employees nationwide:** 150.

WASHINGTON GROUP INTERNATIONAL

7800 East Union Avenue, Suite 100, Denver CO 80237. 303/843-2000. **Contact:** Human Resources. **World Wide Web address:** http://www.wgint.com. **Description:** An engineering and construction firm operating through five major divisions: Government, Industrial/Process, Infrastructure & Mining, Petroleum & Chemicals, and

Power. Washington Group International offers construction, engineering, and program-management services to the environmental, industrial, mining, nuclear-services, power, transportation, and water resources industries. **Positions advertised include:** Estimating Manager; Engineer; Equipment Engineer; Mine Engineer. **Operations at this facility include:** Divisional Headquarters; Service.

WRIGHT WATER ENGINEERS INC.
2490 West 26th Avenue, Suite 100A, Denver CO 80211-4208. 303/480-1700. **Fax:** 303/480-1020. **Contact:** Personnel. **E-mail address:** personnel@wrightwater.com. **World Wide Web address:** http://www.wrightwater.com. **Description:** Specializes in the planning and developing of water resources. **Positions advertised include:** Civil Design Engineer. **Other area locations:** Glenwood Springs CO; Durango CO.

ARTS, ENTERTAINMENT, SPORTS, AND RECREATION

You can expect to find the following types of companies in this section:
Botanical and Zoological Gardens • Entertainment Groups • Motion Picture and Video Tape Production and Distribution • Museums and Art Galleries • Physical Fitness Facilities • Professional Sports Clubs; Sporting and Recreational Camps • Public Golf Courses and Racing and Track Operations • Theatrical Producers and Services

---

ANASAZI HERITAGE CENTER
BUREAU OF LAND MANAGEMENT
27501 Highway 184, Dolores CO 81323-9217. 970/882-4811. **Fax:** 970/882-7035. **Contact:** Human Resources. **World Wide Web address:** http://www.co.blm.gov/ahc. **Description:** An archeological museum that focuses on the interpretation of the Anasazi culture. **Special programs:** Internships. **Corporate headquarters location:** Washington DC. **Parent company:** U.S. Department of the Interior.

ANDERSON RANCH ARTS CENTER
5263 Owl Creek Road, P.O. Box 5598, Snowmass Village CO 81615. 970/923-3181. **Fax:** 970/923-3871. **Contact:** Employment. **World Wide Web address:** http://www.andersonranch.org. **Description:** Offers 100 summer workshops (one or two weeks long) in painting and drawing, ceramics, sculpture, woodworking, furniture design, photography, creative studies, and children's studies. In the winter, the center runs a studio residency program. The center also offers a visiting artists program for professional and emerging artists. **Positions advertised include:** Director of Marketing and Communications. **Special programs:** Internships.

BRECKENRIDGE OUTDOOR EDUCATION CENTER
P.O. Box 697, Breckenridge CO 80424. 970/453-6422. **Fax:** 970/453-4676. **Contact:** Human Resources. **E-mail address:** boec@boec.org. **World Wide Web address:** http://www.boec.org. **Description:** A nonprofit organization offering year-round wilderness and adventure programs and adaptive skiing opportunities for people with disabilities and other special needs. Activities include downhill and cross-country skiing, ropes courses, rafting, rock climbing, camping, and fishing. Founded in 1976. **Special programs:** Internships. **Corporate headquarters location:** This location.

COLORADO HISTORICAL SOCIETY
1300 Broadway, Denver CO 80203. 303/866-3682. **Fax:** 303/866-4464. **Contact:** Alice Rodriguez, Personnel. **World Wide Web address:** http://www.coloradohistory.org. **Description:** A nonprofit organization that collects, preserves, and interprets the history and prehistory of Colorado and the West through educational programs and museum

exhibits. Founded in 1879. **Special programs:** Internships; Summer Jobs. **Corporate headquarters location:** This location. **Number of employees at this location:** 95. **Number of employees nationwide:** 115.

COLORADO ROCKIES
2001 Blake Street, Denver CO 80205. 303/832-8326. **Fax:** 303/312-2028. **Recorded jobline:** 303/312-2490. **Contact:** Human Resources. **World Wide Web address:** http://www.coloradorockies.com. **Description:** The Major League Baseball franchise of the Denver area.

CREEDE REPERTORY THEATRE
124 North Main Street, P.O. Box 269, Creede CO 81130. 719/658-2541. **Fax:** 719/658-2343. **Contact:** Human Resources. **E-mail address:** crt@creederep.com. **World Wide Web address:** http://www.creederep.com. **Description:** A nonprofit theater producing eight plays annually. Founded in 1969. **NOTE:** This location also hires seasonally. **Special programs:** Internships. **Number of employees at this location:** 40.

DENVER BRONCOS
13655 Broncos Parkway, Englewood CO 80112. 203/649-9000. **Contact:** Human Resources. **World Wide Web address:** www.denverbroncos.com. **Description:** The executive office of the NFL franchise and former Super Bowl champions.

DENVER CENTER THEATRE COMPANY
1101 13th Street, Denver CO 80204. 303/893-4000. **Recorded jobline:** 303/446-4873. **Contact:** Human Resources. **World Wide Web address:** http://www.denvercenter.org. **Description:** A professional acting troupe that performs a broad range of theatrical productions year-round. Founded in 1978. **Parent company:** Denver Center for the Performing Arts. **Number of employees at this location:** 300.

THE DENVER ZOO
2300 Steele Street, Denver CO 80205-4899. 303/376-4800. **Fax:** 303/376-4801. **Contact:** Human Resources. **E-mail address:** zoohr@denverzoo.org. **World Wide Web address:** http://www.denverzoo.org. **Description:** A zoo featuring year-round exhibits including Bird World and Tropical Discovery. **Positions advertised include:** Zookeeper; School Programs Specialist.

NATIONAL CINEMEDIA
9110 East Nichols Avenue, Suite 200, Centennial CO 80112-3405. 303/792-3600. **Toll-free phone:** 800/828-2828. **Contact:** Personnel. **World Wide Web address:** http://www.regalcinemas.com. **Description:** A theater-owned cinema programming company representing 1,100 theaters in 43 states. **Parent company:** AMC Theatres and Regal Entertainment Group.

NATIONAL SPORTS CENTER FOR THE DISABLED

P.O. Box 1290, Winter Park CO 80482. 970/726-1540. **Contact:** Human Resources. **World Wide Web address:** http://www.nscd.org. **Description:** Provides outdoor mountain recreational services to children and adults with disabilities. This is a nonprofit company. Founded in 1970. **Positions advertised include:** Recreation Programs Supervisor; National Programs Coordinator. **Special programs:** Internships. **Corporate headquarters location:** This location. **Parent company:** Winter Park Recreation Association. **Annual sales/revenues:** Less than $5 million. **Number of employees at this location:** 55.

NAUTILUS HEALTH AND FITNESS GROUP

1886 Prairie Way, Louisville CO 80027. 303/939-0100. **Fax:** 303/545-1425. **Contact:** Human Resources Department. **World Wide Web address:** http://www.nautilusgroup.com. **Description:** Manufactures and distributes health and fitness products. **Positions advertised include:** Mechanical Engineer. **Special programs:** Internships. **Corporate headquarters location:** Vancouver WA. **Parent company:** The Nautilus Group Inc. **Operations at this facility include:** Administration. **Listed on:** New York Stock Exchange. **Stock exchange symbol:** NLS.

WINTER PARK RESORT

P.O. Box 36, Winter Park CO 80482. 970/726-1536. **Fax:** 303/892-5823. **Recorded jobline:** 888/562-4525. **Contact:** Human Resources. **E-mail address:** wjob@skiwinterpark.com. **World Wide Web address:** http://www.winterparkresort.com. **Description:** A mountain resort offering lodging, skiing, ice-skating, sleigh rides, and hot air balloon rides. **Note:** Applications are accepted online or in-person at the recruiting office in the Administration building. The office is open 7 days a week from 8:00 a.m. to 4:30 p.m. **Positions advertised include:** Lift Electrician; Security Officer; Travel Specialist.

AUTOMOTIVE

You can expect to find the following types of companies in this section:
Automotive Repair Shops • Automotive Stampings • Industrial Vehicles and Moving Equipment • Motor Vehicles and Equipment • Travel Trailers and Campers

---

BESTOP, INC.
P.O. Box 307, Broomfield CO 80038. 303/465-1755. **Physical address:** 2100 West Midway Boulevard, Broomfield CO 80020. **Toll-free phone:** 800/845-3567. **Fax:** 303/466-3436. **Contact:** Human Resources Manager. **World Wide Web address:** http://www.bestop.com. **Description:** Designs and manufactures automotive soft tops and accessories for sport-utility vehicles. **NOTE:** Entry-level positions and second and third shifts are offered. **Office hours:** Monday - Friday, 7:30 a.m. - 5:00 p.m. **Corporate headquarters location:** This location. **Other U.S. locations:** Eastman GA. **International locations:** Ontario, Canada. **Operations at this facility include:** Administration; Manufacturing; Sales; Service. **President:** Ross MacLean. **Annual sales/revenues:** More than $100 million. **Number of employees at this location:** 500. **Number of employees nationwide:** 630.

DAIMLERCHRYSLER CORPORATION
12225 East 39th Avenue, Denver CO 80239. 303/373-8840. **Contact:** Human Resources. **E-mail address:** resume@daimlerchrysler.com. **World Wide Web address:** http://www.daimlerchrysler.com. **Description:** DaimlerChrysler Corporation produces cars, trucks, minivans, and sport-utility vehicles for customers in more than 100 countries. **NOTE:** Please see company Website for instructions on how to apply. **Corporate headquarters location:** Auburn Hills MI. **Operations at this facility include:** This location is a parts depot. **Listed on:** New York Stock Exchange. **Stock exchange symbol:** DCX.

GREASE MONKEY INTERNATIONAL, INC.
7100 East Belleview Avenue, Suite 305, Greenwood Village CO 80111. 303/308-1660. **Fax:** 303/308-5906. **Contact:** Personnel. **World Wide Web address:** http://www.greasemonkeyintl.com. **Description:** The company is a franchiser, owner, and operator of retail quick lube centers. Grease Monkey centers provide customer service and preventive maintenance services for motor vehicles. **NOTE:** Entry-level positions are offered. **Special programs:** Internships. **Corporate headquarters location:** This location. **Other U.S. locations:** Nationwide. **International locations:** Mexico. **Operations at this facility include:** This location provides sales, management, marketing, administrative, accounting, MIS, human resource, franchise support, and real estate services to the organization. **Number of employees at this location:** 50. **Number of employees nationwide:** 350.

McGEE COMPANY
1140 South Jason Street, Denver CO 80223. 303/777-2615. **Contact:** Human Resources. **World Wide Web address:** http://www.mcgeecompany.com. **Description:** Sells automotive equipment and supplies including tire machines, alignment machines, floor jacks, and tire patches. The company mainly sells its products to commercial clients. **CEO:** John Labreche.

NEOPLAN USA CORPORATION
700 Gottlob Auwaeter Drive, Lamar CO 81052. 719/336-3256. **Contact:** Human Resources Department. **World Wide Web address:** http://www.neoplanusa.com. **Description:** Manufactures and markets buses for international distribution. **Corporate headquarters location:** This location. **Other area locations:** Denver CO. **Operations at this facility include:** Manufacturing.

BANKING, SAVINGS & LOANS, AND OTHER DEPOSITORY INSTITUTIONS

You can expect to find the following types of companies in this section:
Banks • Bank Holding Companies and Associations • Lending Firms/Financial Services Institutions

---

AMERICAN NATIONAL BANK
3033 East First Avenue, Denver CO 80206. 303/394-5100. **Contact:** Eileen Terrell, Personnel Director. **World Wide Web address:** http://www.anbbank.com. **Description:** A commercial bank with a complete range of services for private, commercial, and institutional customers. **Positions advertised include:** Corporate Trust Operations Specialist. **Operations at this facility include:** Administration; Sales; Service.

BANK OF THE WEST
2 Steele Street, Denver CO 80206. 303/331-3500. **Contact:** Human Resources. **E-mail address:** Colorado_Careers@commercialfed.com. **World Wide Web address:** http://www.bankofthewest.com. **Description:** A branch location of the multistate bank.

CHASE
9379 North Sheridan Boulevard, Westminster CO 80030. 303/244-5060. **Contact:** Human Resources. **World Wide Web address:** http://www.bankone.com. **Description:** A full-service bank. **NOTE:** Search and apply for positions at http://careers.jpmorganchase.com. **Parent company:** JPMorgan Chase.

COBANK ACB
P.O. Box 5110, Denver CO 80217. 303/740-4000. **Physical address:** 5500 South Quebec Street, Greenwood Village CO 80111. **Fax:** 303/694-5898. **Contact:** Human Resources. **World Wide Web address:** http://www.cobank.com. **Description:** A full-service cooperative bank specializing in cooperative, agribusiness, rural utility, and agricultural export financing. Founded in 1916. **Positions advertised include:** Credit Officer; Lead Financial Analyst; Capital Markets Coordinator; Loan Documentation Specialist; Collateral Documentation Specialist; Application Developer; Credit Information Specialist. **Corporate headquarters location:** This location.

DENVER FEDERAL CREDIT UNION
1075 Acoma Street, Denver CO 80204. 303/573-1170. **Fax:** 303/626-0750. **Contact:** Human Resources. **E-mail address:** careers@dmfcu.org. **World Wide Web address:** http://www.dcfcu.coop. **Description:** A credit union. **Positions advertised include:** Network Administrator.

KEY BANK
100 Broadway, Denver CO 80203. 303/744-3228. **Contact:** Human Resources. **World Wide Web address:** http://www.key.com. **Description:** Offers a wide range of banking and other financial services. **Positions advertised include:** Marketing Professional; Teller; Relationship Manager; Sr. Manager. **Other area locations:** Lakewood CO; Commerce City CO; Littleton CO; Arvada CO; Aurora CO; Thornton CO; Greenwood Village CO; Englewood CO; Golden CO.

PUBLIC SERVICE CREDIT UNION
7055 East Evans Avenue, Denver CO 80224. 303/691-2345. **Fax:** 303/691-8408. **Contact:** Human Resources. **E-mail address:** jobs@pscu.org. **World Wide Web address:** http://www.pscu.org. **Description:** A credit union. Founded in 1938. **Positions advertised include:** Member Service Representative. **Other area locations include:** Canon City CO; Centennial CO; Clifton CO; Colorado Springs CO.

U.S. BANK
918 17th Street, Denver CO 80202. 303/585-7340. **Contact:** Human Resources. **World Wide Web address:** http://www.usbank.com. **Description:** Provides banking and mortgage credit services. **Positions advertised include:** Account Process Coordinator; Operations Manager; Personal Banker; Relationship Business Associate; Retail Support Analyst.

U.S. FEDERAL RESERVE BANK OF KANSAS CITY
1020 16th Street, Denver CO 80202. 303/572-2300. **Contact:** Human Resources. **World Wide Web address:** http://www.kc.frb.org. **Description:** A branch bank of the Federal Reserve System, which consists of 12 regional Federal Reserve banks that, along with the Federal Reserve Board of Governors in Washington DC and the Federal Open Market Committee, comprise the Federal Reserve System, the nation's central bank. As the nation's central bank, the Federal Reserve is charged with three major responsibilities: monetary policy, banking supervision and regulation, and processing payments. **Positions advertised include:** Assistant Examiner; Protection Officer; Research Associate; Sr. Administrative Assistant.

UNIVERSITY OF COLORADO FEDERAL CREDIT UNION
2900 Diagonal Highway, Boulder CO 80301. 303/443-4672. **Fax:** 303/595-0436. **Contact:** Human Resources. **World Wide Web address:** http://www.uofcfcu.com. **Description:** A credit union serving the entire state. **Positions advertised include:** AVP, Consumer Lending; VP, Finance. **Other area locations include:** Longmont CO; Lafayette CO; Denver CO.

WACHOVIA SECURITIES
1200 17th Street, Suite 2500, Denver CO 80202. 303/628-8000. **Contact:** Human Resources. **World Wide Web address:** http://www.wachoviasec.com. **Description:** An investment and securities

firm specializing in real estate investing. **Corporate headquarters location:** Richmond VA.

WELLS FARGO BANK
1740 Broadway, Denver CO 80290. 303/861-8811. **Contact:** Human Resources. **World Wide Web address:** http://www.wellsfargo.com. **Description:** A diversified financial institution with over $234 billion in assets serving over 17 million customers through 5,300 independent locations worldwide. The company also maintains several stand-alone ATMs and branches within retail outlets. Services include community banking, credit and debit cards, home equity and mortgage loans, online banking, student loans, and insurance. Wells Fargo also offers a complete line of commercial and institutional financial services. Founded in 1852. **Corporate headquarters location:** San Francisco CA. **Other U.S. locations:** Nationwide. **International locations:** Worldwide. **Operations at this facility include:** This location is a full-service bank. **Parent company:** Wells Fargo & Company. **Listed on:** New York Stock Exchange. **Stock exchange symbol:** WFC. **Annual sales/revenues:** More than $100 million. **Number of employees worldwide:** 104,000.

WELLS FARGO BUSINESS CREDIT
1700 Lincoln Street, Suite 21, Denver CO 80203. 303/864-6593. **Contact:** Human Resources. **World Wide Web address:** http://www.wellsfargo.com. **Description:** A diversified financial institution with over $234 billion in assets. Wells Fargo serves over 17 million customers through 5,300 independent locations worldwide. The company also maintains several stand-alone ATMs and branches within retail outlets. Services include community banking, credit and debit cards, home equity and mortgage loans, online banking, student loans, and insurance. Wells Fargo also offers a complete line of commercial and institutional financial services. Founded in 1852. **Positions advertised include:** Sr. Business Relationship Manager; Lending Manager; Business Associate. **Corporate headquarters location:** San Francisco CA. **Other U.S. locations:** Nationwide. **International locations:** Worldwide. **Operations at this facility include:** Regional Headquarters; Sales; Service. **Parent company:** Wells Fargo & Company. **Listed on:** New York Stock Exchange. **Stock exchange symbol:** WFC. **Annual sales/revenues:** More than $100 million. **Number of employees worldwide:** 104,000.

BIOTECHNOLOGY, PHARMACEUTICALS, AND SCIENTIFIC R&D

You can expect to find the following types of companies in this section:
Clinical Labs • Lab Equipment Manufacturers • Pharmaceutical Manufacturers and Distributors

AMGEN INC.
4000 Nelson Road, Longmont CO 80503. 303/401-1000. **Contact:** Human Resources. **World Wide Web address:** http://www.amgen.com. **Description:** Researches, develops, manufactures, and markets human therapeutics based on advanced cellular and molecular biology. **Positions advertised include:** Quality Engineer; Sr. Engineer; Validation Engineer; Technical Writer; Sr. IS Project Manager; QA Specialist; Materials Coordinator. **Corporate headquarters location:** Thousand Oaks CA. **Other area locations:** Boulder CO. **Listed on:** NASDAQ. **Stock exchange symbol:** AMGN.

ASPENBIO, INC.
1585 South Perry Street, Castle Rock CO 80104. 303/794-2000. **Contact:** Human Resources. **E-mail address:** info@aspenbioinc.com. **World Wide Web address:** http://www.aspenbioinc.com. **Description:** The company is dedicated to the discovery, development, manufacture and marketing of novel patented products that enhance the reproductive efficiency of animals. The company was founded to produce purified proteins for diagnostic applications and is now a leading supplier of human hormones to many of the nation's largest medical diagnostic companies and research institutions. **Positions advertised include:** Manager of Diagnostic Protein Sales.

BAXTER BIOLIFE PLASMA SERVICES
519 Sable Boulevard, Aurora CO 80011. 303/367-9660. **Contact:** Human Resources. **Description:** BioLife Plasma Services collects high quality plasma that is processed into life-saving plasma-based therapies. **Positions advertised include:** Phlebotomist; Medical Historian. **Corporate headquarters location:** Deerfield IL. **Parent company:** Baxter International, Inc. **Listed on:** New York Stock Exchange. **Stock exchange symbol:** BAX. **Number of employees at this location:** 200. **Number of employees worldwide:** 48,000.

BOLDER BIOTECHNOLOGY, INC.
4056 Youngfield Street, Wheat Ridge CO 80033. 303/420-4420. **Fax:** 303/420-4426. **Contact:** Human Resources. **World Wide Web address:** http://www.bolderbio.com. **Description:** Bolder BioTechnology, Inc. uses advanced protein engineering technologies to create proprietary human protein pharmaceuticals with enhanced therapeutic properties. Products are intended for the treatment of hematological and endocrine disorders,

cancer, and infectious disease. **Positions advertised include:** Scientist; Research Associate.

COLORADO SERUM COMPANY
4950 York Street, P.O. Box 16428, Denver CO 80216. 303/295-7527. **Fax:** 303/295-1923. **Contact:** Joe Huff, President. **E-mail address:** colorado-serum@colorado-serum.com. **World Wide Web address:** http://www.colorado-serum.com. **Description:** Develops and manufactures veterinary serums and biologics.

THE HACH COMPANY
P.O. Box 389, Loveland CO 80539-0389. 970/669-3050. **Fax:** 970/669-2932. **Contact:** Human Resources. **World Wide Web address:** http://www.hach.com. **Description:** Manufactures and sells laboratory instruments, process analyzers, and test kits that analyze the chemical content and other properties of water and other aqueous solutions. The company also produces chemicals for use with its manufactured instruments and test kits. **Positions advertised include:** Key Accounts Manager; Catalog Marketing Manager; Web Manager; Business Development Manager; Export Credit Administrator; Telesales Supervisor; Production Engineer; Project Manager. **Corporate headquarters location:** This location. **Other U.S. locations:** Ames IA. **International locations:** Germany. **Parent company:** Danaher Corporation. **Number of employees at this location:** 500. **Number of employees nationwide:** 800.

HEMOGENIX, INC.
4405 North Chestnut Street, Suite D, Colorado Springs CO 80907. 719/264-6250. **Fax:** 719/264-6253. **Contact:** Human Resources. **World Wide Web address:** http://www.hemogenix.com. **E-mail address:** positions@hemogenix.com. **Description:** Develops stem-cell hemotoxicity testing methods. Founded in 2000.

NATURESMART/NBTY
1500 East 128 Avenue, Thornton CO 80241. 303/474-2300. **Contact:** Personnel. **World Wide Web address:** http://www.nbty.com. **Description:** Develops, manufactures, and markets vitamins, nutrients, and herbal supplements.

OSI PHARMACEUTICALS, INC.
2860 Wilderness Place, Boulder CO 80301. 303/546-7600. **Fax:** 303/444-0672. **Contact:** Human Resources. **E-mail address:** employment@osip.com. **World Wide Web address:** http://www.osip.com. **Description:** A biopharmaceutical company dedicated to the discovery, development, and commercialization of treatments for human diseases. The company's business is focused on making new therapies available to patients, physicians, and health care systems. The company has also developed treatments for diseases caused by HIV, the Hepatitis B virus, the Herpes simplex virus, human papillomavirus, and the influenza virus. **Positions advertised include:** Director, clinical Research; Director, Regulatory Affairs; Director, Clinical

Operations; Clinical Research Associate. **Corporate headquarters location:** Melville NY. **International locations:** UK. **Listed on:** NASDAQ. **Stock exchange symbol:** OSIP

QLT USA, INC.
2579 Midpoint Drive, Fort Collins CO 80525. 970/482-5868. **Contact:** Human Resources. **E-mail address:** recruitingUSA@qltinc.com. **World Wide Web address:** http://www.qltinc.com. **Description:** A global biopharmaceutical company specializing in developing treatments for cancer, eye diseases and dermatological and urological conditions. **Positions advertised include:** Senior Research Associate; Scientist; Engineering Technician; Quality Control Analyst; Material Handler; Quality Assurance Associate. **Corporate headquarters location:** Vancouver British Columbia Canada.

QUEST DIAGNOSTICS INCORPORATED
695 South Broadway, Denver CO 80209. 303/899-6000. **Fax:** 303/899-6123. **Contact:** Human Resources. **World Wide Web address:** http://www.questdiagnostics.com. **Description:** One of the largest clinical laboratories in North America, providing a broad range of clinical laboratory services to health care clients, which include physicians, hospitals, clinics, dialysis centers, pharmaceutical companies, and corporations. The company offers and performs tests on blood, urine, and other bodily fluids and tissues to provide information for health and well-being. **Positions advertised include:** Cytology Supervisor; Billing Coordinator; Medical Technolgist. **Corporate headquarters location:** Teterboro NJ. **Other U.S. locations:** Nationwide. **Listed on:** New York Stock Exchange. **Stock exchange symbol:** DGX.

REPLIDYNE, INC.
1450 Infinite Drive, Louisville CO 80027. 303/996-5500. **Fax:** 303/996-5599. **Contact:** Personnel Department. **E-mail address:** employment@replidyne.com. **World Wide Web address:** http://www.replidyne.com. **Description:** A specialty pharmaceutical company focused on developing and commercializing innovative anti-infective products.

ROCHE COLORADO
2075 North 55th Street, Boulder CO 80301. 303/442-1926. **Fax:** 303/938-6413. **Contact:** Human Resources. **E-mail address:** boulder.hr@roche.com. **World Wide Web address:** http://www.rochecolorado.com. **Description:** An international drug development company focusing on oncology. **Positions advertised include:** Disbursement Accountant; Executive Legal Assistant. **Parent company:** Hoffman-LaRoche Inc.

SANDOZ INC MANUFACTURING
2555 West Midway Boulevard, Broomfield CO 80038-0446. 303/466-2400. **Contact:** Human Resources. **World Wide Web address:** http://www.us.sandoz.com. **Description:** Manufactures and distributes generic pharmaceutical products. **Positions advertised include:** Senior

Distribution Technician; Lead QC Chemist; Tech Services Scientist; Quality Engineer; Packaging Supervisor; QA Support Specialist. **Parent company:** Novartis Group.

SCIONA, INC.
1401 Walnut Street, Suite 203, Boulder CO 80302. 303/442-4300. **Fax:** 303/442-4301. **Contact:** Director of Operations. **E-mail address:** info@sciona.com. **World Wide Web address:** http://www.sciona.com. **Description:** Sciona researches and develops DNA screens for common gene variants that affect an individual's response to food, medications and the environment. Sciona's field of genetic personalization is a discipline aimed at creating products and services tailored to an individual's genetic makeup.

SIRNA THERAPEUTICS, INC.
2950 Wilderness Place, Boulder CO 80301. 303/449-6500. **Fax:** 303/449-6995. **Contact:** Human Resources. **E-mail address:** jobs@sirna.com. **Description:** Sirna Therapeutics is a biotechnology company focused on developing therapeutics based on RNA interference (RNAi) technology, a field of biology and medicine. The Company is using its proprietary nucleic acid technology and expertise to develop a new class of RNAi-based therapeutics that target human diseases and conditions. **Positions advertised include:** Scientist. **Corporate headquarters location:** San Francisco CA.

UNIVERSITY CORPORATION FOR ATMOSPHERIC RESEARCH
NATIONAL CENTER FOR ATMOSPHERIC RESEARCH
P.O. Box 3000, Boulder CO 80307-3000. 303/497-1000. **Physical address:** 1850 Table Mesa Drive, Boulder CO 80305. **Contact:** Human Resources. **World Wide Web address:** http://www.ucar.edu. **Description:** A nonprofit consortium of North American institutions that grants Ph.D. degrees in atmospheric and related sciences. The organization manages the National Center for Atmospheric Research, a research and facilities center sponsored by the National Science Foundation. UCAR also manages over a dozen other programs that enhance the conduct and applications of atmospheric research. **Positions advertised include:** software Engineer/Programmer.

BUSINESS SERVICES & NON-SCIENTIFIC RESEARCH

You can expect to find the following types of companies in this section:
Adjustment and Collection Services • Cleaning, Maintenance, and Pest Control Services • Credit Reporting Services • Detective, Guard, and Armored Car Services • Security Systems Services • Miscellaneous Equipment Rental and Leasing • Secretarial and Court Reporting Services

---

ACS STATE & LOCAL SOLUTIONS, INC.
1999 Broadway, Suite 2700, Denver CO 80202. 303/295-2860. **Contact:** Human Resources. **E-mail address:** recruiter@acs-inc.com. **World Wide Web address:** http://www.acs-inc.com. **Description:** An IT and business services consultancy. Founded in 1988. **Positions advertised include:** Sr. Consultant, Investment Analyst; Business Analyst Manager; Sr. Consultant Retirement Actuary. **Corporate headquarters location:** Dallas TX.

ADT SECURITY SERVICES
14200 East Exposition Avenue, Aurora CO 80012. 303/338-8200. **Contact:** Human Resources. **World Wide Web address:** http://www.adt.com. **Description:** Sells and installs security systems and provides electronic monitoring and maintenance services for homes and businesses. ADT has approximately 170,000 subscribers. Founded in 1993. **Positions advertised include:** Sales Representative. **Other area locations:** Denver CO. **Other U.S. locations:** Miami FL; Atlanta GA; Shreveport LA; Dallas TX; Houston TX. **Number of employees nationwide:** 685.

AON INNOVATIVE SOLUTIONS
13922 Denver West Parkway, Building 54, Golden CO 80401. 303/279-2900. **Contact:** Director of Human Resources. **World Wide Web address:** http://www.aon.com. **Description:** A provider of third-party administrative services including claims adjudication, customer service in-bound call handling, telemarketing, and fulfillment/order taking. **Positions advertised include:** Sr. Programmer/Analyst; Sr. Staff Accountant. **Corporate headquarters location:** Chicago IL. **Other U.S. locations:** Nationwide. **International locations:** Worldwide. **Parent company:** Aon Corporation. **Operations at this facility include:** Administration; Sales; Service. **Listed on:** New York Stock Exchange. **Stock exchange symbol:** AOC. **Number of employees at this location:** 200.

AUTOMATIC LAUNDRY COMPANY
P.O. Box 39365, Denver CO 80239. 303/371-9274. **Contact:** Human Resources. **World Wide Web address:** http://www.automaticlaundry.com.

Description: Leases laundry room space and installs coin-operated laundry equipment in apartment complexes.

BRINK'S INC.
6703 East 47th Avenue Drive, Denver CO 80216. 303/355-2071. **Fax:** 303-355-9954. **Contact:** Human Resources. **World Wide Web address:** www.brinksinc.com. **Description:** An armored security service specializing in transporting currency. **Corporate headquarters location:** Dallas TX.

COMPUTER RESEARCH, INC.
10170 Church Ranch Way, Suite 300, Westminster CO 80021-6061. 303/297-9200. **Contact:** Human Resources. **E-mail address:** crimail@crixnet.com. **World Wide Web address:** http://www.crix.com. **Description:** Provides data processing, accounting, and record-keeping services for approximately 60 investment securities firms and banks throughout the country. Clients use Computer Research, Inc. systems to maintain their customer accounts and firm records in compliance with financial industry and regulatory agency reporting requirements. These systems include a number of proprietary computer programs that the company maintains and operates, linking clients to its data centers in Pittsburgh and Denver (this location.) The programs provide online retrieval, reports, and records on a day-to-day basis using data supplied by the clients. **Positions advertised include:** Mainframe Developer; Applications Developer; CSR.

FIRST DATA CORPORATION
6200 South Quebec Street, Greenwood Village CO 80111. 303/488-8000. **Contact:** Human Resources. **World Wide Web address:** http://www.firstdata.com. **Description:** A holding company. Through its subsidiaries, First Data provides credit card issuing and merchant transaction processing services, e-commerce solutions, money transfers, and other business services. **NOTE:** Apply online. **Positions advertised include:** Sr. Tax Specialist; Manager, Content Management; Project Manager; Sr. Financial Analyst. **Corporate headquarters location:** This location. **Subsidiaries include:** First Data Resources. **Other U.S. locations:** Phoenix AZ; Palo Alto CA; Sunrise FL; Atlanta GA; Omaha NE; Nashville TN. **Listed on:** New York Stock Exchange. **Stock exchange symbol:** FDC.

INFORMATION HANDLING SERVICES (IHS)
15 Inverness Way East, Englewood CO 80112. 303/790-0600. **Contact:** Director of Human Resources. **E-mail address:** info@ihs.com. **World Wide Web address:** http://www.ihs.com. **Description:** Assimilates and indexes technical, engineering, federal, and regulatory information and transfers it to microform and electronic media. **Positions advertised include:** Senior Systems Engineer; Production Clerk. **Corporate headquarters location:** This location. **Parent company:** Information Handling Services Group.

LOOMIS FARGO & COMPANY
600 South Cherry Street, Suite 314, Denver CO 80246. 303/825-0376. **Fax:** 303/355-6383. **Contact:** Personnel. **E-mail address:** employment@loomisfargo.com. **World Wide Web address:** http://www.loomisfargo.com. **Description:** An armored security service specializing in transporting currency. **Corporate headquarters location:** Houston TX. **Other area locations:** Colorado Springs CO; Fort Collins CO; Grand Junction CO; Vail CO. **Other U.S. locations:** Nationwide.

THE MITRE CORPORATION
1155 Academy Park Loop, Colorado Springs CO 80910-3716. 719/574-8000. **Contact:** Human Resources. **World Wide Web address:** http://www.mitre.org. **Description:** The MITRE Corporation is a not-for-profit organization chartered to work in the public interest in the areas of systems engineering, information technology, operational concepts, and enterprise modernization. **Positions advertised include:** Information Security Engineer; Information Systems Engineer. **Number of employees worldwide:** 5,700.

THE PRODUCT LINE, INC.
5000 Lima Street, Denver CO 80239. 720/374-3800. **Fax:** 720/374-3720. **Contact:** Betti Scronce, Director of Human Resources. **E-mail address:** tpljob@tpli.com. **World Wide Web address:** http://www.tpli.com. **Description:** Provides call center services to national and international corporations. Founded in 1982. **Corporate headquarters location:** This location. **Operations at this facility include:** Administration; Sales; Service. **Listed on:** Privately held. **Number of employees at this location:** 300.

RENTAL SERVICE CORP.
481 West 84th Avenue, Thornton CO 80260. 303/428-7466. **Contact:** Human Resources. **World Wide Web address:** http://www.rentalservice.com. **Description:** A general construction equipment rental company. **Parent company:** Atlas Copco Group.

SHAMROCK DELIVERY SERVICES
6484 South Quebec Street, Englewood CO 80111. 303/220-1700. **Fax:** 303/220-0752. **Contact:** Human Resources. **World Wide Web address:** http://www.shamrockdelivery.com. **Description:** A delivery/courier service. Founded in 1989. **Positions advertised include:** Driver.

SOURCE ONE MANAGEMENT, INC.
1225 17th Street, Suite 1500, Denver CO 80202. 303/832-8600. **Fax:** 303/832-1910. **Contact:** Director of Human Resources. **E-mail address:** resumes@sourceone.com. **World Wide Web address:** http://www.sourceone.com. **Description:** Provides staffing for government and private sector management and information technology contracts. **Positions advertised include:** Records Clerk. **Corporate headquarters location:** This location. **Other U.S. locations:** DC; MT; ND; SD; WA. **Operations at this facility include:** Administration;

Service. **Listed on:** Privately held. **Number of employees at this location:** 15. **Number of employees nationwide:** 200.

STARTEK, INC.
100 Garfield Street, Suite 300, Denver CO 80206. 303/262-4500. **Contact:** Human Resources Department. **E-mail address:** jobs@startek.com. **World Wide Web address:** http://www.startek.com. **Description:** Provides process management services to *Fortune* 500 customers and other major corporations worldwide. Services include logistics management, e-commerce support, Internet support, technical support, order processing, packaging, distribution, inventory management, product assembly, manufacturing, fulfillment, and customer support. **Positions advertised include:** Client Service Director; Corporate Procurement Director; Sr. Financial Analyst; Director of Corporate Strategy; Director of Compensation and Benefits. **Corporate headquarters location:** This location. **Other U.S. locations:** LA; TX; VA; IL; WY; OK. **International locations:** Canada. **Listed on:** New York Stock Exchange. **Stock exchange symbol:** SRT.

Z-AXIS CORPORATION
5445 DTC Parkway, Suite 450, Greenwood Village CO 80111. 303/713-0200. **Fax:** 303/713-0299. **Contact:** Heidi O'Neil, Controller. **E-mail address:** jobs@zaxis.com. **World Wide Web address:** http://www.zaxis.com. **Description:** Designs visual evidence for legal cases using computer-generated animation and graphics. **Positions advertised include:** Flash/Lightwave Animator. **Corporate headquarters location:** This location. **Other U.S. locations:** San Francisco CA; Chicago IL; New York NY.

CHARITIES AND SOCIAL SERVICES

You can expect to find the following types of companies in this section:
Social and Human Service Agencies • Job Training and Vocational Rehabilitation Services • Nonprofit Organizations

---

COMPASSION INTERNATIONAL
12290 Voyager Parkway, Colorado Springs CO 80921. 719/487-7000. **Contact:** Recruitment. **World Wide Web address:** http://www.ci.org. **Description:** A Christian organization that aids poverty-stricken children throughout the world. **Positions advertised include:** Corporate Audit Specialist; Editorial Specialist; Feature Writer Specialist; International Communications Specialist; IT Software Development Specialist.

DEVELOPMENTAL DISABILITY RESOURCE CENTER (DDRC)
11177 West 8th Avenue, Suite 300, Westminster CO 80215. 303/233-3363. **Contact:** Human Resources. **World Wide Web address:** http://www.ddrcco.com. **Description:** A nonprofit organization that provides services to individuals with developmental disabilities. **Positions advertised include:** Home Host Provider; Vocational Instructor Supervisor; Early Intervention Speech/Language Therapist.

DIVISION FOR DEVELOPMENTAL DISABILITIES
3824 West Princeton Circle, Denver CO 80236. 303/866-7450. **Fax:** 303/866-7470. **Contact:** Kerry Stern, Acting Director. **Description:** A nonprofit organization that provides services to individuals with developmental disabilities.

EAST DENVER YMCA
3540 East 31st Avenue, Denver CO 80205. 303/322-7761. **Contact:** Human Resources. **World Wide Web address:** http://www.ymca.com. **Description:** One of the nation's largest and most comprehensive nonprofit service organizations. The YMCA provides health and fitness, social and personal development, sports and recreation, education and career development, and camps and conferences to children, youths, adults, the elderly, families, disabled individuals, refugees and foreign nationals, YMCA residents, and community residents through a broad range of specific programs.

GOODWILL INDUSTRIES OF DENVER
6850 North Federal Boulevard, Denver CO 80221. 303/650-7700. **Fax:** 303/650-7749. **Contact:** Human Resources. **E-mail address:** info@goodwilldenver.org. **World Wide Web address:** http://www.goodwilldenver.org. **Description:** Operates 1,400 thrift stores nationwide and provides employment training for the disabled and the disadvantaged. **Other U.S. locations:** Nationwide. **CEO:** Thomas

Welker. **Annual sales/revenues:** $5 - $10 million. **Number of employees at this location:** 290.

MARCH OF DIMES BIRTH DEFECTS FOUNDATION
1325 South Colorado Boulevard, Suite B508, Denver CO 80222. 303/692-0011. **Contact:** Director. **E-mail address:** co611@modimes.org. **World Wide Web address:** http://www.modimes.org. **Description:** March of Dimes operates the Campaign for Healthier Babies that includes programs of research, community services, education, and advocacy. March of Dimes chapters across the country work with their communities to determine and meet the needs of women, babies, and families. Through specially designed programs, women are provided access to prenatal care. **Corporate headquarters location:** White Plains NY.

MILE HIGH UNITED WAY
2505 18th Street, Denver CO 80211-3939. 303/433-8383. **Contact:** Human Resources. **World Wide Web address:** http://www.unitedwaydenver.org. **Description:** A nonprofit organization made up of volunteers and human service professionals. Mile High United Way provides disaster relief, emergency food and shelter, and rehabilitation and development services to needy individuals. Founded in 1887. **NOTE:** Entry-level positions are offered. **Office hours:** Monday - Friday, 8:00 a.m. - 5:00 p.m. **Annual sales/revenues:** $21 - $50 million. **Number of employees at this location:** 65.

PARKPLACE RETIREMENT COMMUNITY
111 Emerson Street, Denver CO 80218. 303/744-0400. **Contact:** Human Resources. **World Wide Web address:** http://www.arclp.com. **Description:** A retirement community. Founded in 1978. **NOTE:** Search and apply for positions online. **Corporate headquarters location:** Brentwood TN. **Parent company:** American Retirement Corporation. **Listed on:** New York Stock Exchange. **Stock exchange symbol:** ACR.

SENIORS INC.
5840 East Evans Avenue, Denver CO 80222. 303/300-6900. **Fax:** 303/300-6950. **Contact:** Human Resources. **World Wide Web address:** http://www.seniorsinc.org. **Description:** Provides programs and services for older persons that promote and enhance independent living. Founded in 1969. **Positions advertised include:** Resource Development Associate Manager. **Special programs:** Internships. **Corporate headquarters location:** This location. **Operations at this facility include:** Administration; Sales; Service. **Number of employees at this location:** 30.

UNITED CEREBRAL PALSY OF COLORADO, INC.
2200 South Jasmine Street, Denver CO 80222. 303/691-9339. **Fax:** 303/691-0846. **Contact:** Human Resources. **World Wide Web address:** http://www.cpco.org. **Description:** A nonprofit organization that provides education, childcare, and employment services, as well as information and referrals. The organization is also engaged in donation pickup.

Corporate headquarters location: This location. **Number of employees at this location:** 30.

THE URBAN LEAGUE OF METROPOLITAN DENVER

5900 East 39th Avenue, Denver CO 80207. 303/388-5861. **Fax:** 303/388-3523. **Contact:** Personnel. **World Wide Web address:** http://www.denverurbanleague.org. **Description:** A nonprofit organization that sponsors a variety of social programs including employment services and career and outplacement counseling. **Corporate headquarters location:** This location.

CHEMICALS, RUBBER, AND PLASTICS

You can expect to find the following types of companies in this section:
Adhesives, Detergents, Inks, Paints, Soaps, Varnishes • Agricultural Chemicals and Fertilizers • Carbon and Graphite Products • Chemical Engineering Firms • Industrial Gases

DIAMOND VOGEL PAINT
4500 East 48th Avenue, P.O. Box 16388, Denver CO 80216-0388. 303/333-4499. **Contact:** Human Resources. **E-mail address:** hrmanager@vogelpaint.com. **World Wide Web address:** http://www.diamondvogel.com. **Description:** Produces a variety of paints, stains, and resins. **Corporate headquarters location:** Orange City IA.

GATES CORPORATION
1551 Wewatta Street, Denver CO 80202. 303/744-1911. **Physical address:** 990 South Broadway, Denver CO 80209. **Contact:** Human Resources Department. **World Wide Web address:** http://www.gates.com. **Description:** An international developer, manufacturer, and distributor of a broad range of rubber and plastic products. The company also operates area subsidiaries engaged in the production of automotive and heavy-duty batteries. **Positions advertised include:** Account Rep; ERP Architect; HSE Specialist. **Corporate headquarters location:** This location.

ORICA LIMITED
33101 East Quincy Avenue, Watkins CO 80137. 303/268-5000. **Fax:** 303/268-5250. **Contact:** Human Resources. **E-mail address:** jobs@orica.com. **World Wide Web address:** http://www.orica.com. **Description:** Manufactures commercial explosives, nitrogen products, paints, fertilizers, chemicals, and plastics. **Corporate headquarters location:** Australia. **International locations:** Worldwide. **Number of employees worldwide:** 10,000.

COMMUNICATIONS:TELECOMMUNICATIONS AND BROADCASTING

You can expect to find the following types of companies in this section:
Cable/Pay Television Services • Communications Equipment • Radio and Television Broadcasting Stations • Telephone, Telegraph, and Other Message Communications

---

ADELPHIA
5619 DTC Parkway, Greenwood Village CO 80111. 303/268-6300. **Contact:** Human Resources. **World Wide Web address:** http://www.adelphia.com. **Description:** The fifth largest U.S. cable television company, serving customers in 31 states and Puerto Rico. **Corporate headquarters location:** This location. **Positions advertised include:** Service Technician; Retention & Sales Specialist; Customer Care Representative; Service Technician.

ANIXTER
14509 East 33rd Place, Suite A, Aurora CO 80011. 303/373-9200. **Contact:** Inside Sales Manager. **World Wide Web address:** http://www.anixter.com. **Description:** A value-added provider of industrial wire and cabling solutions that support voice and data applications. Solutions include customized pre- and postsale services and products from the world's leading manufacturers. Anixter operates delivery through a global distribution network with 160 sales/service locations. Founded in 1957. **Corporate headquarters location:** Skokie IL. **Other U.S. locations:** Nationwide. **International locations:** Worldwide. **Parent company:** Anixter International. **Listed on:** New York Stock Exchange. **Stock exchange symbol:** AXE. **Number of employees nationwide:** 4,100.

AVAYA INC.
1300 West 120th Avenue, Westminster CO 80234-2795. 303/538-1200. **Contact:** Human Resources. **World Wide Web address:** http://www.avaya.com. **Description:** Avaya Inc. manufactures communications products including switching, transmission, fiber-optic cable, wireless systems, and operations systems to supply the needs of telephone companies and other communications services providers. **Positions advertised include:** Software Developer; Software Engineer; System Engineer; Security Consultant; Converged Solutions Expert; Branch Architect; Materials Planner; Product Manager. **Corporate headquarters location:** Basking Ridge NJ. **Other U.S. locations:** Nationwide. **International locations:** Worldwide. **Operations at this facility include:** This location is primarily a research and development facility. **Listed on:** New York Stock Exchange. **Stock exchange symbol:** AV.

BALL CORPORATION
10 Longs Peak Drive, P.O. Box 5000, Broomfield CO 80021-2510. 303/469-3131. **Contact:** Human Resources. **World Wide Web address:** http://www.ball.com. **Description:** Produces metal and plastic packaging products for foods and beverages, and provides aerospace and communications products and services to government and commercial customers. **Positions advertised include:** Sr. Systems Analyst; Sr. Auditor; Manager, Corporate Payroll; Process Engineer. **Corporate headquarters location:** This location. **Listed on:** New York Stock Exchange. **Stock exchange symbol:** BLL.

CBS RADIO
1560 Broadway, Suite 1100, Denver CO 80202. 303/832-5665. **Fax:** 303/832-7000. **Contact:** Personnel. **World Wide Web address:** http://www.cbsradio.com. **Description:** Operates a radio station broadcasting oldies and classical music. **Positions advertised include:** Assistant Controller. **Corporate headquarters location:** New York NY.

CBEYOND COMMUNICATIONS
3131 South Vaughn Way, Suite 400, Aurora CO 80014. 866/424-5415. **Contact:** Human Resources. **World Wide Web address:** http://www.cbeyond.net. **Description:** Provides an integrated package of local and long distance telephony services, high-speed, T-1 Internet access, and Internet-based applications for small business customers. **Positions advertised include:** Sales Associate. **Corporate headquarters location:** Atlanta GA. **Other U.S. locations:** Dallas TX; Houston TX; Oak Brook IL; Los Angeles CA.

CINGULAR WIRELESS
1001 16th Street, Suite C-1, Denver CO 80265-0003. 303/623-0691. **Contact:** Human Resources. **World Wide Web address:** http://www.cingular.com. **Description:** Cingular is a major cellular telephone company providing nationwide service. **Positions advertised include:** Business Care Manager; RF Support Manager; Corporate Account Executive.

GLOBAL CROSSING CONFERENCING
1499 West 121st Avenue, Westminster CO 80234-0076. 303/633-3000. **Contact:** Director of Human Resources. **Description:** A supplier of audio teleconferencing equipment and services in North America and selected overseas markets. Global Crossing Conferencing provides operator-assisted and automatic audio teleconferencing services.

ICG COMMUNICATIONS, INC.
161 Inverness Drive West, Englewood CO 80112. 303/414-5000. **Fax:** 303/414-8805. **Contact:** Human Resources. **World Wide Web address:** http://www.icgcom.com. **Description:** Provides data and voice network communication services. Founded in 1956. **Positions advertised include:** Sr. Account Executive. **Other area locations:** Aurora CO; Colorado Springs CO. **Other U.S. locations:** Nationwide.

ITC TELECOM
12934 Rockbridge Circle, Colorado Springs CO 80921. 877/482-8266. **Fax:** 719/262-9981. **Contact:** Human Resources. **World Wide Web address:** http://www.itctelecom.com. **Description:** Offers services including computer and telephone cabling, business telephone systems (installation, maintenance, troubleshooting, configuration, etc.), computer/telephone integration, voice mail, auto attendant, automatic call distribution, interactive voice response (ivr), wireless communications. **Other U.S. locations:** Bayville NJ.

LEVEL 3 COMMUNICATIONS, INC.
1025 Eldorado Boulevard, Broomfield CO 80021. 720/888-1000. **Contact:** Human Resources. **World Wide Web address:** http://www.level3.com. **Description:** Level 3 is an international communications and information services company. The company operates one of the largest Internet backbones in the world, is one of the largest providers of wholesale dial-up service to ISPs in North America and is the primary provider of Internet connectivity for millions of broadband subscribers. **Positions advertised include:** Director of IT Resource and Portfolio Management; Analyst; Project Manager; Associate, Corporate Strategy; Sr. Analyst; Financial Analyst; Sr. VoIP Network Engineer; Associate, Corporate Development. **Listed on:** NASDAQ. **Stock exchange symbol:** LVLT.

LIBERTY MEDIA CORPORATION
12300 Liberty Boulevard, Englewood CO 80112. 720/875-5400. **Contact:** Human Resources. **World Wide Web address:** http://www.libertymedia.com. **Description:** A holding company that owns electronic retailing, media, communications, and entertainment businesses and investments, including QVC, Encore, and Starz. **Corporate headquarters location:** This location. **Listed on:** New York Stock Exchange. **Stock exchange symbol:** L.

QWEST COMMUNICATIONS
1801 California Street, Denver CO 80202. 303/992-1400. **Recorded jobline:** 303/896-7683. **Contact:** Human Resources. **World Wide Web address:** http://www.qwest.com. **Description:** A long-distance telecommunications carrier that provides a broad array of domestic and international voice, data, and Internet services to commercial and residential customers. Qwest Communications provides service to customers through its network of digital fiber-optic facilities. **Positions advertised include:** Accountant; Sr. Process Analyst; Lead IT Project Manager; Sr. Attorney; Product Manager; Staff Engineer. **Corporate headquarters location:** This location. **Listed on:** New York Stock Exchange. **Stock exchange symbol:** Q.

STARS ENTERTAINMENT GROUP LLC
P.O. Box 6542, Englewood CO 80155. 720/852-7700. **Physical address:** 8900 Liberty Circle, Englewood CO 80112. **Fax:** 720/852-5891. **Contact:** Human Resources. **World Wide Web address:** http://starzencore.com. **Description:** Operates the Encore and Starz!

premium cable movie channels. **Positions advertised include:** Acceptance Testing/System Analyst; Sr. Manager, Marketing; Payroll Administrator; Enterprise Service Business Administrator; Director, E-Marketing and New Media; Sr. Creative Director; Manager, Program Planning and Scheduling; Materials Coordinator.

TIME WARNER TELECOM
P.O. Box 172567, Denver CO 80217-2567. 303/566-1000. **Physical address:** 10475 Park Meadows Drive, Littleton CO 80124. **Fax:** 303/566-1008. **Contact:** Human Resources. **E-mail address:** twtelecom.resumes@twcable.com. **World Wide Web address:** http://www.twtelecom.com. **Description:** Provides telecommunications services and products. Time Warner Telecom is engaged in data communication integration for businesses, local telephone service, and network communication. **Positions advertised include:** Sr. Accounting Manager; Product Manager; Training Coordinator; Sr. Tax Accountant; Sr. Communications Manager; Sr. Internal Auditor; IP Engineer; Sr. Systems Engineer. **Special programs:** Internships. **Corporate headquarters location:** This location. **Other U.S. locations:** Nationwide. **Parent company:** AOL Time Warner. **Listed on:** NASDAQ. **Stock exchange symbol:** AOL.

UNITEDGLOBALCOM, INC.
4643 South Ulster Street, Suite 1300, Denver CO 80237. 303/770-4001. **Fax:** 303/770-4207. **Contact:** Human Resources. **E-mail address:** hr@unitedglobal.com. **World Wide Web address:** http://www.unitedglobal.com. **Description:** UnitedGlobalCom provides integrated broadband television, telephone, and Internet access services. **Corporate headquarters location:** This location. **International locations:** Worldwide. **Listed on:** NASDAQ. **Stock exchange symbol:** UCOMA. **Chairman and CEO:** Gene W. Schneider.

VERIZON WIRELESS
8000 East Belleview Avenue, Greenwood Village CO 80111. 720/489-1223. **Contact:** Personnel. **World Wide Web address:** http://www.verizonwireless.com. **Description:** Verizon offers residential local and long-distance telephone services and Internet access; wireless service plans, cellular phones, and data services; a full-line of business services including Internet access, data services, and telecommunications equipment and services; and government network solutions including Internet access, data services, telecommunications equipment and services, and enhanced communications services. **Positions advertised include:** Assist, Retail Sales. **Corporate headquarters location:** Bedminster NJ. **Parent company:** Verizon Communications. **Listed on:** New York Stock Exchange. **Stock exchange symbol:** VZ.

COMPUTER HARDWARE, SOFTWARE, AND SERVICES

You can expect to find the following types of companies in this section:
Computer Components and Hardware Manufacturers • Consultants and Computer Training Companies • Internet and Online Service Providers • Networking and Systems Services • Repair Services/Rental and Leasing • Resellers, Wholesalers, and Distributors • Software Developers/Programming Services • Web Technologies

---

ADP SECURITIES INDUSTRY SOFTWARE (ADP/SIS)
dba ADP/SIS
4725 Independence Street, Wheat Ridge CO 80033. 303/590-6000. **Fax:** 303/590-6420. **Contact:** Human Resources. **World Wide Web address:** http://www.sis.adp.com. **Description:** Develops financial software for brokerage houses and related companies. **Positions advertised include:** Finance Director; Tandem Technical Consultant; Education Specialist.

AGI
7150 Campus Drive, Suite 260, Colorado Springs CO 80920. 719/573-2600. **Fax:** 719/573-9079. **Contact:** Human Resources. **E-mail address:** hr@agi.com. **World Wide Web address:** http://www.agi.com. **Description:** AGI provides analysis and visualization software to national security and space professionals for integrated analyses of land, sea, air, and space assets. **Corporate headquarters location:** Exton PA.

AT&T GOVERNMENT SOLUTIONS
985 Space Center Drive, Suite 310, Colorado Springs CO 80915. 719/596-5395. **Contact:** Human Resources. **World Wide Web address:** http://www.att.com/gov. **Description:** AT&T Government Solutions provides knowledge-based professional services and technology-based product solutions to government and commercial customers. AT&T Government Solutions also provides studies and analysis capabilities for policy development and planning; modeling and simulation of hardware and software used in real-time testing of sensor, weapon, and battlefield management command, control, and communication systems; and testing and evaluation. **NOTE:** Please see company Website for more details on applying for a position. **Positions advertised include:** Analyst; Intel Analyst; Project Manager. **Corporate headquarters location:** Santa Barbara CA. **Other U.S. locations:** Nationwide. **Operations at this facility include:** This location develops software for the U.S. government. **Parent company:** AT&T Corporation. **Listed on:** New York Stock Exchange. **Stock exchange symbol:** T. **Number of employees worldwide:** 1,300.

ALTIA
5030 Corporate Plaza Drive, Colorado Springs CO 80919. 719/598-4299. **Fax:** 719/598-4392. **Contact:** Human Resources. **E-mail address:** info@altia.com. **World Wide Web address:** http://www.altia.com. **Description:** Manufactures feature prototyping software for engineers and marketing professionals. **Corporate headquarters location:** This location.

ANALYSTS INTERNATIONAL CORPORATION (AIC)
5445 DTC Parkway, Suite 320 A, Englewood CO 80111. 303/721-6200. **Fax:** 303/721-6403. **Contact:** Manager of Human Resources. **World Wide Web address:** http://www.analysts.com. **Description:** AIC is an international, computer consulting firm. The company assists clients in developing systems using various programming languages and software. **Positions advertised include:** Sr. SQL Developer. **Corporate headquarters location:** Minneapolis MN. **Listed on:** NASDAQ. **Stock exchange symbol:** ANLY.

ASPEN SYSTEMS, INC.
3900 Youngfield Street, Wheat Ridge CO 80033-3865. 303/431-4606. **Fax:** 303/431-7196. **Contact:** Personnel. **World Wide Web address:** http://www.aspsys.com. **Description:** A manufacturer of high-performance workstations and servers for the OEM, VAR, and retail industries. **Positions advertised include:** Computer Production Engineer. **Corporate headquarters location:** This location. **Listed on:** Privately held.

AUTO-TROL TECHNOLOGY CORPORATION
12500 North Washington Street, Denver CO 80241-2400. 303/452-4919. **Toll-free phone:** 800/233-2882. **Fax:** 303/252-2249. **Recorded jobline:** 303/252-2007. **Contact:** Human Resources. **E-mail address:** careers@auto-trol.com. **World Wide Web address:** http://www.auto-trol.com. **Description:** Develops and markets software for the CAD/CAM/CAE, technical illustration, network configuration, and technical information management industries. Auto-Trol Technology Corporation integrates computer hardware, operating systems, proprietary graphics software, and applications software into systems for process plant design, civil engineering, discrete manufacturing, facilities layout and design, mechanical design, technical publishing, and network configuration management. **NOTE:** Entry-level positions are offered. **Positions advertised include:** Test Engineer; Consultant/Project Manager; Sales Representative. **Special programs:** Internships. **Corporate headquarters location:** This location. **Other U.S. locations:** Nationwide. **Operations at this facility include:** Administration; Marketing; Research and Development; Sales. **Annual sales/revenues:** $5 - $10 million. **Number of employees at this location:** 200.

BAKER ATLAS
1625 Broadway, Suite 1300, Denver CO 80202. 303/629-9250. **Contact:** Human Resources. **World Wide Web address:** http://www.bakeratlas.com. **Description:** Baker Atlas develops and

markets proprietary computer software, provides management services for the petroleum and mining industries, and provides electronic data processing services. **Positions advertised include:** Well Planner. **Corporate headquarters location:** Houston TX. **Operations at this facility include:** This location develops software for the oil and gas industries. **Parent company:** Baker Hughes. **Listed on:** New York Stock Exchange. **Stock exchange symbol:** BHI.

CGI-AMS
14033 Denver West Parkway, Golden CO 80401. 303/215-3500. **Contact:** Director of Human Resources. **World Wide Web address:** http://www.cgi.com. **Description:** Assists large organizations in solving complex management problems by applying information technology and systems engineering solutions. Industries and markets served include financial service institutions, insurance companies, federal agencies, state and local governments, colleges and universities, telecommunications firms, health care providers, and energy companies. **Listed on:** New York Stock Exchange. **Stock exchange symbol:** GIB.

CHESS INC.
410 Raritan Way, Denver CO 80204. 303/573-5133. **Contact:** Human Resources Department. **World Wide Web address:** http://www.chessinc.com. **Description:** Engaged in the repair and sale of computer equipment and printers. **Other area locations:** Colorado Springs CO. **Positions advertised include:** Account Executive; Parts Administrator; Administrative Assistant; Accounts Receivable Clerk; Service Technician.

CIBER, INC.
5251 DTC Parkway, Suite 600, Greenwood Village CO 80111. 303/779-6242. **Toll-free phone:** 800/242-3799. **Fax:** 303/779-6244. **Contact:** National Recruiting. **World Wide Web address:** http://www.ciber.com. **Description:** Provides consulting for client/server development, mainframe and legacy systems, industry-specific analysis, application-specific analysis, and network development. **Positions advertised include:** Systems Administrator; SQL DBA/ETL Architect; Business Intelligence Developer. **Corporate headquarters location:** This location. **International locations:** Canada; United Kingdom. **Listed on:** New York Stock Exchange. **Stock exchange symbol:** CBR.

COMPUTER SCIENCES CORPORATION (CSC)
460 Wooten Road, Suite 144, Colorado Springs CO 80916. 719/799-2880. **Contact:** Human Resources. **World Wide Web address:** http://www.csc.com. **Description:** An information technology services company offering systems design and integration; IT and business process outsourcing; applications software development; Web and application hosting; and management consulting. **Positions advertised include:** Network Administrator; Network Engineer; Computer Scientist. **Corporate headquarters location:** El Segundo CA. **Other area locations:** Denver CO; Broomfield CO; Greenwood Village CO. **Listed**

on: New York Stock Exchange. **Stock exchange symbol:** CSC. **Number of employees worldwide:** 80,000.

COMSTOR
295 Interlocken Boulevard, Suite 100, Broomfield CO 80021. 303/222-4747. **Toll-free phone:** 800/543-6098. **Fax:** 303/222-4875. **Contact:** Human Resources. **World Wide Web address:** http://www.comstor.com. **Description:** Distributes computers, internetworking products, and peripherals and provides related services. Founded in 1986. **NOTE:** Entry-level positions are offered. **Office hours:** Monday - Friday, 8:00 a.m. - 5:00 p.m. **Corporate headquarters location:** Chantilly VA. **Other U.S. locations:** Tarrytown NY; Pittsburgh PA; Omaha NE. **Number of employees at this location:** 140. **Number of employees nationwide:** 370.

CONVERGYS
10225 Westmoor Drive, Westminster CO 80021. 720/887-7800. **Contact:** Human Resources. **World Wide Web address:** http://www.convergys.com. **Description:** Provides customer care, human resources, and billing services through outsourced solutions, consulting services, and software support to industries including communications, financial services, technology, and consumer products. **Positions advertised include:** Implementation Technical Analyst. **Listed on:** New York Stock Exchange. **Stock exchange symbol:** CVG.

EDS (ELECTRONIC DATA SYSTEMS CORPORATION)
833 Boulder Road Southwest, Louisville CO 80027-2452. 303/665-1500. **Contact:** Human Resources. **World Wide Web address:** http://www.eds.com. **Description:** Provides consulting, systems development, systems integration, and systems management services for large-scale and industry-specific applications. Founded in 1962. **Positions advertised include:** Business Services Analyst. **Corporate headquarters location:** Plano TX. **Other U.S. locations:** Nationwide. **Listed on:** New York Stock Exchange. **Stock exchange symbol:** EDS. **Number of employees nationwide:** 50,000.

EMC CORPORATION
1099 18th Street, 17th Floor, Denver CO 80202. 303/293-9331. **Contact:** Human Resources. **World Wide Web address:** http://www.emc.com. **Description:** Provides products, services, and solutions for information storage and its management with solutions that integrate networked storage technologies, storage systems, software, and services. **Positions advertised include:** Commercial Technology Consultant; Federal Account Manager; Partner Manager; Regional Network Specialist; Sr. Systems Engineer. **Corporate headquarters location:** Hopkinton MA. **Other area locations:** Boulder CO; Englewood CO; Colorado Springs CO.

EAST CENTRAL
NEIGHBORHOOD LINK
2546 15th Street, Denver CO 80211. 303/830-0123. **Contact:** Ted Pinkowitz, President. **World Wide Web address:** http://www.ecentral.com. **Description:** Provides Internet access, e-mail accounts, and home pages on the Web to companies and individuals.

ENSCICON CORPORATION
555 Zang Street, Suite 100, Lakewood CO 80228. 303/980-8600. **Fax:** 303/832-6700. **Contact:** Staffing. **E-mail address:** info@enscicon.com. **World Wide Web address:** http://www.enscicon.com. **Description:** Provides computer science engineering and high-tech consulting services. Founded in 1994. **Positions advertised include:** Project Scheduler; I&C Lead Engineer; Lead Electrical Engineer; Project Geologist; Project Manager; Process Engineer; Mechanical Engineer. **Corporate headquarters location:** This location. **Other U.S. locations:** Portland OR. **Listed on:** Privately held. **President:** William Smith.

EXABYTE CORPORATION
2108 55th Street, Boulder CO 80301. 303/442-4333. **Contact:** Human Resources. **World Wide Web address:** http://www.exabyte.com. **Description:** Designs, manufactures, and markets cartridge tape subsystems for data storage applications. The company's products are used in a broad spectrum of computer systems based on 8mm helical scan, 4mm helical scan, and quarter-inch technologies. Products are used in various computer systems ranging from personal computers to supercomputers. A large majority of its units are used with workstations, network file servers, and minicomputers. **Positions advertised include:** Business Development Rep; Manufacturing Support Engineer; Software Tools Engineer. **Corporate headquarters location:** This location. **Listed on:** NASDAQ. **Stock exchange symbol:** EXBT.

FRONTRANGE SOLUTIONS
1125 Kelly Johnson Boulevard, Colorado Springs CO 80920. 719/531-5007. **Fax:** 719/536-0620. **Contact:** Human Resources Department. **World Wide Web address:** http://www.frontrange.com. **Description:** Develops software for support center markets such as help desks, customer service, and MIS/IS departments. **Positions advertised include:** Consultant; Customer Account Rep; Customer Support Specialist; Inside Sales Rep; Technical Analyst.

GOLDEN SOFTWARE, INC.
809 14th Street, Golden CO 80401-1866. 303/279-1021. **Toll-free phone:** 800/972-1021. **Fax:** 303/279-0909. **Contact:** Human Resources. **World Wide Web address:** http://www.goldensoftware.com. **Description:** Develops contouring, mapping, and graphing software for Windows and DOS operating systems. **Corporate headquarters location:** This location.

HARRIS CORPORATION
1999 Broadway Street, Suite 4000, Denver CO 80202-3050. 303/237-4000. **Contact:** Human Resources. **World Wide Web address:** http://www.broadcast.harris.com. **Description:** Develops software for television and radio stations.

HEWLETT PACKARD
305 Rockrimmon Boulevard South, Colorado Springs CO 80919. 719/548-2000. **Contact:** Human Resources. **World Wide Web address:** http://www.hp.com. **Description:** Designs, manufactures, sells, and services computers, associated peripheral equipment, and related software and supplies. Applications and programs include scientific research, computation, communications, education, data analysis, industrial control, time sharing, commercial data processing, graphic arts, word processing, health care, instrumentation, engineering, and simulation. **NOTE:** Apply online. **Positions advertised include:** ITSM Problem Manager; Associate Consultant; Microsoft Subject Matter Expert; Enterprise Inside Sales Rep; Customer Service Engineer. **Corporate headquarters location:** Palo Alto CA. **Listed on:** New York Stock Exchange. **Stock exchange symbol:** HPQ.

HEWLETT PACKARD
116 Inverness Drive East, Suite 300, Englewood CO 80112. 303/649-3000. **Contact:** Human Resources. **World Wide Web address:** http://www.hp.com. **Description:** Designs, manufactures, sells, and services computers, associated peripheral equipment, and related software and supplies. Applications and programs include scientific research, computation, communications, education, data analysis, industrial control, time sharing, commercial data processing, graphic arts, word processing, health care, instrumentation, engineering, and simulation. **NOTE:** Apply online. **Corporate headquarters location:** Palo Alto CA. **Listed on:** New York Stock Exchange. **Stock exchange symbol:** HPQ.

IBM CORPORATION
6300 Diagonal Highway, Boulder CO 80301. 303/443-9905. **Toll-free phone:** 800/796-9876. **Recorded jobline:** 800/964-4473. **Contact:** Human Resources. **World Wide Web address:** http://www.ibm.com. **Description:** IBM is a developer, manufacturer, and marketer of advanced information processing products including computers and microelectronic technology, software, networking systems, and information technology-related services. The company has operations in the United States, Canada, Europe, Middle East, Africa, Latin America, and Asia. **NOTE:** Search and apply for positions online. **Corporate headquarters location:** Armonk NY. **Operations at this facility include:** This facility is engaged in the manufacture of magnetic discs and tapes. **Subsidiaries include:** IBM Credit Corporation; IBM Instruments, Inc.; IBM World Trade Corporation. **Listed on:** New York Stock Exchange. **Stock exchange symbol:** IBM.

INFOR GLOBAL SOUTIONS
5555 Tech Center Drive, Suite 300, Colorado Springs CO 80919. 719/590-8940. **Fax:** 719/528-1465. **Contact:** Human Resources. **E-mail address:** infor.careers@infor.com. **World Wide Web address:** http://www.infor.com. **Description:** Provider of enterprise business solutions to the manufacturing and distribution industries. **Corporate headquarters location:** Atlanta GA. **Other U.S. locations:** Columbus OH; Grand Rapids MI; East Greenwich RI; Hampton NH; Duluth GA; Malvern PA; Northville MI.

INTRADO, INC.
1600 Dry Creek Road, Longmont CO 80503. 720/494-5800. **Fax:** 720/494-6652. **Contact:** Human Resources. **E-mail address:** HR@intrado.com. **World Wide Web address:** http://www.intrado.com. **Description:** Develops public safety computer software and systems that implement emergency communication networks with telephone service providers. **Positions advertised include:** Incident Administrator; Accounting Manager; Sr. Software Engineer; Product Marketing Manager; Sr. System Administrator; Data Analyst. **Corporate headquarters location:** This location. **Listed on:** NASDAQ. **Stock exchange symbol:** TRDO.

ISYS SEARCH SOFTWARE
8775 East Orchard Road, Suite 811, Englewood CO 80111. 303/689-9998. **Contact:** Human Resources. **E-mail address:** employment@isys-search.com. **World Wide Web address:** http://www.isys-search.com. **Description:** Manufactures text retrieval software. Products include ISYS HindSite Internet utilities; ISYS Web, for online publishing; ISYS Image, for data capture and full-text search; ISYS Electronic Publisher, a retrieval and authoring tool; and ISYS for Adobe Acrobat, a search engine with PDF files.

MANAGED BUSINESS SOLUTIONS (MBS)
1201 Oakridge Drive, Suite 320, Fort Collins CO 80525. 970/224-1016. **Fax:** 970/416-1543. **Contact:** Human Resources. **E-mail address:** careers@mbshome.com. **World Wide Web address:** http://www.mbshome.com. **Description:** MBS specializes in application development, application management and support, and IT resource management. Founded in 1993. **Positions advertised include:** Java Developer; Technical Writer; Tech Solution Specialist; .NET Developer; MPE System Operator.

MAXTOR CORPORATION
2452 Clover Basin Drive, Longmont CO 80503. 303/651-6000. **Fax:** 303/678-2379. **Contact:** Human Resources. **E-mail address:** staffing@maxtor.com. **World Wide Web address:** http://www.maxtor.com. **Description:** Maxtor Corporation produces hard disk drives and related electronic data storage equipment for computers, as well as related components for original equipment manufacturers. **Positions advertised include:** Database Administrator; Product Support Rep. **Corporate headquarters location:** Milpitas CA.

Operations at this facility include: This location is a research and development facility. **Listed on:** New York Stock Exchange. **Stock exchange symbol:** MXO.

McKESSON CORPORATION

285 Century Circle, Louisville CO 80027. 303/926-2000. **Contact:** Human Resources. **World Wide Web address:** http://www.mckesson.com. **Description:** McKesson Corp. is an information solutions company that provides information systems and technology to health care enterprises including hospitals, integrated delivery networks, and managed care organizations. McKesson's primary products are Pathways 2000, a family of client/server-based applications that allows for the integration and uniting of health care providers; STAR, Series, and HealthQuest transaction systems; TRENDSTAR decision support system; and QUANTUM enterprise information system. The company also offers outsourcing services that include strategic information systems planning, data center operations, receivables management, business office administration, and major system conversions. **Positions advertised include:** Technical Support Manager; Cardiology Sales Product Specialist; Technical Support Engineer; Director, Business Analysis. **Corporate headquarters location:** San Francisco CA. **Operations at this facility include:** This location designs and installs software for the medical industry. **Subsidiaries include:** HBO & Company (UK) Limited; HBO & Company Canada Ltd.

OCTAGON SYSTEMS

6510 West 91st Avenue, Suite 110, Westminster CO 80031. 303/430-1500. **Fax:** 303/412-2050. **Contact:** Personnel. **E-mail address:** hrstaffing@octagonsystems.com. **World Wide Web address:** http://www.octagonsystems.com. **Description:** Manufactures personal computers for extreme environments. Founded in 1981. **Positions advertised include:** Director of Operations. **Corporate headquarters location:** This location. **Listed on:** Privately held. **Number of employees at this location:** 70.

1MAGE SOFTWARE INC.

6025 South Quebec Street, Suite 300, Englewood CO 80111. 303/773-1424. **Fax:** 303/796-0587. **Contact:** Human Resources. **E-mail address:** jobs@1mage.com. **World Wide Web address:** http://www.1mage.com. **Description:** Develops and markets image recording and storage systems to convert paper records into electronic format. 1mage Software also offers installation and support services. **Corporate headquarters location:** This location.

ORACLE

12320 Oracle Boulevard, Colorado Springs CO 80921. 719/577-8000. **Fax:** 719/757-2037. **Contact:** Human Resources. **World Wide Web address:** http://www.oracle.com. **Description:** the world's largest enterprise software company. **Positions advertised include:** Contract Renewal Rep; Support Engineer; Sr. Consultant. **Corporate**

headquarters location: Redwood Shores CA. **Other area locations:** Denver CO. **Listed on:** NASDAQ. **Stock exchange symbol:** ORCL.

QUARK, INC.
1800 Grant Street, Suite 800, Denver CO 80203. 303/894-8888. **Fax:** 303/894-3649. **Contact:** Human Resources Department. **E-mail address:** work@quark.com. **World Wide Web address:** http://www.quark.com. **Description:** Develops software including QuarkXPress, one of the leading products in desktop publishing. **Positions advertised include:** VP, Customer Care; VP, Human Resources; VP, Marketing; Project Coordinator; Quality Assurance Engineer; Sr. Software Engineer; Software Architect; Manager, Web Services. **International locations:** Worldwide.

SI INTERNATIONAL
4040 East Bijou Street, Colorado Springs CO 80909. 719/235-4100. **Fax:** 719/380-8702. **Contact:** Human Resources. **World Wide Web address:** http://www.si-intl.com. **Description:** A provider of information technology and network solutions primarily to the federal government, focusing on federal IT modernization, homeland security, and space systems modernization. Founded in 1998. **Positions advertised include:** Manager New Program Development; Principal Contracts Administrator; Video Network Engineer; Systems Engineer; Senior IT Systems Engineer; Associate Network Engineer. **Corporate headquarters location:** Reston VA. **Other area locations:** Denver CO; Fort Collins CO.

SANMINA-SCI CORPORATION
702 Bandley Drive, Fountain CO 80817. 719/382-2000. **Contact:** Human Resources. **World Wide Web address:** http://www.sanmina-sci.com. **Description:** Sanmina-SCI Corporation is an electronics contract manufacturer serving the fastest-growing segments of the global electronics manufacturing services market. Sanmina-SCI provides end-to-end manufacturing solutions to OEMs primarily in the communications, defense and aerospace, industrial and medical instrumentation, multimedia, and computer and server technology sectors. **Positions advertised include:** Quality Engineer; Program Administrator; Buyer; Supply Chain Manager. **Corporate headquarters location:** San Jose CA. **Other U.S. locations:** Nationwide. **International locations:** Canada; France; Ireland; Mexico; Scotland; Singapore; Thailand. **Operations at this facility include:** This location produces a wide range of assemblies for mass storage products including small tape backup devices, large multiple-disk array systems, and high-capacity optical storage units. **Listed on:** NASDAQ. **Stock exchange symbol:** SANM.

SEAGATE TECHNOLOGY
389 Disc Drive, Longmont CO 80503. 720/684-1000. **Contact:** Human Resources. **World Wide Web address:** http://www.seagate.com. **Description:** Designs and manufactures data storage devices and related products including hard drives, tape drives, software, and

systems for many computer-related applications and operating systems. These products include 2.5-inch and 3.5-inch drives with memory storage capacity between 150 megabytes and one gigabyte. **Positions advertised include:** Applications Engineer; Concept Market Development Director; Firmware Engineer; Servo Engineer; Sr. Analyst, Product Marketing; Electrical Design Engineer. **Corporate headquarters location:** Scotts Valley CA.

SPECTRA LOGIC
1700 North 55th Street, Boulder CO 80301-2725. 303/449-6400. **Fax:** 303/939-8844. **Contact:** Human Resources. **E-mail address:** hireme@spectralogic.com. **World Wide Web address:** http://www.spectralogic.com. **Description:** Manufactures backup hardware and automated tape libraries. Founded in 1979. **NOTE:** Entry-level positions are offered. **Positions advertised include:** Disk/RAID Engineer; Firmware Engineer; Project Coordinator; Operations Engineer; Supply Chain Specialist; Hardware Support Technician. **Special programs:** Internships. **Internship information:** For detailed internship information, visit the company's Website. **Corporate headquarters location:** This location. **International locations:** UK; China. **Listed on:** Privately held. **Number of employees at this location:** 150. **Number of employees worldwide:** 300.

SPECTRUM HUMAN RESOURCE SYSTEMS CORPORATION
707 Seventeenth Street, Suite 3800, Denver CO 80202-3438. 303/592-3200. **Toll-free phone:** 800/334-5660. **Fax:** 303/595-9970. **Contact:** Recruiter. **E-mail address:** info@ spectrumhr.com. **World Wide Web address:** http://www.spectrumhr.com. **Description:** Develops computer software for use in human resources management, benefits administration, and training development administration. Founded in 1984. **NOTE:** Entry-level positions are offered. **Positions advertised include:** HR Systems Implementation Programmer. **Corporate headquarters location:** This location. **Listed on:** Privately held. **Annual sales/revenues:** $5 - $10 million. **Number of employees at this location:** 100. **Number of employees nationwide:** 115.

STORAGETEK
One StorageTek Drive, Louisville CO 80028-0001. 303/673-5151. **Contact:** Human Resources. **World Wide Web address:** http://www.stortek.com. **Description:** StorageTek supplies high-performance computer information storage and retrieval systems for mainframe and mid-frame computers and networks. Products include automated cartridge systems, random access subsystems, and fault-tolerant disk arrays. The company also distributes equipment; sells new peripherals, software, and hardware; and offers support services. **Corporate headquarters location:** This location. **Parent company:** Sun Microsystems. **Operations at this facility include:** Administration; Manufacturing; Research and Development.

SUN MICROSYSTEMS, INC.
500 Eldorado Boulevard, Broomfield CO 80021. 303/464-4000. **Contact:** Human Resources. **World Wide Web address:** http://www.sun.com. **Description:** Sun Microsystems Inc. produces high-performance computer systems, workstations, servers, CPUs, peripherals, and operating system software. The company also developed a microprocessor called SPARC. **Corporate headquarters location:** Santa Clara CA. **Operations at this facility include:** This location is a sales office. **Subsidiaries include:** Forte Software Inc. manufactures enterprise application integration software. **Listed on:** NASDAQ. **Stock exchange symbol:** SUNW.

SUNGARD INSURANCE SYSTEMS
14280 East Jewell Avenue, Suite 200, Aurora CO 80012. 303/283-5300. **Contact:** Human Resources. **World Wide Web address:** http://www.sungardinsurance.com. **Description:** Develops financial software for insurance companies. **Parent company:** SunGard Data Systems, Inc. **Listed on:** New York Stock Exchange. **Stock exchange symbol:** SDS.

SYKES ENTERPRISES INC.
777 North Fourth Street, Sterling CO 80751. 970/522-6638. **Contact:** Human Resources. **E-mail address:** careers@sykes.com. **World Wide Web address:** http://www.sykes.com. **Description:** Provides computer outsourcing services, hardware and software technical support, systems consulting and integration, and documentation development. **Corporate headquarters location:** Tampa FL. **Other U.S. locations:** Nationwide. **International locations:** The Netherlands; Philippines. **Listed on:** NASDAQ. **Stock exchange symbol:** SYKE.

T-NETIX, INC.
7108 South Alton Drive, Centennial CO 80112. 720/488-9481. **Contact:** Human Resources Department. **E-mail address:** humanresources@t-netix.com. **World Wide Web address:** http://www.t-netix.com. **Description:** Manufactures software for fraud prevention and advanced call processing. **Corporate headquarters location:** Carrollton TX. **Subsidiaries include:** Cell-Tel, Tampa FL. **Parent company:** Securus.

XAWARE INC.
5555 Tech Center Drive, Suite 200, Colorado Springs CO 80919. 719/884-5400. **Fax:** 719/884-5492. **Contact:** Human Resources. **E-mail address:** careers@xaware.com. **World Wide Web address:** http://www.xaware.com. **Description:** XAware, Inc. is a provider of information integration, conversion, and exchange solutions that helps companies transform and extend existing information assets into standards-based information services. **Positions advertised include:** Professional Services Staff; Sales Operations Specialist.

XI GRAPHICS
1801 Broadway, Suite 1710, Denver CO 80202-3800. 303/298-7478. **Toll-free phone:** 800/946-7433. **Fax:** 303/298-1406. **Contact:**

Employment. **E-mail address:** jobs@xig.com. **World Wide Web address:** http://www.xig.com. **Description:** Develops a line of products that enhance the graphics capabilities of PC hardware. Products include X Windows display servers, OpenGL development, and custom development. **Operations at this facility include:** Customer Service; Financial Offices; Sales; Technical Support. **Listed on:** Privately held.

ZYKRONIX INC.
357 Inverness Drive South, Suite 300C, Englewood CO 80112. 303/799-4944. **Fax:** 303/799-4978. **Contact:** Human Resources. **E-mail address:** hr@zykronix.com. **World Wide Web address:** http://www.zykronix.com. **Description:** Designs and manufactures PCs that are used mainly for industrial applications. Founded in 1990. **President/CEO:** David M. Ghaemi. **Corporate headquarters location:** This location.

EDUCATIONAL SERVICES

You can expect to find the following types of companies in this section:
Business/Secretarial/Data Processing Schools •
Colleges/Universities/Professional Schools • Community
Colleges/Technical Schools/Vocational Schools • Elementary and
Secondary Schools • Preschool and Child Daycare Services

ADAMS STATE COLLEGE
208 Edgemont Boulevard, Alamosa CO 81102. 719/587-7990. **Fax:** 719/587-7938. **Contact:** Human Resources. **World Wide Web address:** http://www.adams.edu. **Description:** A state college with approximately 2,500 students. **Positions advertised include:** Assistant/Associate Professor, Various Departments; Web Application Developer; title V Cooperative Grant Project Specialist. **Number of employees at this location:** 310.

AMERICAN EDUCATIONAL PRODUCTS INC.
401 West Hickory Street, P.O. Box 2121, Fort Collins CO 80522. 970/484-7445. **Contact:** Human Resources. **World Wide Web address:** http://www.amep.com. **Description:** Manufactures and markets a wide variety of educational products including pattern blocks, cubes, geological oddities, puzzles, and arts and crafts supplies. The company also designs, develops, manufactures, markets, and services supplementary educational products including filmstrips and anatomical systems. **Number of employees at this location:** 135.

COLORADO MOUNTAIN COLLEGE
831 Grand Avenue, P.O. Box 10001, Glenwood Springs CO 81602. 970/945-8691. **Fax:** 970/947-8324. **Contact:** Director of Human Resources. **World Wide Web address:** http://www.coloradomtn.edu. **Description:** A two-year college. The school's Associate of Arts and Associate of Science degrees are academic programs designed for students who plan to transfer to a four-year college or university. Colorado Mountain College includes seven campuses in western Colorado. **NOTE:** Applications available online. Resumes accepted only for posted positions. **Positions advertised include:** Dean of Arts and Sciences; Chief Information Officer; Director of Marketing and Communications.

COLORADO MOUNTAIN COLLEGE/EAST
901 South U.S. Highway 24, Leadville CO 80461-9724. 719/486-2015. **Contact:** Human Resources. **World Wide Web address:** http://www.coloradomtn.edu. **Description:** A two-year college. The school's Associate of Arts and Associate of Science degrees are academic programs designed for students who plan to transfer to a four-year college or university. Colorado Mountain College includes seven

campuses in western Colorado. **NOTE:** All hiring is done by the Glenwood campus.

COLORADO SCHOOL OF MINES

1500 Illinois Street, Golden CO 80401. 303/273-3250. **Fax:** 303/384-2025. **Contact:** Human Resources. **World Wide Web address:** http://www.mines.edu. **Description:** Colorado School of Mines is a public research university devoted to engineering and applied science. Founded in 1874. **Positions advertised include:** Assistant/Associate Professor, Various Departments; Program Assistant.

COLORADO STATE UNIVERSITY

Human Resource Services, Fort Collins CO 80523-6004. 970/491-1794. **Fax:** 970/491-2548. **Recorded jobline:** 970/491-3941. **Contact:** Human Resource Services. **World Wide Web address:** http://www.colostate.edu. **Description:** A state university offering undergraduate, graduate, and doctorate programs. **Positions advertised include:** Research Associate; Assistant/Associate Professor; Vice President for Research.

COLORADO STATE UNIVERSITY AT PUEBLO

2200 Bonforte Boulevard, Pueblo CO 81001-4901. 719/549-2100. **Contact:** Human Resources Department. **World Wide Web address:** http://www.colostate-pueblo.edu. **Description:** Colorado State/Pueblo has an enrollment of approximately 4,600 students. The university operates through five divisions: The College of Applied Science & Engineering, The School of Business, The College of Humanities and Social Science, The College of Science and Mathematics, and The Center for Teaching and Learning.

EMILY GRIFFITH OPPORTUNITY SCHOOL

1250 Welton Street, Denver CO 80204. 303/575-4700. **Contact:** Human Resources. **World Wide Web address:** http://www.egos-school.com. **Description:** A trade school offering continuing education (high school diploma, G.E.D.), as well as classes in areas such as medicine, art, aviation, and automotive mechanics.

MESA STATE COLLEGE

1100 North Avenue, Lowell Heiny Hall, Room 237, Grand Junction CO 81502. 970/248-1820. **Contact:** Jan Purin, Human Resources. **E-mail address:** jpurin@mesastate.edu. **World Wide Web address:** http://www.mesastate.edu. **Description:** Mesa State College grants the Bachelor of Business Administration, Bachelor of Science in Nursing, Bachelor of Arts, and Bachelor of Science degrees. The college awards Associate of Arts and Associate of Science degrees, as well as Associate of Applied Science degrees and certificates of proficiency in occupational (vocational-technical) areas. Over 4,500 students are enrolled at the college. Founded in 1925. **Positions advertised include:** Assistant VP for Academic Affairs; Director of Admissions; Grants Specialist; Assistant/Associate Professor, Various Departments.

REGIS UNIVERSITY
3333 Regis Boulevard, Mail Code K-4, Denver CO 80221-1099. 303/458-4161. **Fax:** 303/964-5498. **Recorded jobline:** 303/458-4386. **Contact:** Human Resources. **E-mail address:** resumes@regis.edu. **World Wide Web address:** http://www.regis.edu. **Description:** A four-year, liberal arts/preprofessional, Jesuit university. Six academic divisions offer more than 30 programs of study. Approximately 1,400 students attend Regis University. **Positions advertised include:** Assistant Professor, Various Departments; Programmer/Analyst; Sr. Accountant. **Special programs:** Internships. **Other U.S. locations:** WY. **Number of employees at this location:** 550.

U.S. AIR FORCE ACADEMY
8034 Edgerton Drive, Suite 100, Colorado Springs CO 80840. 719/333-1110. **Contact:** Civilian Personnel Office. **Recorded jobline:** 719/333-2222. **World Wide Web address:** http://www.usafa.af.mil. **Description:** An undergraduate educational institution offering the bachelor of science degree and military training leading to commission in the U.S. Air Force. **NOTE:** Instructions for application for positions are available at the Air Force Personnel Center website: https://ww2.afpc.randolph.af.mil/resweb. **Positions advertised include:** Architect; Budget Technician; Operations Research Analyst.

UNIVERSITY OF COLORADO AT BOULDER
3100 Marine Street, Campus Box 565, Boulder CO 80309. 303/492-6475. **Contact:** Human Resources. **World Wide Web address:** http://www.colorado.edu. **Description:** A four-year state university offering undergraduate and graduate degree programs. Founded in 1876. **Positions advertised include:** Assistant Director for Budget Services; Software System Architect; Education Coordinator; Manager of Information Technology; Director of Operations; Faculty Positions, Various Departments.

UNIVERSITY OF COLORADO AT DENVER
P.O. Box 173364, Campus Box 130, Denver CO 80217-3364. 303/556-2868. **Contact:** Kevin Jacobs, Human Resources. **World Wide Web address:** http://www.ucdhsc.edu. **Description:** A four-year state university offering undergraduate and graduate degree programs. **Positions advertised include:** Computer Technology Coordinator; Grant Specialist Manager; Fiscal Manager; Manager, Academic Technology; Dean, College of Liberal Arts and Sciences; Dean School of Dentistry.

UNIVERSITY OF DENVER
2199 South University Boulevard, Denver CO 80208. 303/871-7420. **Fax:** 303/871-3656. **Contact:** Human Resources. **E-mail address:** hr-postings@du.edu. **World Wide Web address:** http://www.du.edu. **Description:** A four-year university offering undergraduate, graduate, and continuing education programs to more than 8,500 students. **Positions advertised include:** Assistant Professor, Various Departments; Program Counselor; Reference Librarian. **Special**

programs: Internships. **Corporate headquarters location:** This location. **Operations at this facility include:** Administration; Research and Development; Service.

UNIVERSITY OF NORTHERN COLORADO
501 20th Street, Carter Hall, Room 2002, Greeley CO 80639. 970/351-2718. **Contact:** Debbi Rees, Human Resources. **World Wide Web address:** http://www.unco.edu. **Description:** A four-year university offering undergraduate and graduate degree programs to more than 12,000 students. **Positions advertised include:** Director, Center for the Enhancement of Teaching and Learning; Director, Various Schools; Assistant Professor, Various Departments

ELECTRONIC/INDUSTRIAL ELECTRICAL EQUIPMENT AND COMPONENTS

You can expect to find the following types of companies in this section:
Electronic Machines and Systems • Semiconductor Manufacturers

---

AGILENT TECHNOLOGIES, INC.
1900 Garden of the Gods Road, Colorado Springs CO 80907. 877/424-4536. **Contact:** Human Resources. **World Wide Web address:** http://www.agilent.com. **Description:** Agilent Technologies Inc. is a leading manufacturer of scientific instruments and analysis equipment, including data generators, multimeters, and oscilloscopes, serving customers in more than 110 countries. **Positions advertised include:** R&D FPGA Design Engineer; R&D Mechanical Engineer; Hardware Development Engineer; Field Service Technician. **Corporate headquarters location:** Palo Alto CA. **Listed on:** New York Stock Exchange. **Stock exchange symbol:** A.

ATMEL CORPORATION
1150 East Cheyenne Mountain Boulevard, Colorado Springs CO 80906. 719/576-3300. **Fax:** 719/540-1323. **Contact:** Human Resources. **World Wide Web address:** http://www.atmel.com. **Description:** Focusing on consumer, industrial, security, communications, computing, and automotive markets, Atmel designs and manufactures microcontrollers, advanced logic, mixed-signal, nonvolatile memory, and radio frequency (RF) components. Founded in 1984. **Positions advertised include:** Equipment Engineering Services Engineer; Equipment Engineering Services Technician; Integrated Circuit Test Engineer; Sarbanes-Oxley Tester; Sr. Custom Products Design Engineering Technician; Sr. Test Engineer. **Corporate headquarters location:** San Jose CA. **Listed on:** NASDAQ. **Stock exchange symbol:** ATML.

BI INCORPORATED
6400 Lookout Road, Boulder CO 80301. 303/218-1000. **Toll-free phone:** 800/241-2911. **Fax:** 303/218-1250. **Contact:** Human Resources. **E-mail address:** hdhr@bi.com. **World Wide Web address:** http://www.bi.com. **Description:** A provider of electronic home arrest and jail management systems to correctional agencies worldwide. The company also offers a computerized, interactive telephone and monitoring service for its electronic monitoring systems. **Office hours:** Monday - Friday, 8:00 a.m. - 5:30 p.m. **Corporate headquarters location:** This location. **Other U.S. locations:** GA; IL; IN; OH; OR; TX. **International locations:** Puerto Rico. **Number of employees worldwide:** 800.

COLORADO CRYSTAL CORPORATION

2303 West Eighth Street, Loveland CO 80537. 970/667-9248. **Fax:** 970/667-3500. **Contact:** Personnel Director. **E-mail address:** info@coloradocrystal.com. **World Wide Web address:** http://www.coloradocrystal.com. **Description:** Manufactures quartz crystals for a variety of OEMs. **Corporate headquarters location:** This location.

COORSTEK

16000 Table Mountain Parkway, Golden CO 80403. 303/277-4000. **Contact:** Human Resources. **E-mail address:** careers@coorstek.com. **World Wide Web address:** http://www.coorstek.com. **Description:** Manufactures advanced technical ceramics, precision-machined metals, and engineered plastic products. **NOTE:** Apply online. **Positions advertised include:** Ceramic Engineer; International Sourcing Supply Chain Manager; Quality Control Inspector; Production Specialist. **Corporate headquarters location:** This location. **Other area locations:** Grand Junction, CO. **Listed on:** NASDAQ. **Stock exchange symbol:** CRTK.

DENVER DISTRIBUTORS INC.

3301 Mariposa, P.O. Box 11368, Denver CO 80211. 303/433-7463. **Contact:** Mike Selby, President. **Description:** A wholesaler of electrical supplies and equipment to commercial, industrial, and residential contractors.

DIRECTED ENERGY SOLUTIONS (DES)

890 Elkton Dr. Suite 101, Colorado Springs CO 80907. 719/593-7848. **Fax:** 719/593-7846. **Contact:** Human Resources. **Email address:** jobs@denergysolutions.com. **World Wide Web address:** http://www.denergysolutions.com. **Description:** DES develops advanced laser and optical device solutions for research applications, remote sensing, optical communication, chemical/biological defense, directed energy, aircraft self-defense, and medical applications. Founded in 1997. **Positions advertised include:** Director, Advanced Laser Development; Chief Technology Officer; Optomechanical Engineer; Laser System Development Engineer/Project Manager; Precision Mechanical/Cryogenic Systems Engineer.

ENTEGRIS CORPORATION

4405 Arrowswest Drive, Colorado Springs CO 80907. 719/528-2600. **Fax:** 719/528-2749. **Contact:** Human Resources. **World Wide Web address:** http://www.entegris.com. **Description:** Entegris is the world's largest materials integrity management company. Its five business units are wafer handling, finished electronics packaging, liquid microcontamination, liquid systems, and gas microcontamination. It primarily serves the semiconductor industry. **Positions advertised include:** Black Belt; Setup Technician. **Corporate headquarters location:** Chaska MN

FIRST CLASS SECURITY SYSTEMS
3835 West 10th Street, Suite 100C, Greeley CO 80634-1551. 970/339-2449. **Fax:** 970/336-3119. **Contact:** Richard Newman, Office Manager. **Description:** Installs and services burglar and fire alarm, video surveillance, and access control systems. Founded in 1983. **Company slogan:** The best service in the business. **Office hours:** Monday - Friday, 8:00 a.m. - 5:00 p.m. **Corporate headquarters location:** This location. **Owner:** Bob Stewart. **Annual sales/revenues:** Less than $5 million.

ITT INDUSTRIES
4410 East Fountain Boulevard, Colorado Springs CO 80916. 719/591-3600. **Fax:** 719/591-3698. **Contact:** Human Resources. **World Wide Web address:** http://www.ittind.com. **Description:** Serves the defense, energy, and communications markets with research and development services in weapons effects, computer systems, space systems, C3I, SDI, range testing, and instrumentation. **Positions advertised include:** Computer Security Analyst; Director of Marketing; Employment Specialist; Engineer; Environmental Safety and Health Specialist; Lead Software Engineer; Production Design Engineer; Project Engineer. **Corporate headquarters location:** White Plains NY. **Listed on:** New York Stock Exchange. **Stock exchange symbol:** ITT.

LSI LOGIC
2001 Danfield Court, Fort Collins CO 80525. 970/223-5100. **Fax:** 970/206-5549. **Contact:** Personnel. **World Wide Web address:** http://www.lsilogic.com. **Description:** LSI Logic develops, manufactures, markets, and supports complete business information systems for retail, financial, commercial, industrial, medical, educational, and government industries through the production of microelectronics. The company also manufactures and markets business forms and supplies. **Positions advertised include:** Technical Staff; Sr. I/O Cell Design Engineer. **Corporate headquarters location:** Milpitas CA. **Listed on:** New York Stock Exchange. **Stock exchange symbol:** LSI.

LASER TECHNOLOGY, INC. (LTI)
7070 South Tucson Way, Centennial CO 80112. 303/649-1000. **Fax:** 303/649-9710. **Contact:** Human Resources. **World Wide Web address:** http://www.lasertech.com. **Description:** Provides laser-based measurement systems to a wide variety of markets worldwide, as well as laser speed detection systems. Founded in 1985. **NOTE:** Part-time jobs are offered. **Special programs:** Apprenticeships. **Listed on:** American Stock Exchange. **Stock exchange symbol:** LSR.

MESA LABORATORIES, INC.
12100 West Sixth Avenue, Lakewood CO 80228. 303/987-8000. **Contact:** Steve Peterson, Vice President of Finance. **World Wide Web address:** http://www.mesalabs.com. **Description:** Develops, manufactures, and markets computer-based, electronic measurement instruments used across a wide range of industries. Mesa's products include DATARACE patented instruments for measuring and recording

temperature, humidity, and pressure; NUSONICS flow meters and sonic concentration analyzers; and Western Meters and the ECHO Dialyzer Reprocessor are two product lines used in kidney dialysis. **Corporate headquarters location:** This location. **Listed on:** NASDAQ. **Stock exchange symbol:** MLAB. **Number of employees at this location:** 50.

METRON, INC.
1505 West Third Avenue, Denver CO 80223. 303/592-1903. **Fax:** 303/592-1969. **Contact:** Human Resources. **World Wide Web address:** http://www.metroninc.com. **Description:** A manufacturer of fire pump controllers and custom electrical products including switchgear and switchboard equipment. **Corporate headquarters location:** This location. **Number of employees at this location:** 85.

MICROSEMI CORPORATION
800 Hoyt Street, Broomfield CO 80020. 303/469-2161. **Fax:** 303/466-3775. **Contact:** Craig Mullin, Human Resources. **World Wide Web address:** http://www.microsemi.com. **Description:** Microsemi Corporation manufactures and markets semiconductors and similar products and provides related services, principally for the military, aerospace, medical, computer, and telecommunications applications. Major products include high-reliability silicon rectifiers and zener diodes; low-leakage and high-voltage diodes; temperature-compensated zener diodes; and a family of subminiature high-power transient suppresser diodes. **Corporate headquarters location:** Irvine CA. **Operations at this facility include:** This location manufactures rectifiers and diodes. **Listed on:** NASDAQ. **Stock exchange symbol:** MSCC. **Number of employees at this location:** 360. **Number of employees nationwide:** 1,200.

QUANTUM CORPORATION
10125 Federal Drive, Colorado Springs CO 80913. 719/536-5000. **Fax:** 719/536-5952. **Contact:** Human Resources. **World Wide Web address:** http://www.quantum.com. **Description:** Manufactures storage solutions including tape drives and media technologies, autoloaders and libraries, and disk-based backup systems. **Positions advertised include:** Accountant; Business System Analyst; Financial Analyst; MIS Project Manager; Sr. Oracle Developer; Assembler; Sr. Planner/Scheduler; Procurement Specialist. **Corporate headquarters location:** San Jose CA. **Other area locations:** Boulder CO.

RAMTRON INTERNATIONAL CORPORATION
1850 Ramtron Drive, Colorado Springs CO 80921. 719/481-7000. **Fax:** 719/481-9294. **Contact:** Diane Ratliff, Human Resources Manager. **E-mail address:** diane.ratliff@ramtron.com. **World Wide Web address:** http://www.ramtron.com. **Description:** Manufactures semiconductors. **Corporate headquarters location:** This location. **Listed on:** NASDAQ. **Stock exchange symbol:** RMTR.

SAFETRAN TRAFFIC SYSTEMS, INC.
1485 Garden of the Gods Road, Colorado Springs CO 80907. 719/599-5600. **Fax:** 719/599-3853. **Contact:** Human Resources. **World Wide Web address:** http://www.safetran-traffic.com. **Description:** Manufactures traffic control products and systems. **Corporate headquarters location:** This location. **Number of employees at this location:** 100.

SIMTEK CORPORATION
4250 Buckingham Drive, Suite 100, Colorado Springs CO 80907. 719/531-9444. **Fax:** 719/531-9481. **Contact:** Brian Stephens, Director of Quality Assurance. **E-mail address:** resumes@simtek.com. **World Wide Web address:** http://www.simtek.com. **Description:** Develops, produces, and markets nonvolatile semiconductor memories. Simtek's products are targeted for use in commercial electronic equipment markets such as high-density hard drives, modems, smart utility meters, home and commercial security systems, portable telephones, instrumentation, and numerous military systems including communications, radar, sonar, and smart weapons.

SIRENZA MICRODEVICES
303 South Technology Court, Broomfield CO 80021. 303/327-3030. **Fax:** 303/410-7088. **Contact:** Human Resources. **E-mail address:** employ@sirenza.com. **World Wide Web address:** http://www.sirenza.com. **Description:** Sirenza designs, manufactures, and markets a wide range of radio frequency and microwave signal processing components used in the wireless telecommunications industry. These components are used in commercial and military/aerospace applications such as cellular telephones and base stations, wireless local area networking, and satellite communications systems, as well as advanced radar, missile guidance, and navigational systems. The company markets its products primarily to original equipment manufacturers of commercial and defense products. **Positions advertised include:** RF Applications Engineer; RF Engineering Technician.

TELEDYNE BROWN ENGINEERING
1330 Inverness Drive, Suite 350, Colorado Springs CO 80910. 719/574-7270. **Fax:** 719/574-6329. **Contact:** Human Resources. **World Wide Web address:** http://www.tbe.com. **Description:** Engaged in thermoelectric generator development and production. **Positions advertised include:** Maintenance Operations Analyst. **Other U.S. locations:** Nationwide. **Parent company:** Teledyne Technologies Inc. **Listed on:** New York Stock Exchange. **Stock exchange symbol:** TDY.

WALKER COMPONENTS
1795 East 66th Avenue, Denver CO 80216. 303/292-6121. **Contact:** Director of Human Resources. **World Wide Web address:** http://www.walkercomponent.com. **Description:** A distributor of electronic goods to industrial contractors.

ENVIRONMENTAL & WASTE MANAGEMENT SERVICES

**You can expect to find the following types of companies
in this section:**
Environmental Engineering Firms • Sanitary Services

ACURA ENGINEERING
13276 East Fremont Place, Centennial CO 80112. 303/799-8378. **Fax:**
303/799-8392. **Contact:** Human Resources. **E-mail address:**
potential@acurageo.com. **World Wide Web address:**
http://www.acurageo.com. **Description:** Provides geotechnical
engineering and construction materials testing services, Phase 1
environmental site assessments, and forensic investigation services.
Positions advertised include: GEO and CMT Field Tech.

ALLIED WASTE SERVICE OF DENVER
5075 East 74th Avenue, Denver CO 80022. 303/287-8043. **Contact:**
Human Resources. **World Wide Web address:** http://www.awin.com.
Description: Engaged primarily in the collection and disposal of solid
wastes for commercial, industrial, and residential customers. Services
provided include landfill services, waste-to-energy programs, hazardous
waste removal, and liquid waste removal. The company has worldwide
operations at more than 500 facilities. **Corporate headquarters
location:** Scottsdale AZ. **Other U.S. locations:** Nationwide. **Listed on:**
New York Stock Exchange. **Stock exchange symbol:** AW.

ARCADIS
630 Plaza Drive, Suite 200, Highlands Ranch CO 80129. 720/344-3500.
Contact: Corporate Technical Recruiter. **World Wide Web address:**
http://www.arcadis-us.com. **Description:** A consulting firm that provides
environmental and engineering services. The company focuses on the
environmental, building, and infrastructure markets. Founded in 1888.
Positions advertised include: Communications Manager; Regional
Recruiter; Purchasing Assistant. **Other U.S. locations:** Nationwide.
International locations: The Netherlands; United Kingdom. **Parent
company:** Arcadis NV. **Listed on:** NASDAQ. **Stock exchange symbol:**
ARCAF.

COMMODORE ADVANCED SCIENCES, INC.
4251 Kipling Street, Suite 575, Wheat Ridge CO 80033. 303/421-1511.
Contact: Human Resources. **World Wide Web address:**
http://www.commodore.com. **Description:** A technical services
consulting firm that provides waste management, environmental
sciences, advanced technologies, and remediation. Founded in 1977.
NOTE: Entry-level positions are offered. **Corporate headquarters
location:** Alexandria VA. **Other U.S. locations:** Idaho Falls ID; Carlsbad
NM; Los Alamos NM; Oak Ridge TN. **Parent company:** Commodore

Applied Technologies, Inc. **Listed on:** OTC BB. **Stock exchange symbol:** CXIA.

GEOTRANS INC.
363 Centennial Parkway, Suite 210, Louisville CO 80027. 303/665-4390. **Contact:** Human Resources. **World Wide Web address:** http://www.geotransinc.com. **Description:** Provides environmental consulting services. **NOTE:** search and apply for positions online. **Parent company:** Tetra-Tech. **Listed on:** NASDAQ. **Stock exchange symbol:** TTEK.

METRO WASTEWATER RECLAMATION DISTRICT
6450 York Street, Denver CO 80229-7407. 303/286-3000. **Fax:** 303/286-3034. **Contact:** Human Resources. **E-mail address:** resume@mwrd.dst.co.us. **World Wide Web address:** http://www.metrowastewater.com. **Description:** A regional government agency that provides wastewater transmission and treatment services to local governments. **NOTE:** Application required. **Positions advertised include:** Staff Engineer.

SEVERN TRENT LABORATORIES, INC.
4955 Yarrow Street, Arvada CO 80002. 303/736-0100. **Fax:** 303/431-7171. **Contact:** Human Resources. **World Wide Web address:** http://www.stl-inc.com. **Description:** Provides a complete range of environmental testing services to private industry, engineering consultants, and government agencies in support of federal and state environmental regulations. The company also possesses analytical capabilities in the fields of air toxins, field analytical services, radiochemistry/mixed waste, and advanced technology. **NOTE:** Resumes accepted only for open positions. Search and apply for positions online. **Parent company:** Severn Trent Services.

SIEMENS WATER TECHNOLOGIES
1335 Ford Street, Colorado Springs CO 80915-2934. 719/570-5600. **Contact:** Human Resources. **World Wide Web address:** http://www.usfilter.com. **Description:** Siemens Water Technologies provides products, systems, services and automation for water and wastewater treatment. **Positions advertised include:** Drafter/Designer; Engineer; Engineering Director; Manufacturing Supervisor; Project Manager. **Corporate headquarters location:** Warrendale PA. **Parent company:** Siemens.

URS CORPORATION
8181 East Tufts Avenue, Denver CO 80237. 303/694-2770. **Fax:** 303/694-3946. **Contact:** Human Resources. **World Wide Web address:** http://www.urscorp.com. **Description:** Provides regulatory compliance support, site investigation and remediation, air pollution controls, VOC and air toxins control, biotreatment, waste management, ambient and source monitoring, risk management, information management, project chemistry, specialty chemicals, remote sensing services, materials and machinery analysis, and electronic services. Founded in 1969. **Positions**

advertised include: Project CADD Designer; Civil Designer; Contracts Manager; Development Engineer Manager; Electrical Engineer; Environmental Scientist; Geologist; Geotechnical Engineer; Industrial Hygienist; Mechanical Engineer; Principal Claims Analyst. **Corporate headquarters location:** San Francisco CA. **International locations:** Worldwide. **Listed on:** New York Stock Exchange. **Stock exchange symbol:** URS.

WASTE MANAGEMENT COLORADO
2400 West Union Avenue, Englewood CO 80110-5354. 303/797-1600. **Contact:** Human Resources. **World Wide Web address:** http://www.wmcolorado.com. **Description:** A waste disposal company specializing in the hauling of waste materials. **Parent company:** Waste Management, Inc. is an international provider of comprehensive waste management services, as well as engineering and construction, industrial, and related services, with operations in 19 countries. **Listed on:** New York Stock Exchange. **Stock exchange symbol:** WMI.

WASTE MANAGEMENT, INC.
6091 Brighton Boulevard, Commerce City CO 80022. 303/288-5115. **Contact:** Human Resources. **World Wide Web address:** http://www.wm.com. **Description:** A community provider of waste hauling, dumping, and recycling services. **Corporate headquarters location:** Houston TX. **Listed on:** New York Stock Exchange. **Stock exchange symbol:** WMI.

FABRICATED METAL PRODUCTS AND PRIMARY METALS

You can expect to find the following types of companies in this section:
Aluminum and Copper Foundries • Die-Castings • Iron and Steel Foundries • Steel Works, Blast Furnaces, and Rolling Mills

---

BALL CORPORATION
10 Longs Peak Drive, P.O. Box 5000, Broomfield CO 80021-2510. 303/469-3131. **Contact:** Human Resources. **World Wide Web address:** http://www.ball.com. **Description:** Produces metal and plastic packaging products for foods and beverages, and provides aerospace and communications products and services to government and commercial customers. **Positions advertised include:** Sr. Systems Analyst; Sr. Auditor; Manager, Corporate Payroll; Process Engineer. **Corporate headquarters location:** This location. **Listed on:** New York Stock Exchange. **Stock exchange symbol:** BLL.

DYNAMIC MATERIALS CORPORATION
5405 Spine Road, Boulder CO 80301. 303/665-5700. **Fax:** 303/604-1893. **Contact:** Human Resources. **E-mail address:** boom@dynamicmaterials.com. **World Wide Web address:** http://www.dynamicmaterials.com. **Description:** Engaged in the use of explosives to bond and form metals. **NOTE:** Entry-level positions and second and third shifts are offered. **Company slogan:** We strive to live up to our dynamic name. **Special programs:** Internships; Apprenticeships; Training. **Corporate headquarters location:** This location. **Other U.S. locations:** South Windsor CT; Uniontown PA. **Listed on:** NASDAQ. **Stock exchange symbol:** BOOM. **Annual sales/revenues:** $21 - $50 million. **Number of employees at this location:** 80. **Number of employees nationwide:** 135.

EATON METAL PRODUCTS COMPANY
4803 York Street, Denver CO 80216-2237. 303/296-4800. **Contact:** Human Resources. **World Wide Web address:** http://www.eatonmetalsales.com. **Description:** Sells, installs, and services petroleum equipment.

GOLDBERG BROTHERS INC.
8000 East 40th Avenue, P.O. Box 17048, Denver CO 80217. 303/321-1099. **Fax:** 303/388-0749. **Contact:** Human Resources Department. **Description:** Manufactures aluminum and sheet metal products including aluminum castings, sheet metal stampings, and products made from these metals including film canisters, cases, and reels. **Corporate headquarters location:** This location. **Parent company:** J&R Film Co. **Listed on:** Privately held. **Number of employees at this location:** 40.

NICKELS ALUMINUM GOLDEN
P.O. Box 207, Fort Lupton CO 80621-0207. 303/659-9767. **Physical address:** 1405 East 14th Street, Fort Lupton CO 80621. **Contact:** Human Resources. **Description:** An industrial recycler producing coils for aluminum gutters and cans.

NORTHWEST PIPE COMPANY
6030 North Washington Street, Denver CO 80216. 303/289-4080. **Fax:** 303/288-1068. **Contact:** Personnel Administrator. **World Wide Web address:** http://www.nwpipe.com. **Description:** Manufactures welded steel pipes for construction, agricultural, and industrial uses. The company also offers full-service fabricated metal and project engineering services. Founded in 1966. **Corporate headquarters location:** Portland OR. **Listed on:** NASDAQ. **Stock exchange symbol:** NWPX.

QUALITY METAL PRODUCTS
11500 West 13th Avenue, Lakewood CO 80215. 303/232-4242. **Fax:** 303/233-3944. **Contact:** Human Resources. **E-mail address:** skatzman@qualitymetalproducts.com. **World Wide Web address:** http://www.qualitymetalproducts.com. **Description:** Manufactures sheet metal and related products.

RELIANCE METAL CENTER
3855 Silica Drive, Colorado Springs CO 80910. 719/390-4911. **Contact:** Human Resources. **World Wide Web address:** http://www.rsac.com. **Description:** One of the largest Western-based metals service center companies in the United States. Through a network of 20 locations, the company distributes a full line of ferrous and nonferrous metal products, including galvanized, hot-rolled and cold-finished steel, stainless steel, aluminum, brass, copper, and alloy steel. The company sells metal products from locations in nine states and to more than 30,000 customers engaged in a wide variety of industries. **Corporate headquarters location:** Los Angeles CA. **Parent company:** Reliance Steel and Aluminum Company. **Listed on:** New York Stock Exchange. **Stock exchange symbol:** RS.

ROCKY MOUNTAIN STEEL CORPORATION
P.O. Box 316, Pueblo CO 81002. 719/561-6000. **Contact:** Supervisor of Personnel. **World Wide Web address:** http://www.oregonsteel.com. **Description:** Manufactures steel bar products, railroad rails, seamless oil country tubular pipes, and wire. **Corporate headquarters location:** Portland OR. **Parent company:** Oregon Steel Mills. **Listed on:** New York Stock Exchange. **Stock exchange symbol:** OS.

ZIMMERMAN METALS, INC.
201 East 58th Avenue, Denver CO 80216. 303/294-0180. **Toll-free phone:** 800/247-4202. **Fax:** 303/292-5013. **Contact:** Jeanne Klatka, Personnel Manager. **World Wide Web address:** http://www.zimmerman-metals.com. **Description:** Fabricates structural and miscellaneous steel and architectural metals. **Positions advertised include:** Fabrication Fitter; Welder; Supervisor; Producer. **Corporate headquarters location:**

This location. **Operations at this facility include:** Administration; Manufacturing; Research and Development; Sales; Service.

FINANCIAL SERVICES

**You can expect to find the following types of companies
in this section:**
Consumer Financing and Credit Agencies • Investment Specialists •
Mortgage Bankers and Loan Brokers • Security and Commodity Brokers,
Dealers, and Exchanges

AMERICAN CENTURY INVESTMENTS
8300 Fairmount Drive, Denver CO 80247. 303/329-0230. **Contact:**
Human Resources Manager. **World Wide Web address:**
http://www.americancentury.com. **Description:** Provides mutual fund
investment services. Founded in 1958. **Corporate headquarters
location:** Kansas City MO. **Listed on:** Privately held. **Number of
employees at this location:** 350. **Number of employees nationwide:**
2,000. **Number of employees worldwide:** 2,100.

COLUMBIA MANAGEMENT ADVISORS, LLC
12100 East Iliff Avenue, Suite 300, Aurora CO 80014. 303/337-6555.
Fax: 303/743-6341. **Contact:** Personnel. **World Wide Web address:**
http://www.columbiafunds.com. **Description:** Provides investment
products. **Special programs:** Training. **Office hours:** Monday - Friday,
6:00 a.m. - 6:00 p.m. **Corporate headquarters location:** Boston MA.
Parent company: Banc of America Capital Management, LLC.

COUNTRYWIDE FUNDING CORPORATION
8433 Church Ranch Boulevard, Suite 300, Broomfield CO 80021.
303/410-9100. **Fax:** 303/410-9900. **World Wide Web address:**
http://www.countrywide.com. **Contact:** Human Resources. **Description:**
Originates, purchases, sells, and services mortgage loans. The
company's mortgage loans are principally first-lien mortgage loans
secured by single-family residences. **Other U.S. locations:** Nationwide.
Parent company: Countrywide Credit Industries. **Listed on:** New York
Stock Exchange. **Stock exchange symbol:** CCR.

FOUNDERS ASSET MANAGEMENT, LLC
201 University Boulevard, Suite 800, Denver CO 80206. 303/394-4404.
Fax: 303/394-7840. **Contact:** Human Resources. **E-mail address:**
employment@founders.com. **World Wide Web address:**
http://www.founders.com. **Description:** Offers mutual funds including
small-stock, international funds and conservative bond funds. The
company services approximately 125,000 account holders worldwide
and manages assets of approximately $2 billion. Founded in 1938.
Corporate headquarters location: This location. **Parent company:**
Mellon Financial Company.

JANUS CAPITAL GROUP

100 Fillmore Street, Denver CO 80206. 303/333-3863. **Contact:** Recruiting Manager. **World Wide Web address:** http://www.janus.com. **Description:** Manages mutual funds and offers a wide variety of account options and investment services. **Positions advertised include:** Solution Services Specialist; External Wholesaler; Director, Investment Writing; Institutional Marketing Manager; Sr. Audit Manager; Product Manager. **Corporate headquarters location:** This location. **Listed on:** Privately held. **Number of employees at this location:** 700.

SMITH BARNEY

370 17th Street, Suite 2800, Denver CO 80202-1370. 303/572-4025. **Contact:** Human Resources. **World Wide Web address:** http://www.smithbarney.com. **Description:** An investment banking and securities broker. Smith Barney also provides related financial services. **Parent company:** Citigroup, Inc. **Listed on:** New York Stock Exchange. **Stock exchange symbol:** C.

STIFEL NICOLAUS

1125 17th Street, Suite 1500, Denver CO 80202-2032. 303/534-1180. **Contact:** Human Resources. **World Wide Web address:** http://www.stifel.com. **Description:** A securities brokerage firm. **Corporate headquarters location:** St. Louis MO.

UBS FINANCIAL SERVICES INC.

370 17th Street, Suite 4100, Denver CO 80202. 303/436-9000. **Contact:** Human Resources Department. **World Wide Web address:** http://www.financialservicesinc.ubs.com. **Description:** A full-service securities firm with over 300 offices nationwide. Services include investment banking, asset management, merger and acquisition consulting, municipal securities underwriting, estate planning, retirement programs, and transaction management. Clients include corporations, governments, institutions, and individuals. Founded in 1879. **Corporate headquarters location:** New York NY. **Other U.S. locations:** Nationwide. **Annual sales/revenues:** More than $100 million.

FOOD AND BEVERAGES/AGRICULTURE

You can expect to find the following types of companies in this section:
Crop Services and Farm Supplies • Dairy Farms • Food Manufacturers/Processors and Agricultural Producers • Tobacco Products

AMERICAN PRIDE
P.O. Box 98, Henderson CO 80640. 303/659-3643. **Fax:** 303/659-3640. **Contact:** Office Manager. **Description:** Markets bulk and bagged fertilizer, agricultural chemicals, seeds, feed, and veterinary supplies. **Corporate headquarters location:** This location. **Operations at this facility include:** Administration; Sales.

ANHEUSER-BUSCH, INC.
2351 Busch Drive, Fort Collins CO 80524. 970/490-4500. **Toll-free phone:** 800/DIAL-BUD. **Contact:** Human Resources. **World Wide Web address:** http://www.anheuser-busch.com. **Description:** One of the world's largest beer brewers. Brand names include Budweiser, Michelob, and Busch beers. **Positions advertised include:** Maintenance Technician. **Corporate headquarters location:** St. Louis MO. **Parent company:** Anheuser-Busch Companies is engaged in the brewing, entertainment, baking, and manufacturing industries. In addition to its brewing operations, the company also has several related businesses including can manufacturing, paper printing, and barley malting. The company is also involved in real estate and is one of the largest operators of theme parks in the United States, with locations in Florida, Virginia, Texas, Ohio, and California. Through its subsidiary Campbell Taggart Inc., Anheuser-Busch, Inc. is also one of the largest commercial baking companies in the United States, producing foods under the Colonial brand name, among others. **Listed on:** New York Stock Exchange. **Stock exchange symbol:** BUD.

BEVERAGE DISTRIBUTORS CORPORATION
14200 East Moncrieff Place, Suite E, Aurora CO 80011. 303/371-3421. **Contact:** Human Resources. **World Wide Web address:** http://www.beveragedistr.com. **Description:** Provides beverage distribution services. **Number of employees at this location:** 385.

CARGILL INC.
P.O. Box 459, Byers CO 80103. 719/775-2358. **Contact:** Human Resources Department. **E-mail address:** employment@cargill.com. **World Wide Web address:** http://www.cargill.com. **Description:** Cargill Inc., its subsidiaries, and its affiliates are involved in nearly 50 individual lines of business. Cargill Inc. has more than 130 years of service and expertise in commodity trading, handling, transporting, processing, and risk management. Cargill Inc. is a major trader of grains and oilseeds, as well as a marketer of many other agricultural and nonagricultural

commodities. As a transporter, Cargill Inc. uses a network of rail and road systems, inland waterways, and ocean-going routes, combining its own fleet and contracted transportation services to move bulk commodities. As an agricultural supplier, Cargill Inc. is one of the leaders in developing and supplying farm products. Agricultural products include a wide variety of feed, seed, fertilizers, and other goods and services. Cargill Central Research, located at Cargill Inc. headquarters, is dedicated to developing new agricultural products to address the needs of its global customers. The company also provides financial and technical services. Cargill Inc.'s Financial Markets Division (FMD) supports Cargill Inc. and its subsidiaries with financial products including financial instrument trading, emerging markets instrument trading, value investing, and money management. Cargill Inc.'s worldwide food processing businesses supply products ranging from basic ingredients used in food production to recognized name brands. Cargill Inc. also operates a number of industrial businesses, including the production of steel, industrial-grade starches, ethanol, and salt products. **Corporate headquarters location:** Minneapolis MN. **Operations at this facility include:** This facility is an agricultural warehousing and storage location. **Number of employees worldwide:** 70,000.

CEREFORM
1485 East 61st Avenue, P.O. Box 16366, Denver CO 80216. 866/778-7826. **Contact:** Human Resources. **E-mail address:** info@cereformusa.com. **World Wide Web address:** http://www.cereformusa.com. **Description:** Manufactures bakery mixes, jams, jellies, food, and oils. Cereform also sells wholesale bakery supplies and performs some chemical testing. **Parent company:** ABITEC Corporation.

COCA-COLA BOTTLING COMPANY OF DENVER
3825 York Street, Denver CO 80205. 303/292-2653. **Fax:** 303/291-9707. **Contact:** Ron Paxton, Human Resources Director. **World Wide Web address:** http://www.cokecce.com. **Description:** A bottler of soft drink brands including Barq's, Coca-Cola, and Dr. Pepper. **NOTE:** Please check the jobline for available positions before sending a resume. **Positions advertised include:** Employee Relations Manager; Account Manager; Service Technician; Merchandiser. **Corporate headquarters location:** Atlanta GA. **Other U.S. locations:** Nationwide. **Number of employees at this location:** 500.

CONAGRA FLOUR MILLING COMPANY
4545 East 64th Avenue, Commerce City CO 80022. 303/289-6141. **Contact:** Human Resources. **World Wide Web address:** http://www.conagra.com. **Description:** ConAgra Flour Milling Company is a leader in the U.S. flour milling industry with 27 mills in 14 states. Operations also include seven jointly owned mills, three in the United States and four in Canada. **NOTE:** Interested jobseekers must be able to relocate approximately every 18 months to two years. **Office hours:** Monday - Friday, 7:00 a.m. - 4:00 p.m. **Corporate headquarters location:** Omaha NE. **Operations at this facility include:** This location

is engaged in the production and sale of wheat flour products in bulk and bag units to commercial bakeries, wholesale distributors, and retail grocery companies. **Parent company:** ConAgra Foods. **Listed on:** New York Stock Exchange. **Stock exchange symbol:** CAG. **Annual sales/revenues:** More than $100 million. **Number of employees at this location:** 125.

CONAGRA FOODS
149 Kimbark Street, Longmont CO 80501. 303/776-6611. **Contact:** Human Resources. **World Wide Web address:** http://www.conagra.com. **Description:** Engaged in poultry dressing operations. **Corporate headquarters location:** Omaha NE. **Listed on:** New York Stock Exchange. **Stock exchange symbol:** CAG.

HAIN CELESTIAL GROUP
4600 Sleepytime Drive, Boulder CO 80301. 303/530-5300. **Contact:** Stephanie Thibault, Director of Human Resources. **World Wide Web address:** http://www.hain-celestial.com. **Description:** Produces herbal teas and beverages. **Corporate headquarters location:** Melville NY. **Listed on:** NASDAQ. **Stock exchange symbol:** HAIN.

KRAFT FOODS, INC.
OSCAR MAYER & COMPANY
315 Inverness Way South, Englewood CO 80112. 303/784-7500. **Contact:** Human Resources. **World Wide Web address:** http://www.kraft.com. **Description:** Kraft Foods, Inc. is one of the largest producers of packaged grocery products in North America. Major brands include Jell-O, Post, Kool-Aid, Crystal Light, Entenmann's, Miracle Whip, Stove Top, and Shake 'n Bake. Kraft Foods, Inc. markets a number of products under the Kraft brand including natural and processed cheeses and dry packaged dinners. The Oscar Mayer unit markets processed meats, poultry, lunch combinations, and pickles under the Oscar Mayer, Louis Rich, Lunchables, and Claussen brand names. Kraft Foods, Inc. is also one of the largest coffee companies with principal brands including Maxwell House, Sanka, Brim, and General Foods International Coffees. Kraft Foods Ingredients Corporation manufactures private-label and industrial food products for sale to other food processing companies. **Corporate headquarters location:** White Plains NY. **Operations at this facility include:** This location is a sales office of the consumer foods company. **Parent company:** Philip Morris Companies is a holding company whose principal wholly-owned subsidiaries are Philip Morris Inc. (Philip Morris U.S.A.), Philip Morris International Inc., Kraft Foods, Inc., and Philip Morris Capital Corporation. In the tobacco industry, Philip Morris U.S.A. and Philip Morris International together form one of the largest international cigarette operations in the world. U.S. brand names include Marlboro, Parliament, Virginia Slims, Benson & Hedges, and Merit. Philip Morris Capital Corporation is engaged in financial services and real estate. **Listed on:** New York Stock Exchange. **Stock exchange symbol:** KFT.

NATIONAL CATTLEMEN'S BEEF ASSOCIATION

P.O. Box 3469, Englewood CO 80155. 303/694-0305. **Physical address:** 9110 East Nichols Avenue, Suite 300, Centennial CO 80112. **Contact:** Human Resources. **World Wide Web address:** http://www.beef.org. **Description:** An association that operates to improve the economic, political, and social interests of the U.S. cattle industry.

NESTLE PURINA PET CARE COMPANY

4555 York Street, Denver CO 80216. 303/295-0818. **Contact:** Human Resources Department. **World Wide Web address:** http://www.purina.com. **Description:** Produces a line of dog foods, cat foods, and feed for other domestic animals. Founded in 1894. **Office hours:** Monday - Friday, 7:30 a.m. - 4:00 p.m. **Corporate headquarters location:** St. Louis MO. **Number of employees worldwide:** 63,000.

NOBEL/SYSCO FOOD SERVICES COMPANY

1101 West 48th Avenue, Denver CO 80221. 303/458-4000. **Fax:** 303/480-3370. **Recorded jobline:** 303/480-3475. **Contact:** Human Resources. **E-mail address:** jobs@nobelsysco.com. **World Wide Web address:** http://www.nobelsysco.com. **Description:** Markets and distributes a broad line of food products, beverages, and related supplies to restaurants, fast-food operations, schools, and hospitals. **Positions advertised include:** Merchandiser; Sales Associate. **Corporate headquarters location:** Houston TX. **Other U.S. locations:** Nationwide. **Parent company:** SYSCO Corporation. **Listed on:** New York Stock Exchange. **Stock exchange symbol:** SYY. **Number of employees at this location:** 1,000.

PEPSI-COLA BOTTLING COMPANY

3801 Brighton Boulevard, Denver CO 80216. 303/292-9220. **Contact:** Human Resources. **World Wide Web address:** http://www.pepsico.com. **Description:** A division of Pepsi-Cola Company that produces Pepsi, Diet Pepsi, A&W Root Beer, Slice, Orange Slice, and Mountain Dew. **Positions advertised include:** Internal Auditor; Field Engineer. **Office hours:** Monday - Friday, 8:00 a.m. - 4:00 p.m. **Parent company:** PepsiCo, Inc. (Purchase NY) consists of Frito-Lay Company, Pepsi-Cola Company, Quaker Oats Company, and Tropicana Products, Inc. **Listed on:** New York Stock Exchange. **Stock exchange symbol:** PEP.

ROBINSON DAIRY INC.

646 Bryant Street, Denver CO 80204. 303/825-2990. **Contact:** Human Resources. **World Wide Web address:** http://www.robinsondairy.com. **Description:** Produces a complete range of dairy products including milk and ice cream. Robinson Dairy also produces a variety of fruit-flavored drinks. **NOTE:** Fill out application at location. **Corporate headquarters location:** This location.

SINTON DAIRY FOODS COMPANY, INC.

3801 North Sinton Road, Colorado Springs CO 80907. 719/633-3821. **Contact:** Human Resources. **World Wide Web address:** http://www.sintondairy.com. **Description:** Processes dairy products.

U.S. FOODSERVICE

11955 East Peakview Avenue, Englewood CO 80111. 303/792-9230. **Fax:** 303/643-4729. **Contact:** Human Resources. **E-mail address:** recruit-den@allintfs.com. **World Wide Web address:** http://www.usfoodservice.com. **Description:** A broadline distributor of food products, equipment and supplies, cleaning chemicals, and disposables to a variety of food service locations including restaurants, nursing homes, hospitals, and institutional feeders. **Positions advertised include:** District Sales Manager.

THE WESTERN SUGAR COOPERATIVE

7555 East Hampden Avenue, Suite 600, Denver CO 80231. 303/830-3939. **Fax:** 303/830-3941. **Contact:** Human Resources. **E-mail address:** HR@westsernsugar.com. **World Wide Web address:** http://www.westernsugar.com. **Description:** Operates sugar-processing plants in Nebraska, Wyoming, Montana, and Colorado. **Positions advertised include:** Network Analyst/Administrator; Financial Analyst.

GOVERNMENT

You can expect to find the following types of companies in this section:
Courts • Executive, Legislative, and General Government • Public Agencies (Firefighters, Military, Police) • United States Postal Service

---

BUCKLEY AIR FORCE BASE
Aurora CO 720/847-9011. **Recorded jobline:** 800/616-3775. **World Wide Web address:** http://www.buckley.af.mil. **Description:** Home of the Colorado Air National Guard. **NOTE:** Instructions for application for positions are available at the Air Force Personnel Center website: https://ww2.afpc.randolph.af.mil/resweb. **Positions advertised include:** Contract Specialist.

COLORADO COUNCIL ON THE ARTS
1380 Lawrence Street, Denver CO 80204. 303/866-2723. **Fax:** 303/866-4266. **Contact:** Human Resources. **E-mail address:** coloarts@state.co.us. **World Wide Web address:** http://www.coloarts.state.co.us. **Description:** A state agency that awards grants to arts organizations and artists, and promotes the arts in Colorado. Founded in 1967. **Special programs:** Internships.

COLORADO DIVISION OF PARKS AND RECREATION
GOLDEN GATE CANYON STATE PARK
92 Crawford Gulch Road, Golden CO 80403. 303/582-3707. **Contact:** Human Resources Department. **E-mail address:** golden.gate.park@state.co.us. **World Wide Web address:** http://parks.state.co.us. **Description:** An agency overseeing a 14,000-acre mountain park that includes more than 60 miles of hiking trails, 288 picnic sites, 164 campsites, a group camping facility, and a visitor center offering information and sales items related to natural resources. **Special programs:** Internships.

COLORADO HOUSING & FINANCE AUTHORITY
1981 Blake Street, Denver CO 80202-1272. 303/297-2432. **Contact:** Becca Hagen, Human Resources Director. **E-mail address:** resumes@colohfa.org. **World Wide Web address:** http://www.colohfa.org. **Description:** A quasi-governmental organization that provides financing for housing (both rental and home ownership) for low- and moderate-income clients. Colorado Housing & Finance Authority also provides financing for small businesses. **Positions advertised include:** Director of Loan Servicing; Quality Assurance Servicing Auditor; Post Closing Analyst; Operational Support Specialist; Business Development Specialist.

COLORADO MUNICIPAL LEAGUE
1144 Sherman Street, Denver CO 80203-2207. 303/831-6411. **Contact:** Katy Priest, Office Manager. **E-mail address:** kpriest@cml.org. **World**

Wide Web address: http://www.cml.org. **Description:** A non-profit organization consisting of 265 Colorado communities.

COLORADO SPRINGS, CITY OF
P.O. Box 1575, Mail Code 1543, Colorado Springs CO 80901-1575. 719/385-5904. **Contact:** Lauren Kramer, City Manager. **World Wide Web address:** http://www.springsgov.com. **Description:** The administrative offices for the city of Colorado Springs. **NOTE:** Search and apply for jobs at: http://citycareers.SpringsGov.com. **Positions advertised include:** SQL Developer; Sr. Network Engineer; Street Operations Manager; PeopleSoft Developer; Attorney; Sr. Engineering Inspector.

DENVER REGIONAL COUNCIL OF GOVERNMENTS
4500 Cherry Creek Drive South, Suite 800, Denver CO 80246. 303/455-1000. **Fax:** 303/480-6768. **Contact:** Human Resources. **World Wide Web address:** http://www.drcog.org. **Description:** An association of local governments for 39 area cities and eight counties. **NOTE:** Entry-level positions are offered. **Positions advertised include:** Planner. **Special programs:** Internships. **Number of employees at this location:** 80.

FORT CARSON
Civilian Personnel Advisory Center, 6151 Specker, Room 2080, Building 1550, Fort Carson CO 80913-5118. 719/526-4524. **Contact:** Personnel. **World Wide Web address:** http://www.carson.army.mil. **Description:** Organizes the armed forces to defend the nation's security. **NOTE:** Search for open positions at: http://www.cpol.army.mil. **Parent company:** U.S. Department of the Army.

GRAND MESA, UNCOMPAHGRE, AND GUNNISON NATIONAL FOREST
2250 Highway 50, Delta CO 81416. 970/874-6600. **Contact:** Human Resources. **World Wide Web address:** http://www.fs.fed.us/r2/gmug/. **Description:** A division of the United States Department of Agriculture Forest Service. **Special programs:** Internships.

GREELEY, CITY OF
1000 10th Street, Greeley CO 80631. 970/350-9710. **Recorded jobline:** 970/350-9777x200. **Contact:** Human Resources Department. **World Wide Web address:** http://www.ci.greeley.co.us. **Description:** Administrative offices for the city of Greeley. **NOTE:** Application form available online. **Positions advertised include:** Court Clerk; Deputy City Manager; Facilities Coordinator; Recreation Supervisor; Victim Services Coordinator.

LONGMONT, CITY OF
350 Kimbark Street, Longmont CO 80501. 303/776-6050. **Recorded jobline:** 303/651-8710. **Contact:** Human Resources. **E-mail address:** Terry.Rivas@ci.longmont.co.us. **World Wide Web address:** http://www.ci.longmont.co.us. **Description:** Administrative offices for the

city of Longmont. **Positions advertised include:** Recreation Program Supervisor; Librarian; Sr. Police Services Technician; Purchasing and Contracts Manager.

PETERSON AIR FORCE BASE
Colorado Springs CO 719/554-7321. **World Wide Web address:** http://www.peterson.af.mil. **Description:** Home of the 21st Space Wing, which provides missile warning and space control to the North American Aerospace Defense Command and U.S. Strategic Command. **NOTE:** Instructions for application for positions are available at the Air Force Personnel Center website: https://ww2.afpc.randolph.af.mil/resweb.**Positions advertised include:** Acquisition Program Manager; Budget Analyst; Editorial Assistant Office Automation; Human Resources Specialist; Management Analyst; Program Analyst; Security Specialist; Supply Management Specialist; Financial Specialist Supervisor.

PIKES PEAK LIBRARY DISTRICT
P.O. Box 1579, Colorado Springs CO 80901. 719/531-6333. **Contact:** Human Resources. **World Wide Web address:** http://www.ppld.org. **Description:** A system of 12 libraries serving El Paso County, Colorado. **Positions advertised include:** Branch Manager; Branch Monitor.

U.S. BUREAU OF LAND MANAGEMENT
50629 Highways 6 & 24, Glenwood Springs CO 81601. 970/947-2800. **Fax:** 970/947-2829. **Contact:** Volunteers and Interns Coordinator. **World Wide Web address:** http://www.blm.gov. **Description:** A federal agency that is responsible for the management of 261 million acres of public lands and resources including recreation, timber range, wildlife, minerals, watershed, wilderness, and natural, scientific, and cultural values. **Positions advertised include:** Outdoor Recreation Planner; Park Ranger; Biology Technician. **Special programs:** Internships. **Corporate headquarters location:** Washington DC. **Parent company:** U.S. Department of the Interior.

U.S. BUREAU OF RECLAMATION
6th & Kipling, Building 67, P.O. Box 25007, Denver CO 80225-9907. 303/445-2670. **Contact:** Human Resources. **World Wide Web address:** http://www.usbr.gov. **Description:** Engaged in the development and management of water resources in 17 western states. The bureau's primary emphasis is on engineering. **Positions advertised include:** Sr. Advisor, Design, Estimating, and Construction Oversight and Dam Safety. **Parent company:** U.S. Department of the Interior.

U.S. DEPARTMENT OF HOUSING AND URBAN DEVELOPMENT
1670 Broadway, Denver CO 80202-4801. 303/672-5440. **Fax:** 303/672-5004. **Contact:** Human Resources. **World Wide Web address:** http://www.hud.gov. **Description:** Provides comprehensive assistance to help build and rebuild large and small communities; enforces the Fair Housing Act and other civil rights laws; identifies and combats discrimination; helps low- and moderate-income families rent or buy safe,

affordable housing; and helps to create and maintain safe, affordable housing and supportive living environments for the families served by its programs.

U.S. ENVIRONMENTAL PROTECTION AGENCY (EPA)

999 18th Street, Suite 200, Denver CO 80202-2466. 303/312-6312. **Contact:** Human Resources. **World Wide Web address:** http://www.epa.gov. **Description:** The EPA is dedicated to improving and preserving the quality of the environment, both nationally and globally, and protecting human health and the productivity of natural resources. The agency is committed to ensuring that federal environmental laws are implemented and enforced effectively; U.S. policy, both foreign and domestic, encourages the integration of economic development and environmental protection so that economic growth can be sustained over the long term; and public and private decisions affecting energy, transportation, agriculture, industry, international trade, and natural resources fully integrate considerations of environmental quality. Founded in 1970. **NOTE:** Apply online. **Corporate headquarters location:** Washington DC. **Other U.S. locations:** San Francisco CA; Atlanta GA; Chicago IL; Kansas City KS; Boston MA; New York NY; Philadelphia PA; Dallas TX; Seattle WA. **Number of employees nationwide:** 19,000.

U.S. GEOLOGICAL SURVEY
MIDCONTINENT ECOLOGICAL SCIENCE CENTER

Box 25046, Denver Federal Center, Denver CO 80225. 303/236-5900. **Contact:** Personnel. **World Wide Web address:** http://www.usgs.gov. **Description:** Conducts research and develops technologies to improve the understanding and management of biological systems (species, populations, communities, landscapes, and ecosystems) of the interior western United States. The center also develops and implements inventory and monitoring programs for the accurate assessment of biological status and trends, and provides information, technical services, and training related to the management of biological resources. **Positions advertised include:** Interdisciplinary Geographer; Physical Scientist; Cartographer. **Parent company:** U.S. Department of the Interior.

HEALTH CARE SERVICES, EQUIPMENT, AND PRODUCTS

You can expect to find the following types of companies in this section:
Dental Labs and Equipment • Home Health Care Agencies • Hospitals and Medical Centers • Medical Equipment Manufacturers and Wholesalers • Offices and Clinics of Health Practitioners • Residential Treatment Centers/Nursing Homes • Veterinary Services

ACCREDO THERAPEUTICS INC
361 Inverness Drive South, Suite F, Englewood CO 80112-5816. 303/799-6550. **Fax:** 303/799-6551. **Contact:** Human Resources. **World Wide Web address:** http://www.accredohealth.com. **Description:** Accredo Therapeutics provides specialty biopharmaceuticals and services. **Positions advertised include:** Per Diem Nurse; Per Diem Pharmacist. **Corporate headquarters location:** Memphis TN. **Parent company:** Medco Health Solutions, Inc. **Operations at this facility include:** This location offers infusion therapy services.

AIR METHODS CORPORATION
7301 South Peoria Street, Englewood CO 80112. 303/792-7400. **Fax:** 303/790-0499. **Recorded jobline:** 303/792-7508. **Contact:** Human Resources. **World Wide Web address:** http://www.airmethods.com. **Description:** One of the largest providers of air medical emergency services and systems throughout North America. Air Methods Corporation operates a fleet of 41 aircraft, consisting of 29 helicopters and 12 airplanes. The company provides its services to 54 hospitals located in 14 states. The company designs, services, and installs proprietary medical interiors, allowing each aircraft to be operated as an airborne ICU. Founded in 1982. **NOTE:** Drug screening is a mandatory part of the hiring process. **Positions advertised include:** Assembly/Fabrication Supervisor; Avionics Installation Technician; Quality Assurance Inspector; Stress Analyst. **Number of employees at this location:** 250.

AMERICAN MEDICAL RESPONSE
6200 south Syracuse Way, Suite 200, Greenwood Village CO 80111. 303/495-1200. **Contact:** Human Resources. **World Wide Web address:** http://www.amr-inc.com. **Description:** A medical transportation services company. **Corporate headquarters location:** This location. **Other U.S. locations include:** Nationwide.

ARKANSAS VALLEY REGIONAL MEDICAL CENTER
1100 Carson Avenue, La Junta CO 81050. 719/384-5412. **Fax:** 719/383-6062. **Contact:** Director of Human Resources. **World Wide Web address:** http://www.avrmc.org. **Description:** A nonprofit medical center. **Positions advertised include:** Medical Lab Technician;

Occupational Therapist; Physical Therapist; Staff Pharmacist; RN, Various Departments. **Number of employees at this location:** 400.

CSU VETERINARY TEACHING HOSPITAL
300 West Drake Road, Fort Collins CO 80523. 970/221-4535. **Contact:** Human Resources. **World Wide Web address:** http://www.csuvets.colostate.edu. **Description:** A full-service, referral, veterinary, teaching hospital. Departments include cardiology, oncology, ophthalmology, dermatology, neurology, and emergency.

THE CHILDREN'S HOSPITAL
1056 East 19th Street, Denver CO 80218. 303/861-8888. **Fax:** 303/764-8080. **Contact:** Human Resources. **E-mail address:** jobposting@tchden.org. **World Wide Web address:** http://www.childrenshospitalden.org. **Description:** A hospital providing patient care, research, education, and advocacy. **Positions advertised include:** Financial Counselor; Imaging Technician; Patient Service Coordinator; Staff Assistant; Business Systems Analyst; Manager of Accounting; Clinical Nurse Audiologist; Speech Pathologist; Medical Technician; Psychologist.

COLORADO MENTAL HEALTH INSTITUTE AT FORT LOGAN
3550 West Oxford Avenue, Denver CO 80236. 303/866-7100. **Contact:** Human Resources. **World Wide Web address:** http://www.cdhs.state.co.us/ods/mif. **Description:** A 250-bed, state psychiatric hospital. The hospital operates in three divisions: Adolescent; Adult; and Geriatric/Deaf/Aftercare. Treatments include psychotherapy, group therapy, family therapy, behavior modification, occupational and recreational therapy, pastoral counseling, educational services, vocational counseling, and a work therapy program. The hospital is licensed by the Colorado Department of Health and is accredited by the Joint Commission on Accreditation of Hospitals.

CORAM HEALTHCARE CORPORATION
1675 Broadway, Suite 900, Denver CO 80202. 303/672-8745. **Fax:** 303/298-0043. **Contact:** Faye Major, Director, Human Resources. **World Wide Web address:** http://www.coramhc.com. **Description:** One of the largest home health infusion therapy companies in the United States. The company provides a wide range of alternate site delivery services including ambulatory and home infusion therapies, lithotripsy, and institutional pharmacy services. **Corporate headquarters location:** This location. **Other U.S. locations:** Nationwide. **Subsidiaries include:** Coraflex Health Services; HealthInfusion Inc.; Medisys Inc.; T2 Medical. **Listed on:** New York Stock Exchange. **Stock exchange symbol:** CRH. **Annual sales/revenues:** More than $100 million.

CRAIG HOSPITAL
3425 South Clarkson Street, Englewood CO 80113. 303/789-8000. **Recorded jobline:** 303/789-8497. **Contact:** Human Resources. **E-mail address:** humanresources@craighospital.org. **World Wide Web address:** http://www.craighospital.org. **Description:** A hospital for the

care and rehabilitation of patients with injuries to the brain and spinal cord. **NOTE:** Entry-level positions are offered. Please check the jobline for available positions before sending a resume. **Positions advertised include:** Nurse Practitioner/Physician Assistant; Occupational Therapist; Speech Pathologist; Pharmacist; Clerical Coordinator; Operations Manager, HIM. **Special programs:** Internships. **Operations at this facility include:** Administration. **Number of employees at this location:** 500.

CROSSROADS MEDICAL CENTER
1000 Alpine Street, Suite 280, Boulder CO 80304. 303/444-6400. **Contact:** Director of Personnel. **Description:** An ambulatory health care and family practice provider. Crossroads Medical Center also provides pharmacological, laboratory, and physical therapy services, as well as specialist physician services through their own group practice. **Operations at this facility include:** Administration; Divisional Headquarters; Sales.

DAVITA INC.
1057 South Wadsworth Boulevard, Suite 100, Lakewood CO 80226-4360. 800/424-6589. **Contact:** Human Resources. **World Wide Web address:** http://www.davita.com. **Description:** A provider of dialysis services in the United States for patients suffering from chronic kidney failure. The company operates more than 1,200 outpatient dialysis centers in 41 states and the District of Columbia. DaVita also provides acute inpatient dialysis services in over 369 hospitals across the country. **Positions advertised include:** Staff RN; Compliance Auditor; HR - Resource Center Specialist; Director of IT Applications; Disability Specialist; PeopleSoft HRMS Developer; HRIS Analyst; Vascular Access Coordinator; Computer Operator. **Corporate headquarters location:** El Segundo CA.

DEVEREUX CLEO WALLACE CENTERS
8405 Church Ranch Boulevard, Westminster CO 80021. 303/438-2251. **Fax:** 303/438-2290. **Contact:** Human Resources. **E-mail address:** hrcolorado@devereux.org. **World Wide Web address:** http://www.devereux.org. **Description:** A nonprofit, psychiatric treatment center offering both inpatient and outpatient treatments for children and adolescents. **NOTE:** Entry-level positions and second and third shifts are offered. **Positions advertised include:** Financial Manager; Human Resources Director. **Special programs:** Internships.

EASTMAN KODAK COMPANY
9952 Eastman Park Drive, Windsor CO 80551-1386. 970/686-7611. **Contact:** Jean Clark, Director of Personnel. **World Wide Web address:** http://www.kodak.com. **Description:** Eastman Kodak Company has four businesses: Digital & Film Imaging Systems; Health; Graphic Communications; and Display & Components. **NOTE:** Search and apply for positions online. **Positions advertised include:** Production Operator; Assembly/Warehouse Worker; IS Systems Administrator. **Special programs:** Internships. **Corporate headquarters location:** Rochester

NY. **Operations at this facility include:** This location manufactures photographic and medical X-ray films. **Operations at this facility include:** Manufacturing. **Listed on:** New York Stock Exchange. **Stock exchange symbol:** EK. **Number of employees at this location:** 2,300.

EXEMPLA ST. JOSEPH HOSPITAL
1835 Franklin Street, Denver CO 80218. 303/837-7905. **Contact:** Human Resources. **World Wide Web address:** http://www.saintjosephdenver.org. **Description:** A community hospital providing patient care and education. Founded in 1873. **NOTE:** Search and apply for positions online. **Positions advertised include:** RN, Various Departments; Surgical Tech; Laboratory Supervisor; Respiratory Therapist; Radiology Tech; Director of Marketing; Medical Tech; Neonatal Nurse Practitioner.

FISCHER IMAGING CORPORATION
12300 North Grant Street, Denver CO 80241. 303/452-6800. **Fax:** 303/450-4335. **Contact:** Human Resources. **World Wide Web address:** http://www.fischerimaging.com. **Description:** Develops, manufactures, and markets medical imaging systems. Fischer Imaging Corporation provides medical systems for the electrophysiology, fluoroscopic, mammography, and radiographic markets. **NOTE:** Applications accepted only for open positions. **Corporate headquarters location:** This location. **Listed on:** NASDAQ. **Stock exchange symbol:** FIMG. **Number of employees at this location:** 350. **Number of employees nationwide:** 540.

GAMBRO RENAL PRODUCTS, USA
10810 West Collins Avenue, Lakewood CO 80215. **Toll-free phone:** 800/525-2623. **Contact:** Human Resources. **World Wide Web address:** http://www.usa-gambro.com. **Description:** Develops and supplies products, therapies, and services for both in-center and home dialysis, as well as for blood purification in intensive care units. **Positions advertised include:** Accounting Manager; Marketing Manager; Marketing Manager-Water Systems; Vice President of Human Resources GRP Americas.

HEI ADVANCED MEDICAL OPERATIONS
4801 North 63rd Street, Boulder CO 80301. 720/622-4100. **Fax:** 303/530-8291. **Contact:** Human Resources. **World Wide Web address:** http://www.heii.com. **Description:** Manufactures electro-mechanical medical devices, catheters, respiratory diagnostic instruments, MRI (Magnetic Resonance Imaging) systems, and similar medical devices. **Corporate headquarters location:** Victoria MN.

LITTLETON ADVENTIST HOSPITAL
7700 South Broadway, Littleton CO 80122. 303/730-8900. **Fax:** 303/738-2688. **Recorded jobline:** 888/808-8828. **Contact:** Human Resources. **World Wide Web address:** http://www.littletonhosp.org. **Description:** A full service hospital serving Littleton and the surrounding areas. Founded 1989. **Positions advertised include:** Clinical Charge Auditor; Clinical

Coordinator; Certified Nurse Assistant; Nursing Unit Secretary; OR Technician; Pharmacy Technician; Radiology Technician; Respiratory Therapist; Transcriptionist; Ultrasound Technician. **Parent company:** Centura Health.

LONGMONT UNITED HOSPITAL
1950 Mountain View Avenue, Longmont CO 80501. 303/485-4136. **Fax:** 303/485-4137. **Recorded jobline:** 303/651-5241. **Contact:** Human Resources. **World Wide Web address:** http://www.luhcares.org. **Description:** A 143-bed general, acute care, nonprofit, community hospital. Longmont United Hospital offers a cancer care center, a cardiac lab, cardiopulmonary services, a sports rehabilitation center, complimentary medicine, cardiovascular rehabilitation, trauma/emergency center, and behavioral health services. **NOTE:** Second and third shifts are offered. **Positions advertised include:** RN, Various Departments; Respiratory Therapist; CAN; Med Tech; MRI Tech. **Special programs:** Training. **Corporate headquarters location:** This location. **Annual sales/revenues:** $51 - $100 million. **Number of employees at this location:** 930.

THE MEDICAL CENTER OF AURORA
1501 South Potomac Street, Aurora CO 80012. 303/695-2600. **Contact:** Human Resources. **Description:** A medical center with two campuses, and 346 licensed beds. **Positions advertised include:** Sr. Accountant; Clinical Nurse Manager; Director, EMS, Trauma & Disaster; RN; Surgical Tech; Director, Surgical Services. **Parent company:** HealthONE.

MEDTRONIC INC.
826 Coal Creek Circle, Louisville CO 80027. 720/890-3200. **Contact:** Human Resources. **World Wide Web address:** http://www.medtronic.com. **Description:** Develops, manufactures, and markets products, therapies and services used to treat conditions such as diabetes, heart disease, neurological disorders, and vascular illnesses. **Positions advertised include:** Associate Product Manager; Corporate Account Director; Customer Service Rep; Financial Systems Analyst. **Corporate headquarters location:** Minneapolis MN. **Parent company:** Medtronic Inc. **Listed on:** New York Stock Exchange. **Stock exchange symbol:** MOT.

MOUNT SAN RAFAEL HOSPITAL
410 Benedicta Avenue, Trinidad CO 81082. 719/846-9213. **Fax:** 719/846-2752. **Contact:** Human Resources. **World Wide Web address:** http://www.msrhc.org. **Description:** A nonprofit, JCAHO-accredited, acute care hospital with 70 beds offering 24-hour physician coverage; an emergency department; a full laboratory; a pharmacy; X-ray facilities; physical, occupational, and speech therapy; diabetic education; home health care; and prenatal education. **NOTE:** Entry-level positions and second and third shifts are offered. **Special programs:** Training. **Office hours:** Monday - Friday, 8:00 a.m. - 4:30 p.m. **Executive Director:** James D'Agostino. **Annual sales/revenues:** Less than $5 million. **Number of employees at this location:** 144.

NATIONAL JEWISH MEDICAL & RESEARCH CENTER

1400 Jackson Street, G113, Denver CO 80206. 303/388-4461. **Fax:** 303/398-1775. **Recorded jobline:** 800/686-9512. **Contact:** Human Resources Director. **E-mail address:** hr@njc.org. **World Wide Web address:** http://www.njc.org. **Description:** A world leader in the research and treatment of respiratory, immune system, and allergic disorders. National Jewish Medical & Research Center is a nonprofit, nonsectarian institution. Founded in 1899. Positions advertised include: Certified Medical Assistant; Clinical Research Coordinator; Database/Operations Coordinator; Executive Director, Business Development.

NICOLET VASCULAR INC.

720 Corporate Circle, Suite A, Golden CO 80401. 608/441-2266. **Toll-free phone:** 800/525-2519. **Fax:** 608/441-2232. **Contact:** Human Resources. **World Wide Web address:** http://www.viasyshealthcare.com. **Description:** Manufactures diagnostic equipment including fetal heart detectors for determining fetal viability, and systems that aid in the diagnosis of cardiovascular disease. The company also manufactures electronic instrumentation for medical applications in neuro-physiological diagnosis and for monitoring the treatment of brain, muscle, nerve, and sleep disorders, and to test for hearing impairment. **Special programs:** Internships; Summer Jobs. **Corporate headquarters location:** Madison WI. **Parent company:** VIASYS Healthcare. **Listed on:** New York Stock Exchange. **Stock exchange symbol:** VAS. **Annual sales/revenues:** $11 - $20 million. **Number of employees at this location:** 75.

NORTH COLORADO MEDICAL CENTER (NCMC)
BANNER HEALTH COLORADO

1801 16th Street, Greeley CO 80631-5199. 970/352-4121. **Fax:** 970/350-6446. **Recorded jobline:** 970/350-6565. **Contact:** Director of Personnel. **World Wide Web address:** http://www.bannerhealth.com. **Description:** A not-for-profit hospital that serves as the primary full-service tertiary facility for northern and eastern Colorado, southern Wyoming, western Nebraska, and Kansas.. **NOTE:** Apply online. Entry-level positions are offered. **Positions advertised include:** Certified Nursing Assistant; Clinical Nurse Educator; Emergency Department Technician; Infection Control Analyst; Licensed Respiratory Therapist; Medical Technologist; Nuclear Medicine Technologist; Patient Account Representative; Pharmacist; Physical Therapist; Radiology Technologist; RN, Various Departments. **Corporate headquarters location:** Fargo ND. **Other area locations:** Brush CO; Loveland CO; Sterling CO. **Operations at this facility include:** Administration; Regional Headquarters; Service. **Annual sales/revenues:** $21 - $50 million. **Number of employees at this location:** 1,700. **Number of employees nationwide:** 14,000.

NORTH SUBURBAN MEDICAL CENTER (NSMC)

9191 Grant Street, Thornton CO 80229-4341. 303/451-7800. **Contact:** Human Resources. **World Wide Web address:** http://www.northsuburban.com. **Description:** A 157-bed, family-centered health care facility. North Suburban Medical Center offers a full range of services including orthopedics, ICU/CCU, 24-hour emergency coverage, medical and surgical, pediatrics, and oncology. In addition, NSMC also operates a 23-bed Transitional Care Center and a program for inpatient treatment of geriatric, psychiatric disorders. **Positions advertised include:** RN, Various Departments; Cardiovascular Specialist; Clinical Nurse Specialist; Occupational Therapist; Quality Management Coordinator.

PENROSE-ST. FRANCIS HEALTH SERVICES
PENROSE HOSPITAL
2222 North Nevada Avenue, Colorado Springs CO 80907. 719/776-5000. **Contact:** Human Resources. **World Wide Web address:** http://www.centura.org. **Description:** Operates a 300-bed hospital; a cytology laboratory; Huff and Puff, a children's asthma program; The Women's Life Center; ReadyCare clinics; The Penrose Cancer Center; The Namaste Alzheimer Center; The Heart Center at Penrose Hospital; The Center for Health and Nutrition; trauma rehabilitation and comprehensive rehabilitation; and The Clinical Pastoral Education Program. **Positions advertised include:** RN, Various Departments; CNA. **Other area locations:** Green Mountain Falls CO; Woodland Park CO. **Parent company:** Centura Health.

PORTER ADVENTIST HOSPITAL
2525 South Downing Street, Denver CO 80210. 303/778-1955. **Contact:** Human Resources. **World Wide Web address:** http://www.centura.org. **Description:** A 369-bed, nonprofit, acute care hospital. Founded in 1930. **Positions advertised include:** RN, Various Departments; OR Technician; Pharmacy Tech; Physical Therapist; CT Tech. **Parent company:** Centura Health.

POUDRE VALLEY HOSPITAL
1024 South Lemay Avenue, Fort Collins CO 80524. 970/495-7300. **Fax:** 970/495-7629. **Recorded jobline:** 970/495-7310. **Contact:** Patti Oakes, Director of Human Resources. **World Wide Web address:** http://www.pvhs.org. **Description:** A 255-bed hospital providing health care services in northern Colorado, western Nebraska, and southern Wyoming. **NOTE:** Search and apply for positions online. **Positions advertised include:** Clinical Coordinator, Pharmacy; Medical Technologist; Physical Therapist; Supervisor, Clinical Applications **Special programs:** Internships. **Office hours:** Monday - Friday, 7:00 a.m. - 4:30 p.m. **Parent company:** Poudre Valley Health System. **Number of employees at this location:** 1,800.

PRESBYTERIAN/ST. LUKE'S MEDICAL CENTER
1719 East 19th Avenue, Denver CO 80218. 303/839-6000. **Contact:** Human Resources. **World Wide Web address:** http://www.pslmc.com. **Description:** A 680-bed, tertiary care hospital. Presbyterian/St. Luke's Medical Center has comprehensive programs in pediatrics, obstetrics, oncology, cardiology, and orthopedics. The medical center is a leader in tertiary programs such as organ and bone marrow transplantation; high-

risk obstetrical care; diabetes management; wound care; and head, neck, and skull surgery. **Positions advertised include:** Patient Care Director; Apheresis Technologist; Nurse Manager; RN Case Manager; Sonographer; Clinical Education Coordinator; Nurse Recuiter: Manager of Communications. **Parent company:** HealthONE facilities include Medical Center of Aurora, Spalding Rehabilitation Hospital, Swedish Medical Center, Rose Medical Center, and North Suburban Medical Center.

ROCKY MOUNTAIN POISON AND DRUG CENTER
777 Bannock Street, Mail Code 0180, Denver CO 80204. 303/739-1100. **Contact:** Human Resources. **World Wide Web address:** http://www.rmpdc.org. **Description:** Provides rapid and accurate treatment recommendations over the telephone to consumers and health professionals, 24 hours a day. Registered nurses and physicians manage over 120,000 cases per year. Rocky Mountain Poison and Drug Center consults in all areas dealing with chemicals, drugs, and plants. The center's public education program focuses on early intervention and prevention education platforms.

ROSE MEDICAL CENTER
4567 East Ninth Avenue, Denver CO 80220. 303/320-2121. **Contact:** Human Resources. **World Wide Web address:** http://www.rosemed.com. **Description:** A 420-bed medical center that provides inpatient and outpatient services. Founded in 1949. **Positions advertised include:** Controller; Contract Administrator; Ambulatory Surgery Manager; Surgical Tech; Director of Case Management; Oncology Coordinator; Operating Room Manager; RN, Various Departments. **Corporate headquarters location:** This location. **Parent company:** HealthONE. **Listed on:** Privately held. **Number of employees at this location:** 1,600.

ST. ANTHONY CENTRAL HOSPITAL
4231 West 16th Avenue, Denver CO 80204. 303/629-3511. **Contact:** Human Resources. **World Wide Web address:** http://www.centura.org. **Description:** A 593-bed, full-service hospital and the only nonprofit, private Level 1 trauma center in Colorado. **Positions advertised include:** Pharmacy Manager; Case Manager; RN, Various Departments; CT Scan Tech; Occupational Therapist; Mammography Tech. **Parent company:** Centura Health.

ST. ANTHONY NORTH HOSPITAL
2551 West 84th Avenue, Westminster CO 80031. 303/426-2151. **Contact:** Human Resources. **World Wide Web address:** http://www.centura.org. **Description:** A 196-bed hospital. Major medical specialties include family practice, pediatrics, neonatology, cardiology, emergency medicine, obstetrics, oncology, and an adult psychiatric unit. **Positions advertised include:** Clinical Nursing Manager; OR Tech; CT Scan Tech; RN, Various Departments; Ultrasound Tech; Physician Business Liaison. **Parent company:** Centura Health.

ST. MARY-CORWIN REGIONAL MEDICAL CENTER
1008 Minnequa Avenue, Pueblo CO 81004. 719/560-4000. **Contact:** Ms. Jackie Armstrong, Human Resources Services Representative. **World Wide Web address:** http://www.centura.org. **Description:** A hospital. **Positions advertised include:** Director Quality Resources; Physical Therapist; Surgical Tech; Speech Language Pathologist; Registered Respiratory Therapist; Radiation Therapist. **Corporate headquarters location:** Denver CO. **Parent company:** Centura Health. **Operations at this facility include:** Administration. **Number of employees at this location:** 1,300.

SKY RIDGE MEDICAL CENTER
10101 RidgeGate Parkway, Lone Tree CO 80124. 720/225-1000. **Fax:** 303/788-2590. **Contact:** Human Resources. **World Wide Web address:** http://www.skyridgemedcenter.com. **Description:** A health care facility whose services include emergency care, surgical services, cardiac services, and diagnostic and imaging services. **Positions advertised include:** RN; CT Tech; HIM Specialist; CNA; Medical Technologist; Assistant Vice President Surgical Services. **Parent company:** HealthONE.

SPALDING REHABILITATION HOSPITAL
900 Potomac Street, Aurora CO 80011. 303/367-1166. **Contact:** Human Resources. **World Wide Web address:** http://www.spaldingrehab.com. **Description:** One of Denver's leading resources for physical rehabilitation services. In partnership with the HealthONE system, Spalding provides rehabilitation services. Spalding's treatment programs target an array of musculoskeletal problems and neurological disorders, including brain injury; head, neck, and spinal injuries; stroke; multiple sclerosis; and chronic pain. Founded in 1914. **Positions advertised include:** Evening Supervisor; Staff RN; Lead Therapist. **Parent company:** HealthONE.

THE SPECTRANETICS CORPORATION
96 Talamine Court, Colorado Springs CO 80907. 719/633-8333. **Toll-free phone:** 800/633-0960. **Fax:** 719/475-7086. **Contact:** Human Resources. **World Wide Web address:** http://www.spectranetics.com. **Description:** Researches, develops, manufactures, services, supports, and sells medical lasers and attendant catheters used in heart surgery. **Positions advertised include:** Sr. Technician; Sr. Laser Scientist; Engineer; Manufacturing Engineer; Clinical Affairs Manager. **Corporate headquarters location:** This location. **Other U.S. locations:** Nationwide. **International locations:** Worldwide. **Listed on:** NASDAQ. **Stock exchange symbol:** SPNC. **Number of employees at this location:** 75. **Number of employees nationwide:** 140.

U.S. DEPARTMENT OF VETERNS AFFAIRS
DENVER VETERANS ADMINISTRATION MEDICAL CENTER
1055 Clermont Street, Denver CO 80220-3808. 303/399-8020. **Contact:** Human Resources Management Service. **World Wide Web address:** http://www.va.gov. **Description:** A medical center. VA operates medical

centers in each of the 48 contiguous states, Puerto Rico, and the District of Columbia. With approximately 76,000 medical center beds, VA treats nearly 1 million patients in VA hospitals, 75,000 in nursing home care units, and 25,000 in domiciliary residences. **Positions advertised include:** Nurse Manager; Physical Therapist; RN; Chief of Staff. **Corporate headquarters location:** Washington DC. **Parent company:** U.S. Department of Veterans Affairs. **Number of employees at this location:** 1,600.

UNIVERSITY OF COLORADO HOSPITAL
UNIVERSITY OF COLORADO HEALTH SCIENCES CENTER
4200 East 9th Avenue, Campus Box A028, Denver CO 80262. 303/372-2121. **Fax:** 303/372-9650. **Contact:** Human Resources. **World Wide Web address:** http://www.uchsc.edu. **Description:** A regional, tertiary health care and academic medical center. University Hospital is the principal teaching hospital for the University of Colorado Health Sciences Center. Founded in 1921. **Positions advertised include:** Research Assistant; Project Manager; Assistant Professor; Instructor; Senior Instructor. **Special programs:** Internships. **Operations at this facility include:** Administration. **Number of employees at this location:** 2,200.

VALLEYLAB, INC.
5920 Longbow Drive, Boulder CO 80301-3299. 303/530-2300. **Toll-free phone:** 800/255-8522. **Fax:** 303/530-6285. **Contact:** Human Resources Department. **World Wide Web address:** http://www.valleylab.com. **Description:** Develops, manufactures, markets, and services medical equipment and accessories used in hospitals and other medical environments. Principal products are electrosurgical generators, ultrasonic surgical aspirators, and associated disposable products used to perform a variety of surgical and medical procedures. **Positions advertised include:** R&D Engineer; Sr. Research Scientist; Sales Analyst; Associate Product Manager; R&D Director; Design Engineer. **Special programs:** Internships. **Corporate headquarters location:** New York NY. **Parent company:** Tyco Healthcare Group. **Operations at this facility include:** Administration; Divisional Headquarters; Manufacturing; Research and Development; Sales; Service.

VITAL SIGNS - COLORADO
11039 East Lansing Circle, Englewood CO 80112. 303/790-4835. **Contact:** Human Resources. **E-mail address:** humanresources@vital-signs.com. **World Wide Web address:** http://www.vital-signs.com. **Description:** Manufactures disposable medical products such as facemasks, manual resuscitators, anesthesia kits, and related products. **Corporate headquarters location:** Totowa NJ. **Operations at this facility include:** Administration; Manufacturing. **Listed on:** NASDAQ. **Stock exchange symbol:** VITL. **Number of employees at this location:** 250.

HOTELS AND RESTAURANTS

You can expect to find the following types of companies
in this section:
Casinos • Dinner Theaters • Hotel/Motel Operators • Resorts •
Restaurants

ADAM'S MARK HOTEL
1550 Court Place, Denver CO 80202. 303/893-3333. **Contact:** Director
of Human Resources. **World Wide Web address:**
http://www.adamsmark.com. **Description:** A 1,225-room hotel with
restaurant and meeting facilities. **Positions advertised include:**
Assistant Banquet Manager; Director of Advertising and Promotions;
Sales Manager. **Corporate headquarters location:** Minneapolis MN.
Parent company: Ash and Associates, Inc. **Number of employees at
this location:** 375.

BEST WESTERN CENTRAL DENVER
200 West 48th Avenue, Denver CO 80216-1802. 303/296-4000. **Fax:**
303/296-4000. **Contact:** Human Resources Administrator. **World Wide
Web address:** http://www.bestwestern.com. **Description:** A 176-room
hotel. **Corporate headquarters location:** Phoenix AZ. **Listed on:**
Privately held.

BOSTON MARKET, INC.
14103 Denver West Parkway, Golden CO 80401. 303/278-9500. **Fax:**
303/216-5678. **Contact:** Human Resources. **E-mail address:**
SC_Recruiting@bost.com. **World Wide Web address:**
http://www.boston-market.com. **Description:** Operates and franchises
food service stores that specialize in fresh, convenient meals. Boston
Market's menu features home-style entrees, fresh vegetables, salads,
and other side dishes. **Corporate headquarters location:** This location.

THE BROADMOOR HOTEL
1 Lake Avenue, Colorado Springs CO 80906. 719/577-5780. **Fax:**
719/577-5700. **Contact:** Human Resources Office. **World Wide Web
address:** http://www.broadmoor.com. **Description:** A 700-room, five-
star, five-diamond resort. Facilities include 3 championship golf courses,
15 retail outlets, 9 restaurants, 12 tennis courts, and conference rooms.
Founded in 1918. **NOTE:** Entry-level positions, part-time jobs, and
second and third shifts are offered. This location also hires seasonally.
Send resumes to: 15 Lake Circle, Colorado Springs CO 80906. **Special
programs:** Internships; Apprenticeships; Training. **Office hours:**
Monday - Friday, 8:00 a.m. - 5:00 p.m. **Corporate headquarters
location:** This location. **Parent company:** Oklahoma Publishing
Company. **Annual sales/revenues:** $51 - $100 million. **Number of
employees at this location:** 1,500.

BROWN PALACE HOTEL
321 17th Street, Denver CO 80202. 303/297-3111. **Fax:** 303/312-5940. **Contact:** Human Resources. **World Wide Web address:** http://www.brownpalace.com. **Description:** A full-service hotel. **NOTE:** All positions require experience in four- or five-star properties. **Special programs:** Internships. **Corporate headquarters location:** Dallas TX. **Parent company:** Quorum Hotels and Resorts. **Number of employees at this location:** 400.

COLOMEX, INC.
dba TACO BELL
717 North Tejon Street, Colorado Springs CO 80903. 719/633-2500. **Fax:** 719/633-9610. **Contact:** Human Resources. **Description:** Colomex, Inc. owns the largest Taco Bell franchise in Colorado, operating over 30 restaurants. Taco Bell is a leader in the Mexican, fast-food restaurant industry. **Corporate headquarters location:** This location. **Listed on:** Privately held. **Number of employees at this location:** 1,000.

COPPER MOUNTAIN RESORTS, INC.
209 Ten Mile Circle, P.O. Box 3001, Copper Mountain CO 80443. 970/968-2318. **Contact:** Human Resources Department. **World Wide Web address:** http://www.coppersummer.com. **Description:** Operates a resort with ski facilities and a wide range of warm-weather activities. Founded in 1972. **Positions advertised include:** Call Center Sales Agent; Manager of Research and Development; Homeowner Experience Coordinator; IT Business Analyst. **Office hours:** Sunday - Saturday, 8:00 a.m. - 5:00 p.m. **Corporate headquarters location:** This location. **Other area locations:** Dillon CO; Frisco CO; Leadville CO. **COO:** David Barry. **Facilities Manager:** Becky Yessak. **Information Systems Manager:** Doug Feeley. **Purchasing Manager:** Don Jones. **Sales Manager:** Carol Schmidt.

DENVER MARRIOTT TECH CENTER
4900 South Syracuse Street, Denver CO 80237. 303/779-1100. **Recorded jobline:** 303/782-3214. **Contact:** Human Resources Department. **World Wide Web address:** http://www.marriott.com. **Description:** A 625-room hotel. **NOTE:** Entry-level positions, part-time jobs, and second and third shifts are offered. This location also hires seasonally. **Special programs:** Internships; Training; Summer Jobs. **Corporate headquarters location:** Bethesda MD. **Other U.S. locations:** Nationwide. **International locations:** Worldwide. **Parent company:** Marriot International, Inc. **Listed on:** New York Stock Exchange. **Stock exchange symbol:** MAR. **Annual sales/revenues:** More than $100 million. **Number of employees at this location:** 375. **Number of employees nationwide:** 100,000. **Number of employees worldwide:** 150,000.

DOUBLETREE HOTEL DURANGO
501 Camino Del Rio, Durango CO 81301. 970/259-6580. **Fax:** 970/259-4398. **Contact:** Human Resources. **World Wide Web address:**

www.durango.doubletree.com. **Description:** Luxury hotel within walking distance of downtown Durango and restaurants. **Parent Company:** Hilton.

HOLIDAY INN DENVER DOWNTOWN
1450 Glenarm Place, Denver CO 80202. 303/573-1450. **Contact:** Human Resources. **World Wide Web address:** http://www.holiday-inn.com. **Description:** One location of the nationwide hotel chain. **Corporate headquarters location:** Atlanta GA. **Parent company:** Six Continents Hotels, Inc. **Listed on:** New York Stock Exchange. **Stock exchange symbol:** SXC.

HOTEL JEROME
333 East Main Street, Aspen CO 81611. 970/920-1000. **Fax:** 970/925-3112. **Toll-free phone:** 800/331-7213. **Contact:** Human Resources. **E-mail address:** hr@hjerome.com. **World Wide Web address:** www.hoteljerome.com. **Description:** A 91-room landmark hotel located in downtown Aspen with an award winning restaurant.

KEYSTONE RESORT
P.O. Box 38, Keystone CO 80435. 970/496-4157. **Fax:** 970/496-3260. **Contact:** Director of Human Resources. **E-mail address:** keyjobs@vailresorts.com. **World Wide Web address:** http://www.keystoneresort.com. **Description:** A ski resort. **Positions advertised include:** Accountant; Steward; Cook; Front Desk Agent; Lift Mechanic; Lift Electronics Tech. **Parent company:** Vail Resorts Inc. **Listed on:** New York Stock Exchange. **Stock exchange symbol:** MTN.

LIONSHEAD INN
705 West Lionshead Circle, Vail CO 81657. 970/476-2050. **Fax:** 970/476-9265. **Toll-free phone:** 800/283-8245. **Contact:** Human Resources. **World Wide Web address:** www.lionsheadinn.com. **Description:** Luxury inn located minutes from the Eagle Bay Gondola, shops, and restaurants.

MARRIOTT'S MOUNTAIN VALLEY LODGE AT BRECKENRIDGE
655 Columbine Drive, Breckenridge CO 80424. 970/453-8500. **Fax:** 970/453-8110. **Contact:** Human Resources. **World Wide Web address:** http://www.marriott.com. **Description:** A location of the hotel chain. A 111-room hotel within walking distance of shops, restaurants, and golf.

MILLENNIUM HARVEST HOUSE
1345 28th Street, Boulder CO 80302-6899. 303/443-3850. **Toll-free phone:** 800/545-6285. **Fax:** 303/443-1480. **Contact:** Human Resources Department. **E-mail address:** boulder@mhrmail.com. **World Wide Web address:** http://www.millennium-hotels.com. **Description:** A 270-room corporate and leisure hotel with meeting facilities. Founded in 1959. **Special programs:** Internships. **Positions advertised include:** Group Sales Manager; Executive Chef. **Corporate headquarters location:** Denver CO. **Other U.S. locations:** Nationwide. **International locations:** Worldwide. **Parent company:** Millennium & Copthorne Hotels plc.

Operations at this facility include: Administration; Sales; Service. **Listed on:** Privately held. **Annual sales/revenues:** $11 - $20 million. **Number of employees at this location:** 200.

RADISSON HOTELS
3200 South Parker Road, Aurora CO 80014. 303/695-1700. **Contact:** Human Resources. **World Wide Web address:** http://www.radisson.com. **Description:** One location of the nationwide hotel chain.

RADISSON STAPLETON PLAZA HOTEL
3333 Quebec Street, Denver CO 80207. 303/321-3500. **Contact:** Human Resources. **World Wide Web address:** http://www.radisson.com. **Description:** A 300-room hotel whose facilities include a fitness center and a restaurant. **NOTE:** Entry-level positions, part-time jobs, and second and third shifts are offered.

RICHFIELD HOSPITALITY, INC.
7600 East Orchard Road, Suite 230 South, Greenwood Village CO 80111. 303/220-2185. **Contact:** Human Resources. **World Wide Web address:** http://www.swanhost.com. **Description:** A company involved in hotel management and ownership. **Positions advertised include:** Payroll Manager; Director of Revenue Management; Corporate Accounting Manager. **Special programs:** Internships; Co-ops. **Office hours:** Monday - Friday, 8:00 a.m. - 5:00 p.m. **Annual sales/revenues:** More than $100 million. **Number of employees at this location:** 50. **Number of employees nationwide:** 7,000.

ROCK BOTTOM RESTAURANTS, INC.
248 Centennial Parkway, Suite 100, Louisville CO 80027. 303/664-4000. **Fax:** 303/664-4199. **Contact:** Human Resources Department. **World Wide Web address:** http://www.rockbottom.com. **Description:** Owns and operates 29 restaurants and breweries. **NOTE:** Entry-level positions and part-time jobs are offered. **Company slogan:** To run great restaurants with great people. **Positions advertised include:** Restaurant Manager; Sous Chef. **Special programs:** Internships; Training; Summer Jobs. **Corporate headquarters location:** This location. **Other U.S. locations:** Nationwide. **Annual sales/revenues:** More than $100 million. **Number of employees at this location:** 70.

VAIL RESORTS
P.O. Box 7, Vail CO 81658. 970/845-2460. **Fax:** 970/845-2465. **Recorded jobline:** 888/SKI-JOB1. **Contact:** Human Resources. **World Wide Web address:** http://www.vailresorts.com. **Description:** Operates the Vail, Breckenridge, Beaver Creek, Keystone, Heavenly, and other resorts. Founded in 1962. **NOTE:** Entry-level positions and second and third shifts are offered. **Special programs:** Internships; Training; Summer Jobs. **Office hours:** Monday - Friday, 8:00 a.m. - 5:00 p.m. **Corporate headquarters location:** This location. **Listed on:** New York Stock Exchange. **Stock exchange symbol:** MTN.

VICORP RESTAURANTS INC.

400 West 48th Avenue, Denver CO 80216. 303/296-2121. **Contact:** Human Resources. **E-mail address:** h.resources@vicorpinc.com. **World Wide Web address:** http://www.vicorpinc.com. **Description:** Operates Bakers Square and Village Inn restaurant chains and franchises restaurants under the Village Inn name. **Positions advertised include:** Architectural Designer/Sr. Drafter; Site Development Coordinator; Construction Coordinator; Purchasing Specialist; Financial Analyst. **Corporate headquarters location:** This location.

WENDY'S INTERNATIONAL, INC.

6695 West Alameda Avenue, Denver CO 80214. 303/238-9721. **Contact:** Staffing Specialist. **World Wide Web address:** http://www.wendysintl.com. **Description:** One of the world's largest restaurant franchising companies. Wendy's International includes Wendy's, a fast-food restaurant chain, and Tim Hortons, a coffee and baked goods restaurant chain. **Corporate headquarters location:** Dublin OH. **Other U.S. locations:** Nationwide. **Operations at this facility include:** Administration; Divisional Headquarters. **Listed on:** New York Stock Exchange. **Stock exchange symbol:** WEN.

INSURANCE

You can expect to find the following types of companies in this section:
Commercial and Industrial Property/Casualty Insurers • Health Maintenance Organizations (HMO's) • Medical/Life Insurance Companies

---

ALLSTATE INSURANCE COMPANY
5500 South Quebec Street, Suite 250, Englewood CO 80111. 303/779-3700. **Contact:** Human Resources. **World Wide Web address:** http://www.allstate.com. **Description:** A homeowners, automotive, and life insurance firm. **Positions advertised include:** Financial Analyst; Product Consultant.

ANTHEM BLUE CROSS BLUE SHIELD
HMO COLORADO
700 Broadway, Denver CO 80273. 303/831-2131. **Toll-free phone:** 800/654-9338. **Contact:** Human Resources. **World Wide Web address:** http://www.anthem.com. **Description:** A nonprofit health care insurance organization. Anthem Blue Cross Blue Shield provides hospitalization insurance coverage to individuals and groups. The company also provides group and individual insurance coverage performed by professional medical services from doctors, dentists, psychiatrists, and other medical professionals. **Positions advertised include:** Issue Control Specialist; Regional VP, Sales; Project Manager; Director, Nurse Disease Management. **Corporate headquarters location:** Indianapolis IN. **Other area locations:** Colorado Springs CO;. **Parent company:** Anthem, Inc. **Listed on:** New York Stock Exchange. **Stock exchange symbol:** ATH. **CEO/President:** Larry C. Glasscock.

COLORADO BANKERS LIFE INSURANCE COMPANY
5990 Greenwood Plaza Boulevard, Suite 325, Greenwood Village CO 80111. 303/220-8500. **Fax:** 303/220-8056. **Contact:** Human Resources. **World Wide Web address:** http://www.cbl-life.com. **Description:** A financial services institution providing life insurance annuities. **Parent company:** Preferred Financial Group.

FARMERS INSURANCE GROUP
P.O. Box 371078, Denver CO 80231. 303/283-6100. **Physical address:** 7535 East Hampden Avenue, Suite 310, Denver CO 80231-4842. **Contact:** Division Marketing Manager. **World Wide Web address:** http://www.farmersinsurance.com. **Description:** A multiline insurance agency that sells and services insurance policies to individuals, families, and businesses throughout the Denver metropolitan area. **Positions advertised include:** Auto Claims Rep; Worker's Compensation Supervisor; Liability Claims Supervisor. **Corporate headquarters location:** Los Angeles CA. **Other U.S. locations:** Phoenix AZ; Merced CA; Pleasanton CA; Santa Ana CA; Simi Valley CA; Pocatello ID; Aurora

IL; Columbus OH; Portland OR; Austin TX; Vancouver WA. **Parent company:** Zurich. **Number of employees at this location:** 30.

H.R.H.
720 South Colorado Boulevard, North Tower, Galleria Penthouse, P.O. Box 469025, Denver CO 80246. 303/722-7776. **Contact:** Human Resources. **World Wide Web address:** http://www.hrh.com. **Description:** An agency specializing in surety bonds and commercial insurance. **Positions advertised include:** Professional Liability Underwriter; Account Manager. **Corporate headquarters location:** Glen Allen VA.

THE HARTFORD
P.O. Box 5188, Denver CO 80217. 303/645-8500. **Physical address:** 7670 South Chester Street, Suite 300, Englewood CO 80112-3438. **Toll-free phone:** 800/525-7418. **Contact:** Human Resources. **World Wide Web address:** http://www.thehartford.com. **Description:** One of the largest insurance companies in the United States. The Hartford is a *Fortune* 500 company and offers business, farm, home, life, automobile, marine, and health insurance coverage as well as fidelity and surety bonds and reinsurance. Founded in 1810. **NOTE:** Entry-level positions and part-time jobs are offered. **Positions advertised include:** Claims Service consultant; Legal Secretary; Sr. Staff Attorney; Administrative Services Manager; Xpand Underwriter. **Corporate headquarters location:** Hartford CT. **Other U.S. locations:** Nationwide. **International locations:** Worldwide. **Listed on:** New York Stock Exchange. **Stock exchange symbol:** HIG. **Number of employees at this location:** 170. **Number of employees worldwide:** 30,000.

KAISER PERMANENTE
2500 South Havana Street, Aurora CO 80014-1622. 303/338-3800. **Recorded jobline:** 303/338-3949. **Contact:** Human Resources. **World Wide Web address:** http://www.kaiserpermanente.org. **Description:** One of the nation's leading and largest health maintenance organizations. **Positions advertised include:** New Products collection Clerk; Clinical Medicare Reimbursement Manager; Palliative Care Program Manager; Project Manager; Graphic Artist; Sr. Insurance System Coordinator. **Corporate headquarters location:** Oakland CA. **Operations at this facility include:** Regional Headquarters. **Number of employees at this location:** 3,100. **Number of employees nationwide:** 75,000.

METROPOLITAN LIFE INSURANCE COMPANY
1125 17th Street, Suite 809, Denver CO 80202-1019. 303/295-0505. **Contact:** Human Resources. **World Wide Web address:** http://www.metlife.com. **Description:** Offers a wide range of individual and group insurance including life, annuity, disability, and mutual funds. **Positions advertised include:** Business Systems Analyst; Support Analyst. **Corporate headquarters location:** New York NY. **Listed on:** New York Stock Exchange. **Stock exchange symbol:** MET.

NATIONAL FARMER'S UNION INSURANCE
11900 East Cornell Avenue, Aurora CO 80014-3194. 303/337-5500. **Contact:** Human Resources. **World Wide Web address:** http://www.nfuic.com. **Description:** A national insurance company specializing in coverage for farmers. **Corporate headquarters location:** This location.

PROGRESSIVE INSURANCE GROUP
1110 Chapel Hills Drive, Colorado Springs CO 80920. 719/262-5600. **Toll-free phone:** 888/838-7414. **Contact:** Human Resources Manager. **World Wide Web address:** http://www.progressive.com. **Description:** Progressive Insurance Group writes automobile, motorcycle, recreational vehicle, personal water craft, and commercial vehicle insurance in 48 states. Progressive also insures financial institutions. **Positions advertised include:** Sr. Telecom Analyst; Manager, Contact Center; Claims Adjuster; Customer Contact Rep; Quality Assurance Analyst. **Corporate headquarters location:** Baltimore MD. **Other U.S. locations:** Nationwide. **Operations at this facility include:** This location is a customer service center.

VAN GILDER INSURANCE CORPORATION
700 Broadway, Suite 1000, Denver CO 80203. 303/837-8500. **Fax:** 303/831-5295. **Contact:** Human Resources. **World Wide Web address:** http://www.vgic.com. **Description:** Provides a full line of personal and commercial insurance. **Positions advertised include:** Employee Benefits Account Manager; Commercial Lines Account Manager. **Corporate headquarters location:** This location. **Other U.S. locations:** AZ; KS; TX; WY. **Parent company:** Assurex Global.

LEGAL SERVICES

**You can expect to find the following types of companies
in this section:**
Law Firms • Legal Service Agencies

HOLLAND & HART LLP
P.O. Box 8749, Denver CO 80201-8749. 303/295-8000. **Physical
Address:** 555 17th Street, Suite 3200, Denver CO 80202. **Fax:** 303/295-
8261. **Contact:** Julie Carroll, Director of Attorney Recruitment. **E-mail
address:** jcarroll@hollandhart.com. **World Wide Web address:**
http://www.hollandhart.com. **Description:** A law firm. **Other area
locations:** Aspen CO; Boulder CO; Colorado Springs CO; Greenwood
Village CO. **Other U.S. locations:** MT; ID; WY; UT; NM; DC.

KUTAK ROCK LLP
1801 California Street, Suite 3100, Denver CO 80202-2658. 303/297-
2400. **Contact:** Recruitment. **World Wide Web address:**
http://www.kutakrock.com. **Description:** A legal services firm
specializing in corporate law, public and corporate finance, and litigation.
Positions advertised include: Attorney. **Other U.S. locations:**
Nationwide.

NATIVE AMERICAN RIGHTS FUND
1506 Broadway, Boulder CO 80302. 303/447-8760. **Contact:** Rose
Cuny, Office Manager. **World Wide Web address:** http://www.narf.org.
Description: A national legal defense fund for Native American tribes,
villages, groups, and individuals throughout the United States. Founded
in 1970. **Special programs:** Internships. **Other U.S. locations:**
Anchorage AK; Washington DC.

ROTHGERBER JOHNSON & LYONS LLP
1200 17th Street, Suite 3000, Denver CO 80202-5855. 303/623-9000.
Fax: 303/623-9222. **Contact:** Beth Martinez, Recruiting Coordinator.
World Wide Web address: http://www.rothgerber.com. **Description:** A
law firm specializing in all aspects of corporate and government law
including general representation and litigation. Founded in 1903.
Corporate headquarters location: This location. **Other area locations:**
Colorado Springs CO. **Other U.S. locations:** Cheyenne WY.

MANUFACTURING: MISCELLANEOUS CONSUMER

You can expect to find the following types of companies in this section:
Art Supplies • Batteries • Cosmetics and Related Products • Household Appliances and Audio/Video Equipment • Jewelry, Silverware, and Plated Ware • Miscellaneous Household Furniture and Fixtures • Musical Instruments • Tools • Toys and Sporting Goods

---

CAREFREE OF COLORADO
2145 West Sixth Avenue, Broomfield CO 80020. 303/469-3324. **Contact:** Human Resources. **E-mail address:** humanresources@carefreeofcolorado.com. **World Wide Web address:** http://www.carefreeofcolorado.com. **Description:** Manufactures a large line of products for recreational vehicles (RVs). Carefree of Colorado's product line includes awnings, add-a-rooms, and lawn furniture. **Positions advertised include:** Controller; Director of OEM Sales; Accountant; Manufacturing Process Engineer. **Corporate headquarters location:** This location. **Parent company:** Scott Fetzer Company.

COLOREL BLINDS
13802 East 33rd Place, Unit B, Aurora CO 80011. 303/375-8181. **Fax:** 303/574-9182. **Contact:** Human Resources. **Description:** A leading national fabricator and retailer of custom-made window coverings for residential and commercial customers. **NOTE:** Entry-level positions are offered. **Special programs:** Training. **Corporate headquarters location:** This location. **Other U.S. locations:** TX; WA. **Parent company:** Colorel Corporation. **Listed on:** Privately held. **Number of employees nationwide:** 180.

PENTAX CORPORATION
600 12th Street, Suite 300, Golden CO 80401. 303/799-8000. **Fax:** 303/728-0217. **Contact:** Human Resources. **World Wide Web address:** http://www.pentax.com. **Description:** Manufactures cameras, camera supplies, and related photographic products. **Positions advertised include:** Graphic Designer; Service Administrator. **Corporate headquarters location:** This location.

SAMSONITE CORPORATION
11200 East 45th Avenue, Denver CO 80239. 303/373-2000. **Fax:** 303/373-6300. **Contact:** Human Resources. **World Wide Web address:** http://www.samsonite.com. **Description:** Manufactures and markets luggage and business cases. **Corporate headquarters location:** This location. **Operations at this facility include:** Administration; Manufacturing; Research and Development; Service.

SCOTT'S LIQUID GOLD INC.
NEOTERIC COSMETICS
4880 Havana Street, P.O. Box 39-S, Denver CO 80239-0019. 303/576-6049. **Fax:** 303/576-6050. **Recorded jobline:** 800/447-1919 (Option 6.) **Contact:** Shelly Kennison, Director of Human Resources Department. **World Wide Web address:** http://www.scottsliquidgold.com. **Description:** Engaged in the manufacture and distribution of household chemical products as well as disposable cigarette filters. Principal products include Scott's Liquid Gold Wood Cleaner and Preservative, Scott's Liquid Gold Glass Cleaner, and Touch of Scent Air Freshener. Neoteric Cosmetics (also at this location) manufactures a skin care line of alpha-hydroxy products. **Corporate headquarters location:** This location.

TRINIDAD/BENHAM CORPORATION
3650 South Yosemite, Suite 300, P.O. Box 378007, Denver CO 80237. 303/220-1400. **Contact:** Human Resources Manager. **Description:** Engaged in the warehousing, packaging, and wholesaling of dry beans and aluminum foil. **Corporate headquarters location:** This location. **Other U.S. locations:** Chino CA; Murfreesboro TN; Mineola TX. **Operations at this facility include:** Administration; Sales; Service. **Listed on:** Privately held. **Number of employees at this location:** 50. **Number of employees nationwide:** 475.

WATER PIK TECHNOLOGIES, INC.
1730 East Prospect Road, Fort Collins CO 80553-0001. 970/484-1352. **Contact:** Recruiter. **World Wide Web address:** http://www.waterpik.com. **Description:** Manufactures products for consumer and professional use including pulsating showerheads and point-of-use water filtration systems. Brand names include Water-Pik oral irrigators and tooth care products, Shower Massage showerhead units, and Instapure water filters. **Corporate headquarters location:** Newport Beach CA. **Listed on:** New York Stock Exchange. **Stock exchange symbol:** PIK.

WRIGHT & McGILL
4245 East 46th Avenue, P.O. Box 16011, Denver CO 80216-6011. 303/321-1481. **Contact:** Human Resources. **World Wide Web address:** http://www.eagleclaw.com. **Description:** Manufactures a line of fishing rods and tackle. Founded in 1925. **Corporate headquarters location:** This location.

MANUFACTURING: MISCELLANEOUS INDUSTRIAL

You can expect to find the following types of companies in this section:
Ball and Roller Bearings • Commercial Furniture and Fixtures • Fans, Blowers, and Purification Equipment • Industrial Machinery and Equipment • Motors and Generators/Compressors and Engine Parts • Vending Machines

ALFRED MANUFACTURING COMPANY
4398 Elati Street, Denver CO 80216. 303/433-6385. **Contact:** Human Resources. **World Wide Web address:** http://www.alfredmfg.com. **Description:** Manufactures specialty dies and tools, die sets, jigs, fixtures, and industrial molds. Alfred Manufacturing Company is also engaged in machine shop production, metal stamping, welding, and special machinery operation.

BAND-IT INC.
4799 Dahlia Street, P.O. Box 16307, Denver CO 80216-0307. 303/320-4555. **Fax:** 303/333-6549. **Contact:** Human Resources. **E-mail address:** hr.band-it@idexcorp.com. **World Wide Web address:** http://www.band-it-idex.com. **Description:** Manufactures clamps, hose fittings, and brackets. **Corporate headquarters location:** Northbrook IL. **Parent company:** IDEX Corporation. **Listed on:** New York Stock Exchange. **Stock exchange symbol:** IEX.

BREECE HILL LLC
246 South Taylor Avenue, Louisville CO 80027. 303/664-8200. **Fax:** 303/664-8299. **Contact:** Human Resources. **World Wide Web address:** http://www.breecehill.com. **Description:** A developer and manufacturer of Digital Linear Tape (DLT) drive systems. **Corporate headquarters location:** This location. **International locations:** England. **Number of employees at this location:** 100.

EMERSON PROCESS MANAGEMENT
DIETERICH STANDARD, INC.
5601 North 71st Street, Boulder CO 80301. 303/530-9600. **Contact:** Human Resources. **World Wide Web address:** http://www.emersonprocess.com. **Description:** Produces a wide range of flow and process equipment.

ENGINEERING MEASUREMENTS COMPANY (EMCO)
1831 Lefthand Circle, Suite C Longmont CO 80501. 303/682-7060. **Fax:** 303/682-7069. **Contact:** Human Resources Director. **World Wide Web address:** http://www.emcoflow.com. **Description:** Manufactures flow meters. Founded in 1967. **NOTE:** Second and third shifts are offered. **Special programs:** Training. **Parent company:** Spirax Sarco, Inc. **Number of employees at this location:** 90.

HUSSMANN CORPORATION

11929 51st Avenue, Denver CO 80239. 303/371-5447. **Contact:** Plant Manager. **Wide Web address:** http://www.hussmann.com. **Description:** Produces merchandising and refrigeration systems for the food industry. Products include refrigerated display cases, refrigeration systems, beverage coolers, walk-in coolers, and industrial refrigeration equipment. **Parent company:** Ingersoll-Rand Company. **Listed on:** New York Stock Exchange. **Stock exchange symbol:** IR.

MARK VII EQUIPMENT, INC.

5981 Tennyson Street, Arvada CO 80003. 303/423-4910. **Fax:** 303/430-0139. **Contact:** Human Resources. **E-mail address:** jobs@markvii.net. **World Wide Web address:** http://www.mark7inc.com. **Description:** Develops and manufactures products for the automobile-washing industry. **Positions advertised include:** Field Service Technician. **Parent company:** WashTec AG (Germany).

MERRITT EQUIPMENT COMPANY

9339 Highway 85, Henderson CO 80640. 303/289-2286. **Contact:** Human Resources Department. **E-mail address:** merritt@merritt-equip.com. **World Wide Web address:** http://www.merritt-equip.com. **Description:** Manufactures livestock and commodity trailers and aluminum accessories for the trucking industry such as cab guards and toolboxes. **Corporate headquarters location:** This location. **Operations at this facility include:** Administration; Manufacturing; Sales; Service. **Number of employees at this location:** 250.

MICRO MOTION, INC.

7070 Winchester Circle, Boulder CO 80301. 303/527-5200. **Fax:** 303/530-8459. **Recorded jobline:** 303/530-8000. **Contact:** Human Resources. **World Wide Web address:** http://www.micromotion.com. **Description:** Manufactures industrial flow meters. **Positions advertised include:** Systems Engineer; Operations Supervisor; Product Line Business Manager; Manufacturing Specialist; Engineer. **Corporate headquarters location:** This location. **Parent company:** Emerson Process Management. **Number of employees at this location:** 650.

MILE HIGH EQUIPMENT COMPANY
dba ICE-O-MATIC

11100 East 45th Avenue, Denver CO 80239. 303/371-3737. **Fax:** 303/371-6296. **Contact:** Human Resources. **World Wide Web address:** http://www.iceomatic.com. **Description:** Manufactures automatic ice-making and dispensing equipment. **Corporate headquarters location:** Stamford CT. **Parent company:** Enodis Company. **Operations at this facility include:** Administration; Manufacturing; Research and Development; Sales; Service. **Listed on:** New York Stock Exchange. **Stock exchange symbol:** ENO. **Number of employees at this location:** 200.

MOLI INTERNATIONAL
1150 West Virginia Avenue, Denver CO 80223. 303/777-0364. **Contact:** Human Resources. **World Wide Web address:** http://www.moliinternational.com. **Description:** Manufactures a variety of food service equipment including bins and carts.

NER DATA PRODUCTS, INC.
5125 Race Court, Denver CO 80216. 303/297-9900. **Contact:** Manager of Employee Relations. **World Wide Web address:** http://www.nerdata.com. **Description:** A manufacturer of office supplies, primarily ribbons and printing cartridges for typewriters, word processors, and computers. Founded in 1971. **Corporate headquarters location:** Glassboro NJ.

NORGREN
5400 South Delaware Street, Littleton CO 80120. 303/794-2611. **Fax:** 303/795-6200. **Contact:** Martha Parsley, Manager of Human Resources. **World Wide Web address:** http://www.usa.norgren.com. **Description:** Manufactures accessory and component parts for pneumatic systems. **Positions advertised include:** Graduate Engineer; District Sales Manager; Administrative Assistant. **Corporate headquarters location:** This location. **Parent company:** IMI plc (UK).

PUREGAS, LLC
226A Commerce Street, Broomfield CO 80020. 303/427-3700. **Toll-free phone:** 800/521-5351. **Fax:** 303/657-2205. **Contact:** Human Resources. **E-mail address:** Info@puregas.com. **World Wide Web address:** http://www.puregas.com. **Description:** The company manufactures air pressurization systems for the telecommunications industry and well as compressed air dryers and laboratory gas generators.

SILVER WEIBULL
14800 east Moncrieff Place, Aurora CO 80011. 303/373-2311. **Contact:** Employment. **Description:** Fabricators of heavy machinery for the food processing industry. **Parent company:** Ingersoll-Rand (Woodlake NJ.) **Operations at this facility include:** Manufacturing; Sales; Service. **Listed on:** New York Stock Exchange. **Stock exchange symbol:** IR.

SPECIAL PRODUCTS COMPANY
15000 West 44th Avenue, Golden CO 80403. 303/279-5544. **Contact:** Human Resources. **World Wide Web address:** http://www.speeco.com. **Description:** Engaged in custom steel fabrication, the fabrication of screw machine products, the manufacture of agricultural equipment attachments (blades, hitches, tractor accessories, specialized digging equipment), and the fabrication of other metal products. **Corporate headquarters location:** This location.

STAINLESS FABRICATING COMPANY
860 Navajo Street, Denver CO 80204. 303/573-1700. **Toll-free phone:** 800/525-8966. **Fax:** 303/573-3776. **Contact:** Jeff Manion, President/Owner. **Description:** Manufactures custom kitchen equipment

for restaurants and school cafeterias. **Listed on:** Privately held. **Annual sales/revenues:** Less than $5 million. **Number of employees at this location:** 40.

STEWART & STEVENSON
5840 Dahlia Street, Commerce City CO 80022. 303/287-7441. **Fax:** 720/322-7539. **Contact:** Human Resources. **World Wide Web address:** http://www.ssss.com. **Description:** Involved in the assembly of oil pumps, compressors, and engines. **Positions advertised include:** Allison Technician; FAB Laborer; Field Service Technician. **Corporate headquarters location:** Houston TX. **Parent company:** Stewart & Stevenson Power, Inc. **Operations at this facility include:** Administration; Manufacturing; Research and Development; Sales; Service. **Listed on:** NASDAQ. **Stock exchange symbol:** SSSS.

STOLLE MACHINERY COMPANY, LLC
6949 South Potomac Street, Centennial CO 80112. 303/708-9044. **Fax:** 303/708-9045. **Contact:** Human Resources. **World Wide Web address:** http://www.stollemachinery.com. **Description:** Designs, manufactures, and assembles can-making machinery. **Other U.S. locations:** OH .

SUNDYNE CORPORATION
14845 West 64th Avenue, Arvada CO 80007. 303/425-0800. **Fax:** 303/940-3141. **Contact:** Human Resources. **World Wide Web address:** http://www.sundyne.com. **Description:** Manufactures a wide range of pumps and compressors. **Positions advertised include:** Buyer; Engineering Manager; Field Service Engineer; Manufacturing Engineer; Project engineer; Sr. Analyst, Materials. **Parent company:** United Technologies Corporation.

SWISSLOG TRANSLOGIC
10825 East 47th Avenue, Denver CO 80239. 303/371-7770. **Contact:** Human Resources. **E-mail address:** employmentusa@swisslog.com. **World Wide Web address:** http://www.swisslogcom. **Description:** Produces pneumatic-powered conveying systems. **Positions advertised include:** Quality Assurance Technician; Cycle Counter. **Corporate headquarters location:** This location.

A.R. WILFLEY & SONS
P.O. Box 2330, Denver CO 80201. 303/779-1777. **Physical Address:** 7350 East Progress Place, Suite 200, Englewood CO 80111. **Contact:** Bill Wilbur, Director of Communications and Human Resources. **E-mail address:** pumps@wilfley.com. **World Wide Web address:** http://www.wilfley.com. **Description:** Manufactures centrifugal pumps.

WOODWARD GOVERNOR COMPANY
1000 East Drake Road, Fort Collins CO 80525. 970/482-5811. **Contact:** Human Resources. **World Wide Web address:** http://www.woodward.com. **Description:** Designs and manufactures engine control systems and components for engines and other turbomachinery devices for a wide range of industries. **NOTE:** Resumes

are accepted for specific job postings and must reference the specific position. **Corporate headquarters location:** Rockford IL. **Other area locations:** Loveland CO. **Listed on:** NASDAQ. **Stock exchange symbol:** WGOV.

XEROX CORPORATION
4600 South Ulster Street, Suite 1000, Denver CO 80237. 303/796-6200. **Contact:** Human Resources. **E-mail address:** xerox@isearch.com. **World Wide Web address:** http://www.xerox.com. **Description:** Manufactures, markets, services, and finances information processing products including copiers, duplicators, scanners, electronic printing systems, word processing systems, personal computers, and computer peripherals. Xerox does business in over 120 countries. Founded in 1906. **Corporate headquarters location:** Stamford CT. **Other U.S. locations:** Nationwide. **International locations:** Worldwide. **Operations at this facility include:** This location is a regional sales and service office. **Listed on:** New York Stock Exchange. **Stock exchange symbol:** XRX. **Annual sales/revenues:** More than $100 million.

MINING, GAS, PETROLEUM, ENERGY RELATED

You can expect to find the following types of companies in this section:
Anthracite, Coal, and Ore Mining • Mining Machinery and Equipment • Oil and Gas Field Services • Petroleum and Natural Gas

CANYON RESOURCES CORPORATION
14142 Denver West Parkway, Suite 250, Golden CO 80401-3127. 303/278-8464. **Fax:** 303/279-3772. **Contact:** Human Resources Department. **World Wide Web address:** http://www.canyonresources.com. **Description:** Operates an open-pit gold mine in central Montana and other gold properties in mine development including the Briggs project in California and the McDonald Project in Montana. Canyon Resources Corporation operates the Kendall Mine in Montana, which produces gold and silver, and a mine/plant complex in Nevada. The company also conducts exploration and acquisition activities for valuable gold projects throughout the western United States, Latin America, and in select countries in Africa and the Western Pacific. **Corporate headquarters location:** This location. **Listed on:** American Stock Exchange. **Stock exchange symbol:** CAU. **Number of employees at this location:** 120.

COLORADO INTERSTATE GAS COMPANY
Western Pipelines, P.O. Box 1087, Colorado Springs CO 80944. 719/520-4227. **Physical address:** Western Pipelines, 2 North Nevada, Colorado Springs CO 80903. **Contact:** Human Resources. **World Wide Web address:** http://www.cigco.com. **Description:** Gathers, processes, and transports natural gas by pipeline in a six-state Rocky Mountain area to customer utility companies along the eastern front range of Colorado and southern Wyoming. **Corporate headquarters location:** Houston TX. **Other U.S. locations:** KS; OK; TX; UT; WY. **Parent company:** El Paso Corporation. **Listed on:** New York Stock Exchange. **Stock exchange symbol:** EP. **Number of employees nationwide:** 1,200.

CROWN RESOURCES CORPORATION
4251 Kipling Street, Suite 390, Wheat Ridge CO 80033. 303/534-1030. **Contact:** Human Resources. **World Wide Web address:** http://www.crownresources.com. **Description:** Engaged in gold exploration and mining.

FLINT ENERGY SERVICES
P.O. Box 145, 1391 Denver Avenue, Fort Lupton CO 80621-0145. 303/857-2791. **Fax:** 303/892-1820. **Contact:** Human Resources. **World Wide Web address:** http://www.flint-energy.com. **Description:** Provides oil and gas pipeline construction and well servicing. **Corporate headquarters location:** Calgary Alberta, Canada.

FRONTIER OIL REFINERY
4610 South Ulster Street, Suite 200, Denver CO 80237. 303/714-0100. **Contact:** Human Resources. **E-mail address:** hr@frontieroil-den.com. **World Wide Web address:** http://www.frontieroil.com. **Description:** Frontier Oil Corporation manufactures a full line of high-grade fuels from Wyoming crude oils. The company distributes more than one-half of the refinery's products throughout southern Wyoming and also supplies petroleum products to western Nebraska. **Corporate headquarters location:** Houston TX. **Operations at this facility include:** This location is a distributor of petroleum products to the Colorado Front Range. **Listed on:** New York Stock Exchange. **Stock exchange symbol:** FTO. **Number of employees nationwide:** 330.

KINDER MORGAN, INC.
370 Van Gordon Street, P.O. Box 281304, Lakewood CO 80228-8304. 303/989-1740. **Contact:** Human Resources. **World Wide Web address:** http://www.kindermorgan.com. **Description:** A natural gas transmission and distribution company. **Positions advertised include:** Accountant; Insurance Analyst; Network Control Technician; Volume Processor. **Corporate headquarters location:** Houston TX. **Other U.S. locations:** Nationwide. **Listed on:** New York Stock Exchange. **Stock exchange symbol:** KMI.

LUZENAC AMERICA
345 Inverness Drive South, Suite 310, Centennial CO 80112. 303/643-0400. **Fax:** 303/643-0446. **Contact:** Human Resources. **World Wide Web address:** http://www.luzenac.com. **Description:** Luzenac produces talc. **NOTE:** Search for positions on website. Applications accepted only for open positions. **Corporate headquarters location:** This location.

NATIONAL RENEWABLE ENERGY LABORATORIES
1617 Cole Boulevard, Golden CO 80401-3393. 303/275-3000. **Fax:** 303/384-7570. **Contact:** Human Resources. **E-mail address:** nrel_employment@nrel.gov. **World Wide Web address:** http://www.nrel.gov. **Description:** Engaged in the research and development of renewable energy technologies including wind, solar, and biomass electricity. **Positions advertised include:** Scientist; Sr. Scientist; Principal Strategic Analyst; Sr. Engineer; IT Applications Analyst; Sr. Administrator; Master Maintenance Technician.

NEWMONT MINING CORPORATION
1700 Lincoln Street, Denver CO 80203. 303/863-7414. **Fax:** 303/837-5837. **Contact:** Human Resources. **World Wide Web address:** http://www.newmont.com. **Description:** A gold exploration company that also operates, manages, and finances its gold properties in the United States. **Positions advertised include:** Internal Audit Supervisor; Sr. Humna Resources Systems Analyst; Corporate Tax Manager; Accounting System Administrator. **Corporate headquarters location:** This location. **Subsidiaries include:** Newmont Exploration Limited; Newmont Gold Company. **Listed on:** New York Stock Exchange. **Stock exchange symbol:** NEM.

PETRO CANADA

1099 18th Street, Suite 400, Denver CO 80202. 303/297-2100. **Fax:** 303/297-7708. **Contact:** Nancy Hewitt, Human Resources Manager. **E-mail address:** nancy.hewitt@petro-canada.com. **World Wide Web address:** http://www.petro-canada.com. **Description:** An oil and gas company engaged in the exploration, acquisition, development, and production of crude oil and natural gas. Also engaged in oil and gas property operations, oil field services, and natural gas marketing. **Corporate headquarters location:** Calgary Alberta Canada.

ROYAL GOLD, INC.

1660 Wynkoop Street, Suite 1000, Denver CO 80202. 303/573-1660. **Contact:** Controller. **E-mail address:** info@royalgold.com. **World Wide Web address:** http://www.royalgold.com. **Description:** Engaged in the acquisition, exploration, development, and sale of gold and precious metals properties. The company's exploration projects are located in Mono County CA; Eureka County NV; and Yavapai County AZ. Royal Gold also has gold properties located in Elko, White Pine, and Eureka Counties NV. **Corporate headquarters location:** This location. **Subsidiaries include:** Denver Mining Finance Company provides financial, operational, and management services to the mining industry. Environmental Strategies, Inc., a wholly-owned subsidiary of Denver Mining Finance Company, provides environmental consulting services to the mining industry. **Listed on:** NASDAQ. **Stock exchange symbol:** RGLD.

SCHLUMBERGER

6501 South Fiddlers Green Circle, #400, Greenwood Village CO 80111. 303/486-3200. **Fax:** 303/985-4111. **Contact:** Human Resources. **World Wide Web address:** http://www.slb.com. **Description:** Schlumberger develops and sells advanced scientific and engineering services, computer software, and digital mapping products to major oil companies and governments. **Positions advertised include:** Account Manager; Chemical Product Developer; Chemist; Customer Service Representative; Electrical Engineer; Geoscientist; Mechanical Engineer. **Corporate headquarters location:** New York NY. **Operations at this facility include:** This location provides consulting services to the oil and gas industry. **Listed on:** New York Stock Exchange. **Stock exchange symbol:** SLB.

SCOTT SPECIALTY GASES

500 Weaver Park Road, Longmont CO 80501. 303/651-3094. **Fax:** 303/772-7673. **Contact:** Human Resources. **Description:** A manufacturer of specialty gas products for the laboratory, environmental, energy, and chemical industries. **Positions advertised include:** Sales Manager; Customer Service Manager.

TRANSMONTAIGNE, INC.

P.O. Box 5660, Denver CO 80217. 303/626-8200. **Physical address:** 1670 Broadway, Suite 3100, Denver CO 80202. **Contact:** Human

Resources. **E-mail address:** openpositions@transmontaigne.com. **World Wide Web address:** http://www.transmontaigne.com. **Description:** A wholesale petroleum marketer. **Corporate headquarters location:** This location. **Listed on:** American Stock Exchange. **Stock exchange symbol:** TMG.

WESTERN GAS RESOURCES INC.
1099 18th Street, Suite 1200, Denver CO 80202. 303/452-5603. **Fax:** 303/252-6025. **Contact:** Human Resources. **E-mail address:** careers@westerngas.com. **World Wide Web address:** http://www.westerngas.com. **Description:** Owns and operates natural gas gathering and processing facilities. The company also markets and transports natural gas and natural gas liquids. **Positions advertised include:** Project Engineer; Sr. Reservoir Engineer; Internal Auditor; Geological Technician. **Corporate headquarters location:** This location. **Operations at this facility include:** Administration. **Listed on:** New York Stock Exchange. **Listed on:** New York Stock Exchange. **Stock exchange symbol:** WGR. **Number of employees at this location:** 350. **Number of employees nationwide:** 835.

WESTERNGECO
1625 Broadway, Suite 1300, Denver CO 80202. 303/629-9250. **Contact:** Human Resources Department. **World Wide Web address:** http://www.slb.com. **Description:** WesternGeco provides a full range of geophysical services for oil and gas exploration. Services include land and marine seismic surveys, geophysical programming, and data processing and interpretation. **Other U.S. locations:** AK; CA. **International locations:** Australia; Bolivia; Brazil; Canada; Colombia; Egypt; England; Guatemala; Italy; Pakistan; Saudi Arabia; Singapore; Tunisia. **Parent company:** Schlumberger Ltd. **Listed on:** New York Stock Exchange. **Stock exchange symbol:** SLB.

WILLIAMS
1515 Arapahoe Street, Tower 3, Suite 1000, Denver CO 80202. 303/572-3900. **Contact:** Human Resources. **E-mail address:** e-resumes@williams.com. **World Wide Web address:** http://www.williams.com. **Description:** Williams finds, produces, gathers, processes and transports natural gas. The company also manages a wholesale power business. Williams' operations are concentrated in the Pacific Northwest, Rocky Mountains, Gulf Coast, Southern California and Eastern Seaboard. **Positions advertised include:** Measurement Data Specialist; Geoscientist. **Corporate headquarters location:** Tulsa OK.

PAPER AND WOOD PRODUCTS

You can expect to find the following types of companies in this section:
Forest and Wood Products and Services • Lumber and Wood Wholesalers • Millwork, Plywood, and Structural Members • Paper and Wood Mills

CENVEO
8310 South Valley Highway #400, Englewood CO 80112. 303/790-8023. **Fax:** 303/397-7438. **Contact:** Human Resources. **World Wide Web address:** http://www.cenveo.com. **Description:** Cenveo is a leading consolidator in the envelope and specialty printing industries. The company specializes in customized envelopes, filing products, labels, and printed materials. Cenveo operates approximately 70 printing plants and numerous sales offices throughout North America. **Office hours:** Monday - Friday, 7:30 a.m. - 5:00 p.m. **Corporate headquarters location:** This location.

CENVEO
3500 Rockmont Drive, Denver CO 80202. 303/455-3505. **Contact:** Human Resources. **World Wide Web address:** http://www.cenveo.com. **Description:** Cenveo is a leading consolidator in the envelope and specialty printing industries. The company specializes in customized envelopes, filing products, labels, and printed materials. Cenveo operates approximately 70 printing plants and numerous sales offices throughout North America. **Positions advertised include:** Customer Service Rep. **Corporate headquarters location:** Englewood CO. **Operations at this facility include:** This location manufactures and markets envelopes in a wide range of sizes and styles.

INLAND CONTAINER CORPORATION
5000 Oak Street, Wheat Ridge CO 80033-2298. 303/422-7700. **Contact:** Della Nugent, Human Resources Manager. **World Wide Web address:** http://www.templeinland.com. **Description:** A manufacturer of corrugated shipping containers and boxes. **Parent company:** Temple-Inland Inc. **Listed on:** New York Stock Exchange. **Stock exchange symbol:** TIN.

SMURFIT-STONE CONTAINER CORPORATION
5050 East 50th Avenue, Denver CO 80216. 877/772-2999. **Contact:** Human Resources. **World Wide Web address:** http://www.smurfit-stone.com. **Description:** A leading paper-based packaging company. Smurfit-Stone Container Corporation's products include corrugated containers, folding cartons, and multiwall industrial bags. The company is one of the world's largest collectors and processors of recycled products that are then sold to a worldwide customer base. Smurfit-Stone Container Corporation also operates several paper tube, market pulp, and newsprint production facilities. **Corporate headquarters location:**

Chicago IL. **Other U.S. locations:** Nationwide. **Listed on:** NASDAQ. **Stock exchange symbol:** SSCC.

WEYERHAEUSER COMPANY
5995 Greenwood Plaza Boulevard, Greenwood Village CO 80111. 303/770-6262. **Contact:** Human Resources. **World Wide Web address:** http://www.weyerhaeuser.com. **Description:** Weyerhaeuser Company is a diversified, integrated forest products company with 90 plants and mills manufacturing containerboard, bag paper, fine paper, bleached hardwood market pulp, specialty printing papers, corrugated containers, business forms, cut sheet paper, paper bags, inks, lumber, plywood, particleboard, medium-density fiberboard, laminated beams, and value-added wood products. Founded in 1906. **Positions advertised include**: Business Analyst for Structural Frame Software; Technical Sales Rep. **Operations at this facility include:** This facility produces engineered wood products. **Corporate headquarters location:** Tacoma WA. **Listed on:** New York Stock Exchange. **Stock exchange symbol:** WY.

XPEDX
55 Madison Street, Suite 800, Denver CO 80206. 303/329-6644. **Contact:** Director of Human Resources. **World Wide Web address:** http://www.xpedx.com. **Description:** A wholesale distributor of paper and paper-related products. **Special programs:** Training. **Corporate headquarters location:** Covington KY.

PRINTING AND PUBLISHING

You can expect to find the following types of companies in this section:
Book, Newspaper, and Periodical Publishers • Commercial Photographers • Commercial Printing Services • Graphic Designers

THE ASSOCIATED PRESS
1444 Wazee Street, Suite 130, Denver CO 80202. 303/825-0123. **Contact:** Human Resources. **E-mail address:** apjobs@ap.org. **World Wide Web address:** http://www.ap.org. **Description:** One of the largest independent news-gathering organizations in the world. **Corporate headquarters location:** New York NY. **International locations:** Worldwide.

THE BOULDER COUNTY BUSINESS REPORT
3180 Sterling Circle, Suite 201, Boulder CO 80301-2338. 303/440-4950. **Contact:** Jerry Lewis, Editor/Vice President. **World Wide Web address:** http://www.bcbr.com. **Description:** Publishes a monthly business newspaper for the Boulder County area. **Corporate headquarters location:** This location. **Operations at this facility include:** Publishing; Sales. **Number of employees at this location:** 5.

COLORADO SPRINGS BUSINESS JOURNAL
31 East Platte Avenue, Suite 300, Colorado Springs CO 80903. 719/634-5905. **Fax:** 719/634-5157. **Contact:** Publisher. **World Wide Web address:** http://www.csbj.com. **Description:** Publishes a weekly business newspaper. Founded in 1989. **Special programs:** Internships. **Corporate headquarters location:** This location. **Parent company:** Colorado Publishing Company. **Listed on:** Privately held. **Annual sales/revenues:** Less than $5 million. **Number of employees at this location:** 20.

DAILY CAMERA
P.O. Box 4579, Boulder CO 80306. 303/442-1202. **Contact:** Human Resources. **E-mail address:** jobs@thedailycamera.com. **World Wide Web address:** http://www.dailycamera.com. **Description:** Publishes a daily newspaper. **Special programs:** Internships. **Corporate headquarters location:** This location. **Parent company:** E.W. Scripps Company (Cincinnati OH). **Listed on:** New York Stock Exchange. **Stock exchange symbol:** SSP.

DENVER BUSINESS JOURNAL
1700 Broadway, Suite 515, Denver CO 80290-9908. 303/837-3500. **Contact:** Human Resources. **E-mail address:** denver@bizjournals.com. **World Wide Web address:** http://www.denver.bizjournals.com. **Description:** Publishes a business journal.

THE DENVER POST

1560 Broadway, Denver CO 80202. 303/820-1010. **Contact:** Misty Miller, Vice President of Human Resources Department. **World Wide Web address:** http://www.denverpost.com. **Description:** Publishes a daily newspaper with a weekday circulation of more than 280,000 and a Sunday circulation of 450,000. **Special programs:** Internships. **Corporate headquarters location:** Houston TX. **Parent company:** Denver Newspaper Agency. **Operations at this facility include:** Divisional Headquarters.

EAGLE:XM

5105 East 41st Avenue, Denver CO 80216. 303/320-5411. **Fax:** 303/393-6584. **Contact:** Human Resources. **E-mail address:** tdrinkwater@eagledirect.com. **World Wide Web address:** http://www.eagledirect.com. **Description:** A marketing services company.

FREDERIC PRINTING

14701 East 38th Avenue, Aurora CO 80011. 303/371-7990. **Fax:** 303/371-7959. **Contact:** Human Resources Department. **E-mail address:** info@fredericprinting.com. **World Wide Web address:** http://www.fredericprinting.com. **Description:** Provides a wide range of commercial printing services, from camera-ready art to binding. **Corporate headquarters location:** This location. **Parent company:** Consolidated Graphics. **Operations at this facility include:** Administration; Manufacturing; Sales. **Listed on:** New York Stock Exchange. **Stock exchange symbol:** CGX.

THE GAZETTE

P.O. Box 1779, Colorado Springs CO 80901-1779. 719/632-5511. **Physical address:** 30 South Prospect, Colorado Springs CO 80903. **Recorded jobline:** 719/636-0348. **Contact:** Human Resources. **World Wide Web address:** http://www.gazette.com. **Description:** A newspaper with a circulation of approximately 100,000 daily and 125,000 on Sundays. **Parent company:** Freedom Communications, Inc.

GOLDEN BELL PRESS INC.

2403 Champa Street, Denver CO 80205. 303/296-1600. **Contact:** Sherri Simpson, Office Manager. **World Wide Web address:** http://www.goldenbellpress.com. **Description:** Publishes periodicals and operates as an offset printer. Founded in 1936.

GREELEY DAILY TRIBUNE

P.O. Box 1690, Greeley CO 80632. 970/352-0211. **Toll-free phone:** 800/275-0321. **Contact:** Brenda Haines, Human Resources. **World Wide Web address:** http://www.greeleytrib.com. **Description:** Publishes a daily newspaper with a circulation of more than 29,000. Founded in 1870. **Corporate headquarters location:** Reno NV. **Publisher:** Jim Elsberry.

JOHN H. HARLAND COMPANY

4700 South Syracuse Street, Suite 900, Denver CO 80237. 303/770-5190. **Toll-free phone:** 800/937-3799. **Contact:** Human Resources. **World Wide Web address:** http://www.harland.net. **Description:** A financial printing firm. Products include business and personal checks, as well as other forms and documents for the banking industry. **Positions advertised include:** Implementation Manager. **Corporate headquarters location:** Decatur GA. **Listed on:** New York Stock Exchange. **Stock exchange symbol:** JH. **Annual sales/revenues:** More than $100 million. **Number of employees at this location:** 90.

THE HIBBERT GROUP

2399 Blake Street, Suite 120, Denver CO 80205. 303/297-1601. **Fax:** 303/672-7320. **Contact:** Deena Lowe, Human Resources. **E-mail address:** HrDenver@hibbertgroup.com. **World Wide Web address:** http://www.hibbertgroup.com. **Description:** Provides marketing services. **Positions advertised include:** Customer Service Rep. **Corporate headquarters location:** This location. **Other U.S. locations include:** Trenton NJ. **Parent company:** Hibbert Company (Trenton NJ).

IHS ENERGY GROUP

15 Inverness Way East, MSB106, Englewood CO 80112-5776. 303/736-3000. **Contact:** Employment Coordinator. **E-mail address:** careers@ihs.com. **World Wide Web address:** http://www.ihsenergy.com. **Description:** Publishes oil activity information including reports, maps, and well data. **Positions advertised include:** International Tax Director; Database Marketing Manager; Sr. Product Manager; Sr. Business Solutions Architect; Sr. Treasury Analyst; Sr. Manager Finance. **Listed on:** New York Stock Exchange. **Stock exchange symbol:** IHS.

JEPPESEN SANDERSON INC.

55 Inverness Drive East, Englewood CO 80112-5498. 303/799-9090. **Fax:** 303/328-4121. **Contact:** Human Resources. **E-mail address:** jobs@jeppesen.com. **World Wide Web address:** http://www.jeppesen.com. **Description:** Publishes and distributes flight information manuals, flight training supplies, and informational products. **NOTE:** If you are faxing your resume, please specify the position that you are interested in and specify a desired salary. **Positions advertised include:** IT Procurement Specialist; Project Manager; Strategic Account Manager; Software Test Engineer; Business Analyst; Requirements Analyst; HR Generalist; Instructional Designer; Technical Writer. **Other U.S. locations:** San Jose CA; Wilsonville OR; Washington DC; Atlanta GA. **International locations:** Australia; Germany; Russia; United Kingdom; China. **Operations at this facility include:** Administration; Divisional Headquarters; Manufacturing; Research and Development; Sales; Service. **Number of employees at this location:** 800. **Number of employees worldwide:** 1,100.

JOHNSON PRINTING

1880 South 57th Court, Boulder CO 80301. 303/443-1576. **Contact:** Human Resources. **World Wide Web address:** http://www.jpcolorado.com. **Description:** Provides commercial printing services (prepress, offset, binding, digital, and postproduction).

LEXISNEXIS

555 Middlecreek Parkway, Colorado Springs CO 80921. 719/488-3000. **Contact:** Human Resources. **World Wide Web address:** http://www.lexisnexis.com. **Description:** A full-service, multimedia publisher that develops legal information products and citations products in all forms of media including online and CD-ROM. **Positions advertised include:** Manager, Lexis Caselaw and Citations. **Number of employees at this location:** 850.

MEDIANEWS GROUP, INC.

1560 Broadway, Suite 2100, Denver CO 80202. 303/563-6360. **Contact:** Human Resources. **World Wide Web address:** http://www.medianewsgroup.com. **Description:** A newspaper holding company, operating 40 daily newspapers in nine states. **Positions advertised include:** Business Development Manager; Internal Auditor.

PENTON TECHNOLOGY MEDIA

221 East 29th Street, Loveland CO 80538. 970/663-4700. **Contact:** Recruiter. **World Wide Web address:** http://www.pentontech.com. **Description:** Publishes technical information for IBM AS/400 and Windows NT users and financial analysts. The company produces numerous magazines, books, and textbooks. **Positions advertised include:** eMedia Business Systems Manager; Strategic Marketing Manager; Web Designer. **Corporate headquarters location:** Cleveland OH. **Other area locations:** Lakewood CO. **International locations:** United Kingdom. **Parent company:** Penton Media, Inc. **Listed on:** New York Stock Exchange. **Stock exchange symbol:** PME. **Number of employees at this location:** 80.

PRIMEDIA BUSINESS

5680 Greenwood Plaza Boulevard, Suite 100, Greenwood Village CO 80111. 303/741-2901. **Contact:** Personnel. **World Wide Web address:** http://www.primedia.com. **Description:** A publisher of business-to-business magazines and newsletters. PRIMEDIA also produces 450 technical books and valuation guides. **Parent company:** PRIMEDIA Specialty Magazines. **Listed on:** New York Stock Exchange. **Stock exchange symbol:** PRM.

THE PUEBLO CHIEFTAIN

P.O. Box 4040, Pueblo CO 81003. 719/544-3520. **Physical address:** 825 West 6th Street, Pueblo CO 81003. **Contact:** Executive Editor. **World Wide Web address:** http://www.chieftain.com. **Description:** Publishes the *Pueblo Chieftain*, a newspaper with a circulation of 51,000. **Corporate headquarters location:** This location.

ROCKY MOUNTAIN NEWS
100 Gene Amole Way, Denver CO 80204. 303/892-5173. **Contact:** Administrative Services Department. **World Wide Web address:** http://www.rockymountainnews.com. **Description:** Publishes a newspaper with a daily circulation of more than 344,000. **Positions advertised include:** Internet Site Developer; Internet Content Producer. **Special programs:** Internships. **Office hours:** Monday - Friday, 8:00 a.m. - 5:00 p.m. **Other U.S. locations:** Nationwide. **Parent company:** E.W. Scripps Company (Cincinnati OH.) **Operations at this facility include:** Administration; Sales; Service. **Listed on:** New York Stock Exchange. **Stock exchange symbol:** SSP. **Number of employees at this location:** 1,600.

REAL ESTATE

You can expect to find the following types of companies in this section:
Land Subdividers and Developers • Real Estate Agents, Managers, and Operators • Real Estate Investment Trusts

BURNS REALTY & TRUST
1625 Broadway, World Trade Center, Penthouse Suite, Denver CO 80202. 303/629-1899. **Contact:** Mark Gritz, Treasurer/Controller. **Description:** Engaged in real estate and investments, as well as owning and operating apartments and nonresidential buildings.

COLDWELL BANKER MOORE & COMPANY
8490 East Crescent Parkway, Greenwood Village CO 80111. 303/409-1500. **Fax:** 303/409-6352. **Contact:** Sue Senter-Reed, Director of Human Resources. **E-mail address:** Sue.Senter-Reed@nrtinc.com. **World Wide Web address:** http://www.coloradohomes.com. **Description:** A real estate sales company.

GRUBB & ELLIS COMPANY
One Tabor Center, 1200 17th Street, Suite 2000, Denver CO 80202-5841. 303/572-7700. **Contact:** Administrative Manager. **World Wide Web address:** http://www.grubb-ellis.com. **Description:** A commercial real estate brokerage firm offering a full range of services including transaction, management, and consulting services. Founded in 1973. **Positions advertised include:** Administrative Assistant. **Special programs:** Internships. **Corporate headquarters location:** Northbrook IL. **Other area locations:** Colorado Springs CO. **Other U.S. locations:** Nationwide. **Listed on:** New York Stock Exchange. **Stock exchange symbol:** GBE.

PRUDENTIAL COLORADO REAL ESTATE
9635 Maroon Circle, Suite 400, Englewood CO 80112. 303/750-3475. **Fax:** 303/369-3455. **Contact:** Human Resources. **Description:** Markets residential and commercial real estate throughout metropolitan Denver.

ROSENBERG MANAGEMENT INC.
3400 East Bayaud Avenue, Suite 390, Denver CO 80209. 303/320-6067. **Contact:** Manager. **Description:** A real estate investment company involved in operating apartment buildings.

FREDERICK ROSS COMPANY
717 17th Street, Suite 2000, Denver CO 80202. 303/892-1111. **Contact:** Human Resources. **World Wide Web address:** http://www.frederickross.com. **Description:** A full-service commercial real estate firm. **Corporate headquarters location:** This location. **Parent company:** Oncor International. **Operations at this facility**

include: Administration; Research and Development; Sales; Service.
Listed on: Privately held. **Number of employees at this location:** 150.

WALKER ASSOCIATES
420 East 58th Avenue, Denver CO 80216. 303/292-5537. **Contact:**
Human Resources. **Description:** A real estate agency whose dealings
include electronic component distributor banks, ranches, and commercial
properties.

RETAIL

You can expect to find the following types of companies in this section:
Catalog Retailers • Department Stores, Specialty Stores • Retail Bakeries • Supermarkets

---

ALPINE LUMBER COMPANY
5800 North Pecos, Denver CO 80221. 303/458-8733. **Contact:** General Manager. **World Wide Web address:** http://www.alpinelumber.com. **Description:** A retail lumberyard. Founded in 1963. **Corporate headquarters location:** This location. **Other area locations include:** Brighton CO; Denver CO.

AUTOZONE
1108 Bonforte Boulevard, Pueblo CO 81001-1805. 719/542-9000. **Contact:** Human Resources. **World Wide Web address:** http://www.autozone.com. **Description:** A do-it-yourself, retail auto parts chain, specializing in foreign and domestic parts. **Corporate headquarters location:** Memphis TN. **Listed on:** New York Stock Exchange. **Stock exchange symbol:** AZO.

BMC WEST
6400 Arapahoe Avenue, Boulder CO 80303. 303/442-5382. **Contact:** General Manager. **World Wide Web address:** http://www.bmcwest.com. **Description:** A lumber and hardware retailer. **Corporate headquarters location:** Boise ID. **Parent company:** Building Materials Holding Corporation. **Listed on:** NASDAQ. **Stock exchange symbol:** BMHC.

BARNES & NOBLE BOOKSTORES
960 South Colorado Boulevard, Glendale CO 80246. 303/691-2998. **Fax:** 303/691-9193. **Contact:** Manager. **World Wide Web address:** http://www.bn.com. **Description:** Barnes & Noble Bookstores is a bookstore chain operating nationwide. **Corporate headquarters location:** New York NY. **Operations at this facility include:** This location houses the district headquarters as well as a bookstore. **Listed on:** New York Stock Exchange. **Stock exchange symbol:** BKS.

BURT CHEVROLET, INC.
5200 South Broadway, Englewood CO 80110. 303/761-0333. **Contact:** Employment Administrator. **E-mail address:** jobs@burt.com. **World Wide Web address:** http://www.burt.com. **Description:** A new and used automobile dealership. **NOTE:** Send resumes to: Burt Automotive Network, Attn: Employment Administrator, 10301 East Arapahoe Road, Centennial CO 80112.

CHRISTY SPORTS, LLC

875 Parfet Street, Lakewood CO 80215. 303/237-6321. **Fax:** 303/274-4589. **Contact:** Human Resources. **World Wide Web address:** http://www.christysports.com. **Description:** Operates Christy Sports, SportStalker, and Powder Tools sporting goods stores. The company specializes in retail skiing, snowboarding, and sport clothing. In addition, Christy Sports offers patio furniture and several golf retail stores. **NOTE:** Entry-level positions are offered. **Special programs:** Training; Summer Jobs. **Corporate headquarters location:** This location. **Other U.S. locations:** UT. **Number of employees at this location:** 75. **Number of employees nationwide:** 500.

CURRENT, INC.

1005 East Woodman Road, Colorado Springs CO 80920. 719/594-4100. **Contact:** Personnel. **World Wide Web address:** http://www.currentinc.com. **Description:** Prints and markets greeting cards, stationery, and checks. **Corporate headquarters location:** St. Paul MN. **Other U.S. locations:** Nationwide. **Parent company:** Deluxe Corporation.

EMPIRE OLDSMOBILE/HONDA

P.O. Box 200336, Denver CO 80220. 303/399-1950. **Physical address:** 6160 East Colfax Avenue, Denver CO 80220. **Contact:** Judy Grinestaff, Payroll Supervisor. **Description:** An automobile dealership.

THE FOSS COMPANY

1224 Washington Avenue, Golden CO 80401. 303/279-3373. **Contact:** Personnel Manager. **World Wide Web address:** http://www.fossco.com. **Description:** A general store, post office, pharmacy, and liquor store. This location is also headquarters for Ski Country Decanters, H.J. Foss Apparel, and The Golden Ram Restaurant. **Corporate headquarters location:** This location. **Operations at this facility include:** Administration; Sales; Service.

FURNITURE ROW COMPANY

13333 East 37th Avenue, Denver CO 80239. 303/371-8560. **Contact:** Human Resources. **World Wide Web address:** http://www.furniturerow.com. **Description:** A retail furniture dealer with 270 stores in 31 states. **Corporate headquarters location:** This location.

GALLERIA LIGHTING & DESIGN

239-B Detroit Street, Denver CO 80206. 303/592-1223. **Toll-free phone:** 800/332-2066. **Fax:** 303/534-2566. **Contact:** Human Resources. **World Wide Web address:** http://www.dbwrite.com. **Description:** Galleria Lighting & Design sells lighting fixtures in both retail and wholesale markets. **Positions advertised include:** Sales Executive. **Parent company:** QED. **Listed on:** Privately held. **Annual sales/revenues:** $51 - $100 million. **Number of employees at this location:** 30. **Number of employees nationwide:** 200.

IKON OFFICE SOLUTIONS

7173 South Havana Street, Suite A, Englewood CO 80112. 720/875-8300. **Contact:** Lynn Hannblom, Director of Human Resources. **World Wide Web address:** http://www.ikon.com. **Description:** Engaged in the retail sale and service of Canon office equipment and supplies. **Positions advertised include:** Sales Manager; Account Executive. **Corporate headquarters location:** Valley Forge PA. **Other U.S. locations:** Nationwide. **Operations at this facility include:** Administration; Regional Headquarters; Sales; Service. **Listed on:** New York Stock Exchange. **Stock exchange symbol:** IKN.

LEWAN & ASSOCIATES, INC.

1400 South Colorado Boulevard, P.O. Box 22855, Denver CO 80222. 303/759-5440. **Contact:** Human Resources. **World Wide Web address:** http://www.lewan.com. **Description:** A retail office products dealer. **Positions advertised include:** Enterprise Solution Sales Account Executive; New Business Development Representative. **Corporate headquarters location:** This location.

MOUNTAIN STATES MOTORS

1260 South Colorado Boulevard, Denver CO 80246. 303/757-7751. **Contact:** Frank Murray, Office Manager. **World Wide Web address:** http://www.vwdenver.com. **Description:** An automobile dealership specializing in Volkswagen sales and service.

ROCKY MOUNTAIN CHOCOLATE FACTORY, INC.

265 Turner Drive, Durango CO 81303. 970/247-4943. **Fax:** 970/382-7371. **Contact:** Jamie Callies, Human Resource Supervisor. **E-mail address:** employment@rmcf.com. **World Wide Web address:** http://www.rmcf.com. **Description:** A retail distributor of candy products including chocolate covered fruit, fudge, and caramel apples. The company operates over 200 retail stores worldwide. Founded in 1981. **NOTE:** Part-time jobs and second and third shifts are offered. This location also hires seasonally. **Special programs:** Internships; Summer Jobs. **Office hours:** Monday - Friday, 8:00 a.m. - 5:00 p.m. **Corporate headquarters location:** This location. **Other U.S. locations:** Nationwide. **International locations:** Canada; Taiwan; United Arab Emirates. **Listed on:** NASDAQ. **Stock exchange symbol:** RMCF. **Number of employees at this location:** 120. **Number of employees nationwide:** 400.

THE SANBORN MAP COMPANY

1935 Jamboree Drive, Suite 100, Colorado Springs CO 80920. 719/593-0093. **Fax:** 719/528-5093. **Contact:** Human Resources. **E-mail address:** employment@sanborn.com. **World Wide Web address:** http://www.sanbornmap.com. **Description:** The Sanborn Map Company produces high-quality, detailed maps. Founded in 1866. **Positions advertised include:** GIS Technicians; System Administrator.

7-ELEVEN, INC.

7167 South Alton Way, Englewood CO 80112. 303/740-9333. **Fax:** 303/220-1062. **Recorded jobline:** 800/711-5627. **Contact:** Human Resources. **World Wide Web address:** http://www.7-eleven.com. **Description:** The 7-Eleven convenience store chain is one of the largest store chains in the world. **Corporate headquarters location:** Dallas TX. **Operations at this facility include:** This location serves as the regional headquarters of 7-Eleven convenience stores in Colorado and Utah. **Listed on:** New York Stock Exchange. **Stock exchange symbol:** SE. **Number of employees at this location:** 3,500.

SPORTS AUTHORITY

705 West Hampden Avenue, Englewood CO 80110. 303/789-5266. **Fax:** 303/863-2243. **Contact:** Human Resources. **World Wide Web address:** http://www.sportsauthority.com. **Description:** Operates a chain of retail sporting goods stores. **Positions advertised include:** Department Manager. **Other U.S. locations:** Nationwide. **Listed on:** NASDAQ.

SUN ENTERPRISES INC.

8877 North Washington Street, Thornton CO 80229. 303/287-7566. **Fax:** 303/287-7716. **Contact:** Gerald Bieker, Controller. **E-mail address:** sun@sunent.com. **World Wide Web address:** http://www.sunent.com. **Description:** A retailer of motorcycles, ATVs, watercraft, snowmobiles, power equipment, and related parts and accessories. **Office hours:** Tuesday - Saturday, 9:00 a.m. - 6:00 p.m. **Vice President:** Ronald Lang. **Annual sales/revenues:** $11 - $20 million. **Number of employees at this location:** 45.

ULTIMATE ELECTRONICS, INC.

321 West 84th Avenue, Suite A, Thornton CO 80260. 303/412-2500. **Toll-free phone:** 800/260-2660. **Fax:** 303/412-2501. **Contact:** Human Resources. **World Wide Web address:** http://www.ultimateelectronics.com. **Description:** A specialty retailer of home entertainment and consumer electronics. The company operates stores under the SoundTrack, Audio King, and Ultimate Electronics names. Founded in 1968. **NOTE:** Entry-level positions and second and third shifts are offered. **Positions advertised include:** Accounting Manager; Financial Analyst; General Manager; Graphic Designer; Copywriter. **Special programs:** Training. **Corporate headquarters location:** This location. **Other area locations:** Arvada CO; Aurora CO; Boulder CO; Colorado Springs CO; Denver CO; Fort Collins CO; Littleton CO. **Other U.S. locations:** Albuquerque NM; Las Vegas NV; Murray UT; Orem UT; Salt Lake City UT. **Listed on:** NASDAQ. **Stock exchange symbol:** ULTE. **Annual sales/revenues:** More than $100 million. **Number of employees at this location:** 700. **Number of employees nationwide:** 1,600.

WAL-MART STORES, INC.

7455 West Colfax Avenue, Lakewood CO 80214. 303/274-5211. **Contact:** Human Resources. **World Wide Web address:** http://www.walmartstores.com. **Description:** Wal-Mart Stores is a retail merchandise chain operating full-service discount department stores, combination grocery and discount stores, and warehouse stores requiring membership. Founded in 1962. **Corporate headquarters location:** Bentonville AR. **Listed on:** New York Stock Exchange. **Stock exchange symbol:** WMT.

WILD OATS MARKETS
3375 Mitchell Lane, Boulder CO 80301. 303/440-5220. **Contact:** Human Resources. **World Wide Web address:** http://www.wildoats.com. **Description:** Owns and operates more than 100 health food supermarkets in the U.S. and Canada. **Positions advertised include:** Communications Manager; Compensation Analyst; Director of Design; HR Management systems Manager; Plan Development Manager; Pricing Specialist. **Corporate headquarters location:** This location. **Other U.S. locations:** Nationwide. **Listed on:** NASDAQ. **Stock exchange symbol:** OATS.

STONE, CLAY, GLASS, AND CONCRETE PRODUCTS

You can expect to find the following types of companies in this section:
Cement, Tile, Sand, and Gravel • Crushed and Broken Stone • Glass and Glass Products • Mineral Products

AGGREGATE INDUSTRIES
1707 Cole Boulevard, Suite 100, Golden CO 80401. 303/777-3058. **World Wide Web address:** http://www.aggregate.com. **Contact:** Human Resources. **Description:** Manufactures ready-mix concrete and other aggregate products. **NOTE:** Resumes accepted only for posted positions. **Positions advertised include:** Contracting Accountant; Estimator/Project Manager; Human Resources Generalist; VP/General Manager, Aggregates. **Corporate headquarters location:** Rockville MD.

BRANNAN SAND AND GRAVEL COMPANY
2500 East Brannan Way, Denver CO 80229. 303/534-1231. **Fax:** 303/534-1236. **World Wide Web address:** http://www.brannan1.com. **Contact:** Judy Carpenter, Employee Relations Manager. **E-mail address:** judycarp@qwest.net. **Description:** Manufactures asphalt products used in construction, as well as other rock products. **Positions advertised include:** CDL Driver; Estimator; Project Superintendent; Laborer; Mechanic; Equipment Operator; Office Personnel. **Corporate headquarters location:** This location.

CARDER CONCRETE PRODUCTS COMPANY
8311 West Carder Court, Littleton CO 80125. 303/791-1600. **Contact:** Human Resources. **E-mail address:** info@carderconcrere.com. **World Wide Web address:** http://www.carderconcrete.com. **Description:** Produces concrete products including culverts, storm and drainage pipes, and box culverts. Founded in 1968. **Operations at this facility include:** Administration; Manufacturing; Regional Headquarters; Sales.

COORS BREWING COMPANY
P.O. Box 4030, 13th and Ford Street, Golden CO 80401-0030. 303/279-6565. **Contact:** Human Resources. **Description:** Coors Brewing Company is the third largest brewer in the U.S. **Positions advertised include:** Finance Manager; Channel Development Manager; Plant Maintenance Mechanic; Sourcing Manager; Internal Communications Project Manager; Capital Planning Analyst. **Parent company:** Molson Coors Brewing Company. **Listed on:** New York Stock Exchange. **Stock exchange symbol:** TSX-TAP.

GATES & SONS, INC.
90 South Fox Street, Denver CO 80223. 303/744-6185. **Fax:** 303/744-6192. **Contact:** Employment Manager. **E-mail address:** info@gatesconcreteforms.com. **World Wide Web address:**

http://www.gatesconcreteforms.com. **Description:** Produces concrete forms for walls, seating, columns, prefabricated buildings, elevator shafts, and various other uses. **Corporate headquarters location:** This location.

JOHNS MANVILLE CORPORATION

717 17th Street, Denver CO 80202. 303/978-2000. **Contact:** Human Resources. **E-mail address:** humanresources@jm.com. **World Wide Web address:** http://www.jm.com. **Description:** A fiberglass manufacturer. The company produces and markets insulation products for buildings and equipment, high-efficiency air filtration media, and commercial roofing systems and textile glass used as reinforcements in buildings and industrial applications. **Positions advertised include:** Audit Manager; Director Strategic Sourcing; Global Innovation Leader; Interactive Web Designer; Manager Network Solutions; Product Manager; Technical Writer. **Corporate headquarters location:** This location. **Parent company:** Berkshire Hathaway. **Listed on:** New York Stock Exchange. **Stock exchange symbol:** BRK. **Number of employees nationwide:** 8,500.

LAFARGE NORTH AMERICA INC.

1400 West 64th Avenue, Denver CO 80021. 303/657-4200. **Contact:** Human Resources. **World Wide Web address:** http://www.lafargenorthamerica.com. **Description:** Material supplier of ready-mix concrete aggregates and admixtures. Lafarge is a general contractor for the heavy construction industry. **Corporate headquarters location:** Herndon VA. **International locations:** Canada. **Listed on:** New York Stock Exchange. **Stock exchange symbol:** LAF.

MONIERLIFETILE LLC

10121 Dallas Street, Henderson CO 80640. 303/286-3856. **Contact:** Operations Manager. **World Wide Web address:** http://www.monierlifetile.com. **Description:** Manufactures concrete, clay, and synthetic roof tiles. **Positions advertised include:** Plant Manager. **Corporate headquarters location:** Irvine CA. **Other U.S. locations:** Nationwide.

ROBINSON BRICK COMPANY

1845 West Dartmouth Avenue, Denver CO 80110-1308. 303/781-9002. **Contact:** Human Resources. **E-mail address:** hr@robinsonbrick.com. **World Wide Web address:** http://www.robinsonbrick.com. **Description:** Produces and markets a variety of brick and tile materials including paving brick and clay brick. Founded in 1880. **Positions advertised include:** Maintenance Mechanic. **Office hours:** Monday - Friday, 7:00 a.m. - 5:00 p.m. **Corporate headquarters location:** This location. **Operations at this facility include:** Administration; Manufacturing; Research and Development; Sales; Service.

ROCKY MOUNTAIN PRESTRESS

5801 Pecos, P.O. Box 21500, Denver CO 80221. 303/480-1111. **Fax:** 303/433-0451. **Contact:** Joe Slobojan, Personnel. **E-mail address:**

SlobojanJ@rmpprestress.com. **World Wide Web address:** http://www.rmpprestress.com. **Description:** Manufactures and sells prestressed structural concrete building materials, primarily used in heavy construction projects. **Positions advertised include:** Project Engineer; Project Drafter; Safety Coordinator; Estimator. **Corporate headquarters location:** This location. **Operations at this facility include:** Administration; Manufacturing; Research and Development; Sales; Service. **Number of employees at this location:** 300.

STRESSCON CORPORATION
P.O. Box 15129, Colorado Springs CO 80935. 719/390-5041. **Physical address:** 3210 Astrozon Boulevard, Colorado Springs CO 80910. **Contact:** Human Resources Department. **E-mail address:** careers@stresscon.com. **World Wide Web address:** http://www.stresscon.com. **Description:** Stresscon manufactures and distributes precast/prestressed structural concrete, architectural concrete, and concrete used in other large-scale construction projects. **Corporate headquarters location:** This location. **President:** H.W. Reinking.

TRANSPORTATION AND TRAVEL

You can expect to find the following types of companies in this section:
Air, Railroad, and Water Transportation Services • Courier Services • Local and Interurban Passenger Transit • Ship Building and Repair • Transportation Equipment • Travel Agencies • Trucking • Warehousing and Storage

---

AMERICOLD LOGISTICS, LLC
4475 East 50th Avenue, Denver CO 80216. 303/320-0333. **Recorded jobline:** 866/KOOL-JOB. **Contact:** Personnel. **E-mail address:** employment@amclog.com. **World Wide Web address:** http://www.americold.net. **Description:** Operates refrigerated warehouse facilities that store frozen and refrigerated food products for various food distributing and processing companies. **Corporate headquarters location:** Atlanta GA. **Other U.S. locations:** Portland OR.

ASPEN DISTRIBUTION INC.
11075 East 40th Avenue, Denver CO 80239. 303/371-2511. **Contact:** Personnel. **World Wide Web address:** http://www.aspendistribution.com. **Description:** A local trucking company and public warehouse.

ASSOCIATED GLOBAL SYSTEMS
16075 East 32nd Avenue, Aurora CO 80011. 720/858-0200. **Contact:** Human Resources. **E-mail address:** careers@agsystems.com. **World Wide Web address:** http://www.agsystems.com. **Description:** An air transportation company offering domestic, international, and same-day services. **Corporate headquarters location:** New Hyde Park NY.

BAX GLOBAL
16075 East 32nd Avenue, Suite B, Aurora CO 80011. 720/859-6240. **Fax:** 720/859-6298. **Toll-free phone:** 800/525-3720. **Contact:** Human Resources. **World Wide Web address:** http://www.baxglobal.com. **Description:** Bax Global offers business-to-business freight delivery through a worldwide network of offices in 124 countries, with 155 offices in the U.S. **Other area locations:** Grand Junction CO. **Other U.S. locations:** Nationwide. **International locations:** Worldwide. **Parent company:** The Brink's Company.

GRAND VALLEY TRANSIT
201 South Avenue, Grand Junction CO 81501. 970/256-7433. **Contact:** Ralph Power, Executive Director. **World Wide Web address:** http://www.grandvalleytransit.com. **Description:** Provides transportation services to people with disabilities.

GREYHOUND BUS LINES

12881 Highway 61, Sterling CO 80751. 970/522-5522. **Contact:** Human Resources. **World Wide Web address:** http://www.greyhound.com. **Description:** Greyhound is a major nationwide bus route service operator, with more than 3,000 stop facilities throughout the United States. Greyhound also offers passenger express bus service, sightseeing services, airport ground transportation, and independent charter bus services. **Corporate headquarters location:** Dallas TX. **Operations at this facility include:** This location is a local bus terminal.

GROUP VOYAGERS, INC.
dba GLOBUS & COSMOS

5301 South Federal Circle, Littleton CO 80123. 303/703-7000. **Toll-free phone:** 800/851-0728. **Fax:** 303/795-6615. **Contact:** Jackie Boyd, Recruiter. **Description:** Provides travel packages to more than 70 countries on all seven continents. **NOTE:** Entry-level positions and part-time jobs are offered. **Positions advertised include:** Oracle Financial Programmer; C+ Developer; Air Associate. **Special programs:** Training. **Office hours:** Monday - Friday, 7:00 a.m. - 6:00 p.m. **Corporate headquarters location:** This location. **Other U.S. locations:** Pasadena CA. **International locations:** Worldwide. **Number of employees at this location:** 290.

LAIDLAW TRANSIT SERVICES, INC.

6345 North Colorado Boulevard, Commerce City CO 80022. 303/288-1939. **Contact:** Human Resources. **World Wide Web address:** http://www.laidlawtransit.com. **Description:** Provides urban busing services. **Corporate headquarters location:** Overland Park KS. **Parent company:** Laidlaw, Inc. provides solid waste collection, compacting, transportation, treatment, transfer, and disposal services; provides hazardous waste services; operates hazardous waste facilities and wastewater treatment plants; and operates passenger and school buses, transit systems buses, and tour and charter buses.

UTILITIES: ELECTRIC, GAS, AND WATER

You can expect to find the following types of companies in this section:
Gas, Electric, and Fuel Companies • Other Energy-Producing Companies • Public Utility Holding Companies • Water Utilities

COLORADO SPRINGS UTILITIES
P.O. Box 1103, Colorado Springs CO 80947. 719/448-4800. **Contact:** Human Resources. **E-mail address:** hrservicecenter@csu.org. **World Wide Web address:** http://www.csu.org. **Description:** Provides public utility services. **NOTE:** Apply online. **Positions advertised include:** Administrative Technician; Instrumentation, Electrical & Control Specialist; Maintenance Superintendent.

DUKE ENERGY
1324 North Seventh Avenue, Greeley CO 80631. 970/454-3366. **Contact:** Human Resources. **World Wide Web address:** http://www.duke-energy.com. **Description:** Provides electric service to approximately 2 million customers, operates pipelines that deliver 12 percent of the natural gas consumed in the United States, and is a leading maker of electricity, natural gas, and natural gas liquids. **Corporate headquarters location:** Charlotte NC. **Listed on:** New York Stock Exchange. **Stock exchange symbol:** DUK.

MISCELLANEOUS WHOLESALING

You can expect to find the following types of companies in this section:
Exporters and Importers • General Wholesale Distribution Companies

---

CORPORATE EXPRESS
One Environmental Way, Broomfield CO 80021. 303/664-2000. **Fax:** 303/664-3474. **Contact:** Personnel. **World Wide Web address:** http://www.corporateexpress.com. **Description:** A business-to-business supplier of office and computer products and services. The company supplies products through a direct sales staff and direct mail catalogs. **Corporate headquarters location:** This location. **International locations:** Worldwide. **Parent company:** Buhrmann. **Listed on:** New York Stock Exchange. **Stock exchange symbol:** BUH.

JHB INTERNATIONAL INC.
1955 South Quince Street, Denver CO 80231. 303/751-8100. **Contact:** Personnel Coordinator. **World Wide Web address:** http://www.jhbinternational.snapmonkey.net. **Description:** Wholesales and exports buttons and thimbles.

ACCOUNTING AND MANAGEMENT CONSULTING

AMERICAN ACCOUNTING ASSOCIATION
5717 Bessie Drive, Sarasota FL 34233-2399. 941/921-7747. **Fax:** 941/923-4093. **E-mail address:** Office@aaahq.org. **World Wide Web address:** http://aaahq.org. **Description:** A voluntary organization founded in 1916 to promote excellence in accounting education, research and practice.

AMERICAN INSTITUTE OF CERTIFIED PUBLIC ACCOUNTANTS
1211 Avenue of the Americas, New York NY 10036. 212/596-6200. **Toll-free phone:** 888/777-7077. **Fax:** 212/596-6213. **World Wide Web address:** http://www.aicpa.org. **Description:** A non-profit organization providing resources, information, and leadership to its members.

AMERICAN MANAGEMENT ASSOCIATION
1601 Broadway, New York NY 10019. 212/586-8100. **Fax:** 212/903-8168. **Toll-free phone:** 800/262-9699. **E-mail address:** info@amanet.org. **World Wide Web address:** http://www.amanet.org. **Description:** A non-profit association providing its members with management development and educational services.

ASSOCIATION OF GOVERNMENT ACCOUNTANTS
2208 Mount Vernon Avenue, Alexandria VA 22301. 703/684-6931. **Toll-free phone:** 800/AGA-7211. **Fax:** 703/548-9367. **World Wide Web address:** http://www.agacgfm.org. **Description:** A public financial management organization catering to the professional interests of financial managers at the local, state and federal governments and public accounting firms.

ASSOCIATION OF MANAGEMENT CONSULTING FIRMS
380 Lexington Avenue, Suite 1700, New York NY 10168. 212/551-7887. **Fax:** 212/551-7934. **E-mail address:** info@amcf.org. **World Wide Web address:** http://www.amcf.org. **Description:** Founded in 1929 to provide a forum for confronting common challenges; increasing the collective knowledge of members and their clients; and establishing a professional code conduct.

CONNECTICUT SOCIETY OF CERTIFIED PUBLIC ACCOUNTANTS
845 Brook Street, Building Two, Rocky Hill CT 06067-3405. 860/258-4800. **Fax:** 860/258-4859. **E-mail address:** info@cs-cpa.org. **World Wide Web address:** http://www.cs-cpa.org. **Description:** A statewide professional membership organization catering to CPAs.

INSTITUTE OF INTERNAL AUDITORS
247 Maitland Avenue, Altamonte Springs FL 32701-4201. 407-937-1100. **Fax:** 407-937-1101. **E-mail address:** iia@theiia.org. **World Wide Web address:** http://www.theiia.org. **Description:** Founded in 1941 to serves members in internal auditing, governance and internal control, IT audit, education, and security worldwide.

INSTITUTE OF MANAGEMENT ACCOUNTANTS
10 Paragon Drive, Montvale NJ 07645-1718. 201/573-9000. **Fax:** 201/474-1600. **Toll-free phone:** 800/638-4427. **E-mail address:** ima@imanet.org. **World Wide Web address:** http://www.imanet.org. **Description:** Provides members personal and professional development opportunities in management accounting, financial management and information management through education and association

with business professionals and certification in management accounting and financial management.

INSTITUTE OF MANAGEMENT CONSULTANTS
2025 M Street, NW, Suite 800, Washington DC 20036-3309. 202/367-1134. **Toll-free phone:** 800/221-2557. **Fax:** 202/367-2134. **E-mail address:** office@imcusa.org. **World Wide Web address:** http://www.imcusa.org. **Description** Founded in 1968 as the national professional association representing management consultants and awarding the CMC (Certified Management Consultant) certification mark.

NATIONAL ASSOCIATION OF TAX PROFESSIONALS
720 Association Drive, PO Box 8002, Appleton WI 54912-8002. 800/558-3402. **Fax:** 800/747-0001. **E-Mail address:** natp@natptax.com. **World Wide Web address:** http://www.natptax.com. **Description:** Founded in 1979 as a nonprofit professional association dedicated to excellence in taxation with a mission to serve professionals who work in all areas of tax practice.

NATIONAL SOCIETY OF PUBLIC ACCOUNTANTS
1010 North Fairfax Street, Alexandria VA 22314. 703/549-6400. **Toll-free phone:** 800/966-6679. **Fax:** 703/549-2984. **Email address:** members@nsacct.org. **World Wide Web address:** http://www.nsacct.org. **Description:** For more than 50 years, NSA has supported its members with resources and representation to protect their right to practice, build credibility and grow the profession. NSA protects the public by requiring its members to adhere to a strict Code of Ethics.

ADVERTISING, MARKETING, AND PUBLIC RELATIONS

ADVERTISING RESEARCH FOUNDATION
641 Lexington Avenue, New York NY 10022. 212/751-5656. **World Wide Web address:** http://www.thearf.com. **Description:** Founded in 1936 by the Association of National Advertisers and the American Association of Advertising Agencies, the Advertising Research Foundation (ARF) is a nonprofit corporate-membership association, which is today the preeminent professional organization in the field of advertising, marketing and media research. Its combined membership represents more than 400 advertisers, advertising agencies, research firms, media companies, educational institutions and international organizations.

AMERICAN ASSOCIATION OF ADVERTISING AGENCIES
405 Lexington Avenue, 18th Floor, New York NY 10174-1801. 212/682-2500. **Fax:** 212/682-8391. **World Wide Web address:** http://www.aaaa.org. **Description:** Founded in 1917 as the national trade association representing the advertising agency business in the United States.

AMERICAN MARKETING ASSOCIATION
311 South Wacker Drive, Suite 5800, Chicago IL 60606. 312/542-9000. **Fax:** 312/542-9001. **Toll-free phone:** 800/AMA-1150. **E-mail address:** info@ama.org. **World Wide Web address:** http://www.marketingpower.com. **Description:** A professional associations for marketers providing relevant marketing information that experienced marketers turn to everyday.

DIRECT MARKETING ASSOCIATION
1120 Avenue of the Americas, New York NY 10036-6700. 212/768-7277. **Fax:** 212/302-6714. **E-mail address:** info@the-dma.org. **World Wide Web address:** http://www.the-dma.org. **Description:** Founded in 1917 as a non-profit organization representing professionals working in all areas of direct marketing.

INTERNATIONAL ADVERTISING ASSOCIATION
521 Fifth Avenue, Suite 1807, New York NY 10175. 212/557-1133. **Fax:** 212/983-0455. **E-mail address:** iaa@iaaglobal.org. **World Wide Web address:** http://www.iaaglobal.org. **Description:** A strategic partnership that addresses the common interests of all the marketing communications disciplines ranging from advertisers to media companies to agencies to direct marketing firms to individual practitioners.

MARKETING RESEARCH ASSOCIATION
1344 Silas Deane Highway, Suite 306, PO Box 230, Rocky Hill CT 06067-0230. 860/257-4008. **Fax:** 860/257-3990. **E-mail address:** email@mra-net.org. **World Wide Web address:** http://www.mra-net.org. **Description:** MRA promotes excellence in the opinion and marketing research industry by providing members with a variety of opportunities for advancing and expanding their marketing research and related business skills. To protect the marketing research environment, we will act as an advocate with appropriate government entities, other associations, and the public.

PUBLIC RELATIONS SOCIETY OF AMERICA
33 Maiden Lane, 11th Floor, New York NY 10038-5150. 212/460-1400. **Fax:** 212/995-0757. **E-mail address:** info@prsa.org. **World Wide Web address:** http://www.prsa.org. **Description:** A professional organization for public relations

practitioners. Comprised of nearly 20,000 members organized into 116 Chapters represent business and industry, counseling firms, government, associations, hospitals, schools, professional services firms and nonprofit organizations.

AEROSPACE

AMERICAN INSTITUTE OF AERONAUTICS AND ASTRONAUTICS
1801 Alexander Bell Drive, Suite 500, Reston VA 20191-4344. 703/264-7500.
Toll-free phone: 800/639-AIAA. **Fax:** 703/264-7551. **E-mail address:**
info@aiaa.org. **World Wide Web address:** http://www.aiaa.org. **Description:**
The principal society of the aerospace engineer and scientist.

NATIONAL AERONAUTIC ASSOCIATION OF USA
1815 N. Fort Myer Drive, Suite 500, Arlington VA 22209. 703/527-0226. **Fax:**
703/527-0229. **E-mail address:** naa@naa-usa.org. **World Wide Web address:**
http://www.naa-usa.org. **Description:** A non-parochial, charitable organization
serving all segments of American aviation whose membership encompass all
areas of flight including skydiving, models, commercial airlines, and military
fighters.

PROFESSIONAL AVIATION MAINTENANCE ASSOCIATION
717 Princess Street, Alexandria VA 22314. 703/683-3171. **Toll-free phone:**
866/865-PAMA. **Fax:** 703/683-0018. **E-mail address:** hq@pama.org. **World
Wide Web address:** http://www.pama.org. **Description:** A non-profit
organization concerned with promoting professionalism among aviation
maintenance personnel; fostering and improving methods, skills, learning, and
achievement in aviation maintenance. The association also conducts regular
industry meetings and seminars.

APPAREL, FASHION, AND TEXTILES

AMERICAN APPAREL AND FOOTWEAR ASSOCIATION
1601 North Kent Street, Suite 1200, Arlington VA 22209. 703/524-1864. **Fax:** 703/522-6741. **World Wide Web address:** http://apparelandfootwear.org. **Description:** The national trade association representing apparel, footwear and other sewn products companies, and their suppliers. Promotes and enhances its members' competitiveness, productivity and profitability in the global market.

THE FASHION GROUP
8 West 40th Street, 7th Floor, New York NY 10018. 212/302-5511. **Fax:** 212/302-5533. **E-mail address:** info@fgi.org. **World Wide Web address:** http://www.fgi.org. **Description:** A non-profit association representing all areas of the fashion, apparel, accessories, beauty and home industries.

INTERNATIONAL ASSOCIATION OF CLOTHING DESIGNERS AND EXECUTIVES
124 West 93rd Street, Suite 3E, New York NY 10025. 603/672-4065. **Fax:** 603/672-4064. **World Wide Web address:** http://www.iacde.com. **Description:** Founded in 1911, with the mission to serve as a global network for the sharing of information by its members on design direction and developments, fashion and fiber trends, and technical innovations affecting tailored apparel, designers, their suppliers, retailers, manufacturing executives and educational institutions for the purpose of enhancing their professional standing and interests.

NATIONAL COUNCIL OF TEXTILE ORGANIZATIONS
1776 I Street, NW, Suite 900, Washington DC 20006. 202/756-4878. **Fax:** 202/756-1520. **World Wide Web address:** http://www.ncto.org. **Description:** The national trade association for the domestic textile industry with members operating in more than 30 states and the industry employs approximately 450,000 people.

ARCHITECTURE, CONSTRUCTION, AND ENGINEERING

AACE INTERNATIONAL: THE ASSOCIATION FOR TOTAL COST MANAGEMENT
209 Prairie Avenue, Suite 100, Morgantown WV 26501. 304/296-8444. **Fax:** 304/291-5728. **E-mail address:** info@aacei.org. **World Wide Web address:** http://www.aacei.org. **Description:** Founded 1956 to provide its approximately 5,500 worldwide members with the resources to enhance their performance and ensure continued growth and success. Members include cost management professionals: cost managers and engineers, project managers, planners and schedulers, estimators and bidders, and value engineers.

AMERICAN ASSOCIATION OF ENGINEERING SOCIETIES
1828 L Street, NW, Suite 906, Washington DC 20036. 202/296-2237. **Fax:** 202/296-1151. **World Wide Web address:** http://www.aaes.org. **Description:** A multidisciplinary organization of engineering societies dedicated to advancing the knowledge, understanding, and practice of engineering.

AMERICAN CONSULTING ENGINEERS COMPANIES
1015 15th Street, 8th Floor, NW, Washington DC, 20005-2605. 202/347-7474. **Fax:** 202/898-0068. **E-mail address:** acec@acec.org. **World Wide Web address:** http://www.acec.org. **Description:** Engaged in a wide range of engineering works that propel the nation's economy, and enhance and safeguard America's quality of life. These works allow Americans to drink clean water, enjoy a healthy life, take advantage of new technologies, and travel safely and efficiently. The Council's mission is to contribute to America's prosperity and welfare by advancing the business interests of member firms.

AMERICAN INSTITUTE OF ARCHITECTS
1735 New York Avenue, NW, Washington DC 20006. 202/626-7300. **Fax:** 202/626-7547. **Toll-free phone:** 800/AIA-3837. **E-mail address:** infocentral@aia.org. **World Wide Web address:** http://www.aia.org. **Description:** A non-profit organization for the architecture profession dedicated to: Serving its members, advancing their value, improving the quality of the built environment. Vision Statement: Through a culture of innovation, The American Institute of Architects empowers its members and inspires creation of a better-built environment.

AMERICAN INSTITUTE OF CONSTRUCTORS
P.O. Box 26334, Alexandria VA 22314. 703/683-4999. **Fax:** 703/683-5480. **E-mail address:** admin@aicenet.org. **World Wide Web address:** http://www.aicnet.org. **Description:** Founded to help individual construction practitioners achieve the professional status they deserve and serves as the national qualifying body of professional constructor. The Institute AIC membership identifies the individual as a true professional. The Institute is the constructor's counterpart of professional organizations found in architecture, engineering, law and other fields.

AMERICAN SOCIETY FOR ENGINEERING EDUCATION
1818 N Street, NW, Suite 600, Washington DC, 20036-2479. 202/331-3500. **Fax:** 202/265-8504. **World Wide Web address:** http://www.asee.org. **Description:** A nonprofit member association, founded in 1893, dedicated to promoting and improving engineering and technology education.

AMERICAN SOCIETY OF CIVIL ENGINEERS
1801 Alexander Bell Drive, Reston VA 20191-4400. 703/295-6300. **Fax:** 703/295-6222. **Toll-free phone:** 800/548-2723. **World Wide Web address:** http://www.asce.org. **Description:** Founded to provide essential value to its members, their careers, partners and the public by developing leadership, advancing technology, advocating lifelong learning and promoting the profession.

AMERICAN SOCIETY OF HEATING, REFRIGERATION, AND AIR CONDITIONING ENGINEERS
1791 Tullie Circle, NE, Atlanta GA 30329. 404/636-8400. **Fax:** 404/321-5478. **Toll-free phone:** 800/527-4723. **E-mail address:** ashrae@ashrae.org. **World Wide Web address:** http://www.ashrae.org. **Description:** Founded with a mission to advance the arts and sciences of heating, ventilation, air conditioning, refrigeration and related human factors and to serve the evolving needs of the public and ASHRAE members.

AMERICAN SOCIETY OF MECHANICAL ENGINEERS
Three Park Avenue, New York, NY 10016-5990. 973-882-1167. **Toll-free phone:** 800/843-2763. **E-mail address:** infocentral@asme.org. **World Wide Web address:** http://www.asme.org. **Description:** Founded in 1880 as the American Society of Mechanical Engineers, today ASME International is a nonprofit educational and technical organization serving a worldwide membership of 125,000.

AMERICAN SOCIETY OF NAVAL ENGINEERS
1452 Duke Street, Alexandria VA 22314-3458. 703/836-6727. **Fax:** 703/836-7491. **E-mail address:** asnehq@navalengineers.org. **World Wide Web address:** http://www.navalengineers.org. **Description:** Mission is to advance the knowledge and practice of naval engineering in public and private applications and operations, to enhance the professionalism and well being of members, and to promote naval engineering as a career field.

AMERICAN SOCIETY OF PLUMBING ENGINEERS
8614 Catalpa Avenue, Suite 1007, Chicago IL 60656-1116. 773/693-2773. **Fax:** 773/695-9007. **E-mail address:** info@aspe.org. **World Wide Web address:** http://www.aspe.org. **Description:** The international organization for professionals skilled in the design, specification and inspection of plumbing systems. ASPE is dedicated to the advancement of the science of plumbing engineering, to the professional growth and advancement of its members and the health, welfare and safety of the public.

AMERICAN SOCIETY OF SAFETY ENGINEERS
1800 E Oakton Street, Des Plaines IL 60018. 847/699-2929. **Fax:** 847/768-3434. **E-mail address:** customerservice@asse.org. **World Wide Web address:** http://www.asse.org. **Description:** A non-profit organization promoting the concerns of safety engineers.

ASSOCIATED BUILDERS AND CONTRACTORS
4250 N. Fairfax Drive, 9th Floor, Arlington VA 22203-1607. 703/812-2000. **E-mail address:** gotquestions@abc.org. **World Wide Web address:** http://www.abc.org. **Description:** A national trade association representing more than 23,000 merit shop contractors, subcontractors, material suppliers and related firms in 80 chapters across the United States. Membership represents all specialties within the U.S. construction industry and is comprised primarily of firms that perform work in the industrial and commercial sectors of the industry.

ASSOCIATED GENERAL CONTRACTORS OF AMERICA, INC.
333 John Carlyle Street, Suite 200, Alexandria VA 22314. 703/548-3118. **Fax:** 703/548-3119. **E-mail address:** info@agc.org. **World Wide Web address:** http://www.agc.org. **Description:** A construction trade association, founded in 1918 on a request by President Woodrow Wilson.

THE ENGINEERING CENTER (TEC)
One Walnut Street, Boston MA 02108-3616. 617/227-5551. **Fax:** 617/227-6783. **E-mail address:** tec@engineers.org. **World Wide Web address:** http://www.engineers.org. **Description:** Founded with a mission to increase public awareness of the value of the engineering profession; to provide current information affecting the profession; to offer administrative facilities and services to engineering organizations in New England; and to provide a forum for discussion and resolution of professional issues.

ILLUMINATING ENGINEERING SOCIETY OF NORTH AMERICA
120 Wall Street, Floor 17, New York NY 10005. 212/248-5000. **Fax:** 212/248-5017(18). **E-mail address:** iesna@iesna.org. **World Wide Web address:** http://www.iesna.org. **Description:** To advance knowledge and to disseminate information for the improvement of the lighted environment to the benefit of society.

JUNIOR ENGINEERING TECHNICAL SOCIETY
1420 King Street, Suite 405, Alexandria VA 22314. 703/548-5387. **Fax:** 703/548-0769. **E-mail address:** info@jets.org. **World Wide Web address:** http://www.jets.org. **Description:** JETS is a national non-profit education organization that has served the pre-college engineering community for over 50 years. Through competitions and programs, JETS serves over 30,000 students and 2,000 teachers, and holds programs on 150 college campuses each year.

NATIONAL ACTION COUNCIL FOR MINORITIES IN ENGINEERING
440 Hamilton Avenue, Suite 302, White Plains NY 10601-1813. 914/539-4010. **Fax:** 914/539-4032. **E-mail address:** webmaster@nacme.org. **World Wide Web address:** http://www.nacme.org. **Description:** Founded in 1974 to provide leadership and support for the national effort to increase the representation of successful African American, American Indian and Latino women and men in engineering and technology, math- and science-based careers.

NATIONAL ASSOCIATION OF BLACK ENGINEERS
1454 Duke Street, Alexandria VA 22314. 703/549-2207. **Fax:** 703/683-5312. **E-mail address:** info@nsbe.org. **World Wide Web address:** http://www.nsbe.org. **Description:** A non-profit organization dedicated to increasing the number of culturally responsible Black engineers who excel academically, succeed professionally and positively impact the community.

NATIONAL ASSOCIATION OF HOME BUILDERS
1201 15th Street, NW, Washington DC 20005. 202/266-8200. **Toll-free phone:** 800/368-5242. **World Wide Web address:** http://www.nahb.org. **Description:** Founded in 1942, NAHB has been serving its members, the housing industry, and the public at large. A trade association that promotes the policies that make housing a national priority.

NATIONAL ASSOCIATION OF MINORITY ENGINEERING PROGRAM ADMINISTRATORS
1133 West Morse Boulevard, Suite 201, Winter Park FL 32789. 407/647-8839. **Fax:** 407/629-2502. **E-mail address:** namepa@namepa.org **World Wide Web**

address: http://www.namepa.org. **Description:** Provides services, information, and tools to produce a diverse group of engineers and scientists, and achieve equity and parity in the nation's workforce.

NATIONAL ELECTRICAL CONTRACTORS ASSOCIATION
3 Bethesda Metro Center, Suite 1100, Bethesda MD 20814. 301/657-3110. **Fax:** 301/215-4500. **World Wide Web address:** http://www.necanet.org. **Description:** Founded in 1901 as representative segment of the construction market comprised of over 70,000 electrical contracting firms.

NATIONAL SOCIETY OF PROFESSIONAL ENGINEERS
1420 King Street, Alexandria VA 22314-2794. 703/684-2800. **Fax:** 703/836-4875. **World Wide Web address:** http://www.nspe.org. **Description:** An engineering society that represents engineering professionals and licensed engineers (PEs) across all disciplines. Founded in 1934 to promote engineering licensure and ethics, enhance the engineer image, advocate and protect legal rights, publish industry news, and provide continuing education.

SOCIETY OF FIRE PROTECTION ENGINEERS
7315 Wisconsin Avenue, Suite 620E, Bethesda MD 20814. 301/718-2910. **Fax:** 301/718-2242. **E-mail address:** sfpehqtrs@sfpe.org. **World Wide Web address:** http://www.sfpe.org. **Description:** Founded in 1950 and incorporated as in independent organization in 1971, the professional society represents professionals in the field of fire protection engineering. The Society has approximately 3500 members in the United States and abroad, and 51 regional chapters, 10 of which are outside the US.

ARTS, ENTERTAINMENT, SPORTS, AND RECREATION

AMERICAN ASSOCIATION OF MUSEUMS
1575 Eye Street NW, Suite 400, Washington DC 20005. 202/289-1818. **Fax:** 202/289-6578. **World Wide Web address:** http://www.aam-us.org. **Description:** Founded in 1906, the association promotes excellence within the museum community. Services include advocacy, professional education, information exchange, accreditation, and guidance on current professional standards of performance.

AMERICAN FEDERATION OF MUSICIANS
1501 Broadway, Suite 600, New York NY 10036. 212/869-1330. **Fax:** 212/764-6134. **World Wide Web address:** http://www.afm.org. **Description:** Represents the interests of professional musicians. Services include negotiating agreements, protecting ownership of recorded music, securing benefits such as health care and pension, or lobbying our legislators. The AFM is committed to raising industry standards and placing the professional musician in the foreground of the cultural landscape.

AMERICAN MUSIC CENTER
30 West 26th Street, Suite 1001, New York NY 10010. 212/366-5260. **Fax:** 212/366-5265. **World Wide Web address:** http://www.amc.net. **Description:** Dedicated to fostering and composition, production, publication, and distribution of contemporary (American) music.

AMERICAN SOCIETY OF COMPOSERS, AUTHORS, AND PUBLISHERS (ASCAP)
One Lincoln Plaza, New York NY 10023. 212/621-6000. **Fax:** 212/724-9064. **E-mail address:** info@ascap.com. **World Wide Web address:** http://www.ascap.com. **Description:** A membership based association comprised of composers, songwriters, lyricists, and music publishers across all genres of music.

AMERICAN SYMPHONY ORCHESTRA LEAGUE
33 West 60th Street, 5th Floor, New York NY 10023-7905. 212/262-5161. **Fax:** 212/262-5198. **E-mail address:** league@symphony.org. **World Wide Web address:** http://www.symphony.org. **Description:** Founded in 1942 to exchange information and ideas with other orchestra leaders. The league also publishes the bimonthly magazine.

AMERICAN ZOO AND AQUARIUM ASSOCIATION
8403 Colesville Road, Suite 710, Silver Spring MD 20910-3314. 301/562-0777. **Fax:** 301/562-0888. **World Wide Web address:** http://www.aza.org. **Description:** Dedicated to establishing and maintaining excellent professional standards in all AZA Institutions through its accreditation program; establishing and promoting high standards of animal care and welfare; promoting and facilitating collaborative conservation and research programs; advocating effective governmental policies for our members; strengthening and promoting conservation education programs for our public and professional development for our members, and; raising awareness of the collective impact of its members and their programs.

ASSOCIATION OF INDEPENDENT VIDEO AND FILMMAKERS

304 Hudson Street, 6th floor, New York NY 10013. 212/807-1400. **Fax:** 212/463-8519. **E-mail address:** info@aivf.org. **World Wide Web address:** http://www.aivf.org. **Description:** A membership organization serving local and international film and videomakers including documentarians, experimental artists, and makers of narrative features.

NATIONAL ENDOWMENT FOR THE ARTS
1100 Pennsylvania Avenue, NW, Washington DC 20506. 202/682-5400. **E-mail address:** webmgr@arts.endow.com. **World Wide Web address:** http://www.nea.gov. **Description:** Founded in 1965 to foster, preserve, and promote excellence in the arts, to bring art to all Americans, and to provide leadership in arts education.

NATIONAL RECREATION AND PARK ASSOCIATION
22377 Belmont Ridge Road, Ashburn VA 20148-4150. 703/858-0784. **Fax:** 703/858-0794. **E-mail address:** info@nrpa.org. **World Wide Web address:** http://www.nrpa.org. **Description:** Works "to advance parks, recreation and environmental conservation efforts that enhance the quality of life for all people."

WOMEN'S CAUCUS FOR ART
P.O. Box 1498, Canal Street Station, New York NY 10013. 212/634-0007. **E-mail address:** info@nationalwca.com. **World Wide Web address:** http://www.nationalwca.com. **Description:** Founded in 1972 in connection with the College Art Association (CAA), as a national organization unique in its multi-disciplinary, multicultural membership of artists, art historians, students /educators, museum professionals and galleries in the visual arts.

AUTOMOTIVE

NATIONAL AUTOMOBILE DEALERS ASSOCIATION
8400 Westpark Drive, McLean VA 22102. 703/821-7000. **Toll-free phone:** 800/252-6232. **E-mail address:** nadainfo@nada.org. **World Wide Web address:** http://www.nada.org. **Description:** NADA represents America's franchised new-car and -truck dealers. Today there are more than 19,700 franchised new-car and -truck dealer members holding nearly 49,300 separate new-car and light-, medium-, and heavy-duty truck franchises, domestic and import. Founded in 1917.

NATIONAL INSTITUTE FOR AUTOMOTIVE SERVICE EXCELLENCE
101 Blue Seal Drive, SE, Suite 101, Leesburg VA 20175. 703/669-6600. **Toll-free phone:** 877/ASE-TECH. **World Wide Web address:** http://www.ase.com. **Description:** An independent, non-profit organization established in 1972 to improve the quality of vehicle repair and service through the testing and certification of repair and service professionals. More than 420,000 professionals hold current ASE credentials.

SOCIETY OF AUTOMOTIVE ENGINEERS
400 Commonwealth Drive, Warrendale PA 15096-0001. 724/776-4841. **E-mail address:** customerservice@sae.org. **World Wide Web address:** http://www.sae.org. **Description:** An organization with more than 84,000 members from 97 countries who share information and exchange ideas for advancing the engineering of mobility systems.

BANKING

AMERICA'S COMMUNITY BANKERS
900 Nineteenth Street, NW, Suite 400, Washington DC 20006. 202/857-3100. **Fax:** 202/296-8716. **World Wide Web address:** http://www.acbankers.org. **Description:** Represents the nation's community banks of all charter types and sizes providing a broad range of advocacy and service strategies to enhance their members' presence and contribution to the marketplace.

AMERICAN BANKERS ASSOCIATION
1120 Connecticut Avenue, NW, Washington DC 20036. 800/BANKERS. **World Wide Web address:** http://www.aba.com. **Description:** Founded in 1875 and represents banks on issues of national importance for financial institutions and their customers. Members include all categories of banking institutions, including community, regional and money center banks and holding companies, as well as savings associations, trust companies and savings banks.

BIOTECHNOLOGY, PHARMACEUTICALS, AND SCIENTIFIC R&D

AMERICAN ASSOCIATION FOR CLINICAL CHEMISTRY
2101 L Street, NW, Suite 202, Washington DC 20037-1558. 202/857-0717. **Fax:** 202/887-5093. **Toll-free phone:** 800/892-1400. **World Wide Web address:** http://www.aacc.org. **Description:** Founded in 1948 as an international scientific/medical society of clinical laboratory professionals, physicians, research scientists and other individuals involved with clinical chemistry and other clinical laboratory science-related disciplines. The society has 10,000 members.

AMERICAN ASSOCIATION OF COLLEGES OF PHARMACY
1426 Prince Street, Alexandria VA 22314. 703/739-2330. **Fax:** 703/836-8982. **E-mail address:** mail@aacp.org. **World Wide Web address:** http://www.aacp.org. **Description:** Founded in 1900 as the national organization representing the interests of pharmaceutical education and educators. Comprising all 89 U.S. pharmacy colleges and schools including more than 4,000 faculty, 36,000 students enrolled in professional programs, and 3,600 individuals pursuing graduate study, AACP is committed to excellence in pharmaceutical education.

AMERICAN ASSOCIATION OF PHARMACEUTICAL SCIENTISTS
2107 Wilson Boulevard, Suite 700, Arlington VA 22201-3042. 703/243-2800. **Fax:** 703/243-9650. **E-mail address:** aaps@aaps.org. **World Wide Web address:** http://www.aaps.org. **Description:** Founded in 1986 as professional, scientific society of more than 10,000 members employed in academia, industry, government and other research institutes worldwide. The association advances science through the open exchange of scientific knowledge; serves as an information resource; and contributes to human health through pharmaceutical research and development.

AMERICAN COLLEGE OF CLINICAL PHARMACY (ACCP)
3101 Broadway, Suite 650, Kansas City MO 64111. 816/531-2177. **Fax:** 816/531-4990. **E-mail address:** accp@accp.com **World Wide Web address:** http://www.accp.com. **Description:** A professional and scientific society providing leadership, education, advocacy, and resources enabling clinical pharmacists to achieve excellence in practice and research.

AMERICAN PHARMACISTS ASSOCIATION
2215 Constitution Avenue, NW, Washington DC 20037-2985. 202/628-4410. **Fax:** 202/783-2351. **E-mail address:** info@aphanet.org. **World Wide Web address:** http://www.aphanet.org. **Description:** Founded in 1852 as the national professional society of pharmacists. Members include practicing pharmacists, pharmaceutical scientists, pharmacy students, pharmacy technicians, and others interested in advancing the profession.

AMERICAN SOCIETY FOR BIOCHEMISTRY AND MOLECULAR BIOLOGY
9650 Rockville Pike, Bethesda MD 20814-3996. 301/634-7145. **Fax:** 301/634-7126. **E-mail address:** asbmb@asbmb.faseb.org. **World Wide Web address:** http://www.asbmb.org. **Description:** A nonprofit scientific and educational organization with over 11,900 members. Most members teach and conduct research at colleges and universities. Others conduct research in various government laboratories, nonprofit research institutions and industry. The Society's student members attend undergraduate or graduate institutions.

AMERICAN SOCIETY OF HEALTH-SYSTEM PHARMACISTS
7272 Wisconsin Avenue, Bethesda MD 20814. 301/657-3000. **Toll-free phone:** 866/279-0681. **World Wide Web address:** http://www.ashp.org. **Description:** A national professional association representing pharmacists who practice in hospitals, health maintenance organizations, long-term care facilities, home care, and other components of health care systems.

NATIONAL PHARMACEUTICAL COUNCIL
1894 Preston White Drive, Reston VA 20191-5433. 703/620-6390. **Fax:** 703/476-0904. **E-mail address:** main@npcnow.com. **World Wide Web address:** http://www.npcnow.org. **Description:** Conducts research and education programs geared towards demonstrating that the appropriate use of pharmaceuticals improves both patient treatment outcomes and the cost effective delivery of overall health care services.

NATIONAL SPACE BIOMEDICAL RESEARCH INSTITUTE
One Baylor Plaza, NA-425, Houston TX 77030. 713/798-7412. **Fax:** 713/798-7413. **E-mail address:** info@www.nsbri.org. **World Wide Web address:** http://www.nsbri.org. **Description:** Conducts research into health concerns facing astronauts on long missions.

BUSINESS SERVICES & NON-SCIENTIFIC RESEARCH

AMERICAN SOCIETY OF APPRAISERS
555 Herndon Parkway, Suite 125, Herndon VA 20170. 703/478-2228. **Fax:** 703/742-8471. **E-mail address:** asainfo@appraisers.org. **World Wide Web address:** http://www.appraisers.org. **Description:** Fosters professional excellence through education, accreditation, publication and other services. Its goal is to contribute to the growth of its membership and to the appraisal profession.

EQUIPMENT LEASING ASSOCIATION OF AMERICA
4301 North Fairfax Drive, Suite 550, Arlington VA 22203-1627. 703/527-8655. **Fax:** 703/527-2649. **World Wide Web address:** http://www.elaonline.com. **Description:** Promotes and serves the general interests of the equipment leasing and finance industry.

NATIONAL ASSOCIATION OF PERSONNEL SERVICES
The Village at Banner Elk, Suite 108, P.O. Box 2128, Banner Elk NC 28604. 828/898-4929. **Fax:** 828/898-8098. **World Wide Web address:** http://www.napsweb.org. **Description**: Serves, protects, informs, and represents all facets of the personnel services industry regarding federal legislation and regulatory issues by providing education, certification, and member services which enhance the ability to conduct business with integrity and competence.

CHARITIES AND SOCIAL SERVICES

AMERICAN COUNCIL FOR THE BLIND
1155 15th Street, NW, Suite 1004, Washington DC 20005. 202/467-5081. **Fax:** 202/467-5085. **Toll-free phone:** 800/424-8666. **World Wide Web address:** http://www.acb.org. **Description:** The nation's leading membership organization of blind and visually impaired people. It was founded in 1961.

CATHOLIC CHARITIES USA
1731 King Street, Alexandria VA 22314. 703/549-1390. **Fax:** 703/549-1656. **World Wide Web address:** http://www.catholiccharitiesusa.org. **Description:** A membership association of social service networks providing social services to people in need.

NATIONAL ASSOCIATION OF SOCIAL WORKERS
750 First Street, NE, Suite 700, Washington DC 20002-4241. 202/408-8600. **E-mail address:** membership@naswdc.org. **World Wide Web address:** http://www.naswdc.org. **Description:** A membership organization comprised of professional social workers working to enhance the professional growth and development of its members, to create and maintain professional standards, and to advance sound social policies.

NATIONAL COUNCIL ON FAMILY RELATIONS
3989 Central Avenue, NE, #550, Minneapolis MN 55421. 763/781-9331. **Fax:** 763/781-9348. **Toll-free phone:** 888/781-9331. **E-mail address:** info@ncfr.org. **World Wide Web address:** http://www.ncfr.org. **Description:** Provides a forum for family researchers, educators, and practitioners to share in the development and dissemination of knowledge about families and family relationships, establishes professional standards, and works to promote family well-being.

NATIONAL FEDERATION OF THE BLIND
1800 Johnson Street, Baltimore MD 21230-4998. 410/659-9314. **Fax:** 410/685-5653. **World Wide Web address:** http://www.nfb.org. **Description:** Founded in 1940, the National Federation of the Blind (NFB) is the nation's largest membership organization of blind persons. With fifty thousand members, the NFB has affiliates in all fifty states plus Washington D.C. and Puerto Rico, and over seven hundred local chapters. As a consumer and advocacy organization, the NFB is a leading force in the blindness field today.

NATIONAL MULTIPLE SCLEROSIS SOCIETY
733 Third Avenue, New York NY 10017. **Toll-free phone:** 800/344-4867. **World Wide Web address:** http://www.nmss.org. **Description:** Provides accurate, up-to-date information to individuals with MS, their families, and healthcare providers is central to our mission.

CHEMICALS, RUBBER, AND PLASTICS

AMERICAN CHEMICAL SOCIETY
1155 Sixteenth Street, NW, Washington DC 20036. 202/872-4600. **Fax:** 202/872-6067. **Toll-free phone:** 800/227-5558. **E-mail address:** help@acs.org. **World Wide Web address:** http://www.acs.org. **Description:** A self-governed individual membership organization consisting of more than 159,000 members at all degree levels and in all fields of chemistry. The organization provides a broad range of opportunities for peer interaction and career development, regardless of professional or scientific interests. The Society was founded in 1876.

AMERICAN INSTITUTE OF CHEMICAL ENGINEERS
3 Park Avenue, New York NY 10016-5991. 212/591-8100. **Toll-free phone:** 800/242-4363. **Fax:** 212/591-8888. **E-mail address:** xpress@aiche.org. **World Wide Web address:** http://www.aiche.org. **Description:** Founded in 1908 and provides leadership in advancing the chemical engineering profession; fosters and disseminates chemical engineering knowledge, supports the professional and personal growth of its members, and applies the expertise of its members to address societal needs throughout the world.

THE ELECTROCHEMICAL SOCIETY
65 South Main Street, Building D, Pennington NJ 08534-2839. 609/737-1902. **Fax:** 609/737-2743. **World Wide Web address:** http://www.electrochem.org. **Description:** Founded in 1902, The Electrochemical Society has become the leading society for solid-state and electrochemical science and technology. ECS has 8,000 scientists and engineers in over 75 countries worldwide who hold individual membership, as well as roughly 100 corporate members.

SOCIETY OF PLASTICS ENGINEERS
14 Fairfield Drive, PO Box 403, Brookfield CT 06804-0403. 203/775-0471. **Fax:** 203/775-8490. **E-mail address:** info@4spe.org. **World Wide Web address:** http://www.4spe.org. **Description:** A 25,000-member organization promoting scientific and engineering knowledge relating to plastics. Founded in 1942.

THE SOCIETY OF THE PLASTICS INDUSTRY, INC.
1667 K Street, NW, Suite 1000, Washington DC 20006. 202/974-5200. **Fax:** 202/296-7005. **World Wide Web address:** http://www.socplas.org. **Description:** Founded in 1937, The Society of the Plastics Industry, Inc., is the trade association representing one of the largest manufacturing industries in the United States. SPI's members represent the entire plastics industry supply chain, including processors, machinery and equipment manufacturers and raw materials suppliers. The U.S. plastics industry employs 1.4 million workers and provides more than $310 billion in annual shipments.

COMMUNICATIONS:TELECOMMUNICATIONS AND BROADCASTING

ACADEMY OF TELEVISION ARTS & SCIENCES
5220 Lankershim Boulevard, North Hollywood CA 91601-3109. 818/754-2800. **Fax:** 818/761-2827. **World Wide Web address:** http://www.emmys.com. **Description:** Promotes creativity, diversity, innovation and excellence though recognition, education and leadership in the advancement of the telecommunications arts and sciences.

AMERICAN DISC JOCKEY ASSOCIATION
20118 North 67th Avenue, Suite 300-605, Glendale AZ 85308. 888/723-5776. **E-mail address:** office@adja.org. **World Wide Web address:** http://www.adja.org. **Description:** Promotes ethical behavior, industry standards and continuing education for its members.

AMERICAN WOMEN IN RADIO AND TELEVISION, INC.
8405 Greensboro Drive, Suite 800, McLean VA 22102. 703/506-3290. **Fax:** 703/506-3266. **E-mail address:** info@awrt.org. **World Wide Web address:** http://www.awrt.org. **Description:** A non-profit, professional organization of women and men who work in the electronic media and allied fields.

COMPTEL/ASCENT
1900 M Street, NW, Suite 800, Washington DC 20036. 202/296-6650. **Fax:** 202/296-7585. **World Wide Web address:** http://www.comptelascent.org. **Description:** An association representing competitive telecommunications companies in virtually every sector of the marketplace: competitive local exchange carriers, long-distance carriers of every size, wireless service providers, Internet service providers, equipment manufacturers, and software suppliers.

MEDIA COMMUNICATIONS ASSOCIATION-INTERNATIONAL
7600 Terrace Avenue, Suite 203, Middleton WI 53562. 608/827-5034. **Fax:** 608/831-5122. **E-mail address:** info@mca-i.org. **World Wide Web address:** http://www.itva.org. **Description:** A not-for-profit, member-driven organization that provides opportunities for networking, forums for education and the resources for information to media communications professionals.

NATIONAL ASSOCIATION OF BROADCASTERS
1771 N Street, NW, Washington DC 20036. 202/429-5300. **Fax:** 202/429-4199. **E-mail address:** nab@nab.org. **World Wide Web address:** http://www.nab.org. **Description:** A trade association that represents the interests of free, over-the-air radio and television broadcasters.

NATIONAL CABLE & TELECOMMUNICATIONS ASSOCIATION
1724 Massachusetts Avenue, NW, Washington DC 20036. 202/775-3550. **E-mail address:** webmaster@ncta.com. **World Wide Web address:** http://www.ncta.com. **Description:** The National Cable and Telecommunications Association is the principal trade association of the cable and telecommunications industry. Founded in 1952, NCTA's primary mission is to provide its members with a strong national presence by providing a single, unified voice on issues affecting the cable and telecommunications industry.

PROMAX & BDA
9000 West Sunset Boulevard, Suite 900, Los Angeles CA 90069. 310/788-7600.
Fax: 310/788-7616. **World Wide Web address:** http://www.promax.org.
Description: A non-profit association dedicated to advancing the role and effectiveness of promotion, marketing, and broadcast design professionals in the electronic media.

U.S. TELECOM ASSOCIATION
1401 H Street, NW, Suite 600, Washington DC 20005-2164. 202/326-7300. **Fax:** 202/326-7333. **E-mail address:** membership@usta.org. **World Wide Web address:** http://www.usta.org. **Description:** A trade association representing service providers and suppliers for the telecom industry. Member companies offer a wide range of services, including local exchange, long distance, wireless, Internet and cable television service.

COMPUTER HARDWARE, SOFTWARE, AND SERVICES

ASSOCIATION FOR COMPUTING MACHINERY
1515 Broadway, New York NY, 10036. 212/626-0500. 212/626-0500. **Toll-free phone:** 800/342-6626. **World Wide Web address:** http://www.acm.org. **Description:** A 75-000-member organization founded in 1947 to advance the skills of information technology professionals and students worldwide.

ASSOCIATION FOR MULTIMEDIA COMMUNICATIONS
PO Box 10645, Chicago IL 60610. 773/276-9320. **E-mail address:** info@amcomm.org. **World Wide Web address:** http://www.amcomm.org. **Description:** A networking and professional organization for people who create New Media, including the Web, CD-ROMs and DVDs, interactive kiosks, streaming media, and other digital forms. The association promotes understanding of technology, e-learning, and e-business.

ASSOCIATION FOR WOMEN IN COMPUTING
41 Sutter Street, Suite 1006, San Francisco CA 94104. 415/905-4663. **Fax:** 415/358-4667. **E-mail address:** info@awc-hq.org. **World Wide Web address:** http://www.awc-hq.org. **Description:** A not-for-profit, professional organization for individuals with an interest in information technology. The association is dedicated to the advancement of women in the computing fields, in business, industry, science, education, government, and the military.

BLACK DATA PROCESSING ASSOCIATES
6301 Ivy Lane, Suite 700, Greenbelt MD 20770. 301/220-2180. **Fax:** 301/220-2185. **Toll-free phone:** 800/727-BDPA. **World Wide Web address:** http://www.bdpa.org. **Description:** A member-focused organization that positions its members at the forefront of the IT industry. BDPA is committed to delivering IT excellence to our members, strategic partners, and community.

INFORMATION TECHNOLOGY ASSOCIATION OF AMERICA
1401 Wilson Boulevard, Suite 1100, Arlington VA 22209. 703/522-5055. **Fax:** 703/525-2279. **Wide Web address:** http://www.itaa.org. **Description:** A trade association representing the U.S. IT industry and providing information about its issues, association programs, publications, meetings, and seminars.

INTERNATIONAL WEBMASTER'S ASSOCIATION- HTML WRITERS GUILD
119 E. Union Street, Suite F, Pasadena CA 91030. **World Wide Web address:** http://www.hwg.org. **Description:** Provides online web design training to individuals interested in web design and development.

NETWORK PROFESSIONAL ASSOCIATION
17 South High Street, Suite 200, Columbus OH 43215. 614/221-1900. **Fax:** 614/221-1989. **E-mail address:** npa@npa.org. **World Wide Web address:** http://www.npa.org. **Description:** A non-profit association for professionals in Network Computing.

SOCIETY FOR INFORMATION MANAGEMENT
401 North Michigan Avenue, Chicago IL 60611. 312/527-6734. **E-mail address:** sim@simnet.org **World Wide Web address:** http://www.simnet.org. **Description:** With 3,000 members, SIM is a network for IT leaders including CIOs, senior IT executives, prominent academicians, consultants, and others. SIM is a community of thought leaders who share experiences and knowledge, and who explore future IT direction. Founded in 1968.

SOCIETY FOR TECHNICAL COMMUNICATION
901 North Stuart Street, Suite 904, Arlington VA 22203-1822. 703/522-4114. **Fax:** 703/522-2075. **World Wide Web address:** http://www.stc.org. **Description:** A 25,000-member organization dedicated to advancing the arts and sciences of technical communication

SOFTWARE & INFORMATION INDUSTRY ASSOCIATION
1090 Vermont Avenue, NW, Sixth Floor, Washington DC 20005-4095. 202/289-7442. **Fax:** 202/289-7097. **World Wide Web address:** http://www.siia.net. **Description:** The SIIA is the principal trade association for the software and digital content industry. SIIA provides services in government relations, business development, corporate education and intellectual property protection to leading companies.

USENIX ASSOCIATION
2560 Ninth Street, Suite 215, Berkeley CA, 94710. 510/528-8649. **Fax:** 510/548-5738. **E-mail address:** office@usenix.org. **World Wide Web address:** http://www.usenix.org. **Description:** Founded in 1975 the association fosters technical excellence and innovation, supports and disseminates practical research, provides a neutral forum for discussion of technical issues, and encourages computing outreach to the community. USENIX brings together engineers, system administrators, scientists, and technicians working on the cutting edge of the computing world.

EDUCATIONAL SERVICES

AMERICAN ASSOCIATION OF SCHOOL ADMINISTRATORS
801 North Quincy Street, Suite 700, Arlington VA 22203-1730. 703/528-0700. **Fax:** 703/841-1543. **E-mail address:** info@aasa.org. **World Wide Web address:** http://www.aasa.org. **Description:** The professional organization for more than 14,000 educational leaders in the U.S. and other countries. The association supports and develops effective school system leaders who are dedicated to the highest quality public education for all children.

AMERICAN ASSOCIATION FOR HIGHER EDUCATION
One Dupont Circle, Suite 360, Washington DC 20036-1143. 202/293-6440. **Fax:** 202/293-0073. **E-mail address:** info@aahe.org. **World Wide Web address:** http://www.aahe.org. **Description:** An independent, membership-based, nonprofit organization dedicated to building human capital for higher education.

AMERICAN FEDERATION OF TEACHERS
555 New Jersey Avenue, NW, Washington DC 20001. 202/879-4400. **E-mail address:** online@aft.org. **World Wide Web address:** http://www.aft.org. **Description:** Improves the lives of its members and their families, gives voice to their professional, economic and social aspirations, brings together members to assist and support one another and to promote democracy, human rights and freedom.

COLLEGE AND UNIVERSITY PROFESSIONAL ASSOCIATION FOR HUMAN RESOURCES
Tyson Place, 2607 Kingston Pike, Suite 250, Knoxville TN 37919. 865/637-7673. **Fax:** 865/637-7674. **World Wide Web address:** http://www.cupa.org. **Description:** Promotes the effective management and development of human resources in higher education and offers many professional development opportunities.

NATIONAL ASSOCIATION FOR COLLEGE ADMISSION COUNSELING
1631 Prince Street, Alexandria VA 22314-2818. 703/836-2222. **Fax:** 703/836-8015. **World Wide Web address:** http://www.nacac.com. **Description:** Founded in 1937, NACAC is an organization of 8,000 professionals dedicated to serving students as they make choices about pursuing postsecondary education. NACAC supports and advances the work of college admission counseling professionals.

NATIONAL ASSOCIATION OF COLLEGE AND UNIVERSITY BUSINESS OFFICERS
2501 M Street, NW, Suite 400, Washington DC 20037. 202/861-2500. **Fax:** 202/861-2583. **World Wide Web address:** http://www.nacubo.org. **Description:** A nonprofit professional organization representing chief administrative and financial officers at more than 2,100 colleges and universities across the country.

NATIONAL SCIENCE TEACHERS ASSOCIATION
1840 Wilson Boulevard, Arlington VA 22201-3000. 703/243-7100. **World Wide Web address:** http://www.nsta.org. **Description:** Promotes excellence and innovation in science teaching and learning.

ELECTRONIC/INDUSTRIAL ELECTRICAL EQUIPMENT AND COMPONENTS

AMERICAN CERAMIC SOCIETY
P.O. Box 6136, Westerville OH 43086-6136. 614/890-4700. **Fax:** 614/899-6109. **E-mail address:** info@ceramics.org. **World Wide Web address:** http://www.acers.org. **Description:** Provides technical, scientific and educational information to its members and others in the ceramics and related materials field, structures its services, staff and capabilities to meet the needs of the ceramics community, related fields, and the general public.

ELECTRONIC INDUSTRIES ALLIANCE
2500 Wilson Boulevard, Arlington VA 22201. 703/907-7500. **World Wide Web address:** http://www.eia.org. **Description:** A national trade organization including 2,500 U.S. manufacturers. The Alliance is a partnership of electronic and high-tech associations and companies whose mission is promoting the market development and competitiveness of the U.S. high-tech industry through domestic and international policy efforts.

ELECTRONICS TECHNICIANS ASSOCIATION, INTERNATIONAL
5 Depot Street, Greencastle IN 46135. 765/653-8262. **Fax:** 765/653-4287. **Toll-free phone:** 800/288-3824. **E-mail address:** eta@tds.net. **World Wide Web address:** http://www.eta-sda.org. **Description:** A not-for-profit, worldwide professional association founded by electronics technicians and servicing dealers in 1978. Provides professional credentials based on an individual's skills and knowledge in a particular area of study.

FABLESS SEMICONDUCTOR ASSOCIATION
Three Lincoln Center, 5430 LBJ Freeway, Suite 280, Dallas TX 75240. 972/866-7579. **Fax:** 972/239-2292. **World Wide Web address:** http://www.fsa.org. **Description:** An industry organization aimed at achieving an optimal balance between wafer supply and demand.

INSTITUTE OF ELECTRICAL AND ELECTRONICS ENGINEER (IEEE)
3 Park Avenue, 17th Floor, New York NY 10016-5997. 212/419-7900. **Fax:** 212/752-4929. **E-mail address:** ieeeusa@ieee.org. **World Wide Web address:** http://www.ieee.org. **Description:** Advances the theory and application of electrotechnology and allied sciences, serves as a catalyst for technological innovation and supports the needs of its members through a wide variety of programs and services.

INTERNATIONAL SOCIETY OF CERTIFIED ELECTRONICS TECHNICIANS
3608 Pershing Avenue, Fort Worth TX 76107-4527. 817/921-9101. **Fax:** 817/921-3741 **Toll-free phone:** 800/946-0201 **E-mail address:** info@iscet.org **World Wide Web address:** http://www.iscet.org. **Description:** Prepares and tests technicians in the electronics and appliance service industry. Designed to measure the degree of theoretical knowledge and technical proficiency of practicing technicians.

NATIONAL ELECTRONICS SERVICE DEALERS ASSOCIATION
3608 Pershing Avenue, Fort Worth TX 76107-4527. 817/921-9061. **Fax:** 817/921-3741. **World Wide Web address:** http://www.nesda.com. **Description:** A trade organization for professionals in the business of repairing consumer electronic equipment, appliances, or computers.

ENVIRONMENTAL & WASTE MANAGEMENT SERVICES

AIR & WASTE MANAGEMENT ASSOCIATION
One Gateway Center, 3rd Floor, 420 Fort Duquesne Boulevard, Pittsburgh PA 15222-1435. 412/232-3444. **Fax:** 412/232-3450. **E-mail address:** info@awma.org. **World Wide Web address:** http://www.awma.org. **Description:** A nonprofit, nonpartisan professional organization providing training, information, and networking opportunities to thousands of environmental professionals in 65 countries.

AMERICAN ACADEMY OF ENVIRONMENTAL ENGINEERS
130 Holiday Court, Suite 100, Annapolis MD 21401. 410/266-3311. **Fax:** 410/266-7653. **World Wide Web address:** http://www.aaee.net. **Description:** AAEE was founded in 1955 for the principal purpose of serving the public by improving the practice, elevating the standards, and advancing public recognition of environmental engineering through a program of specialty certification of qualified engineers.

INSTITUTE OF CLEAN AIR COMPANIES
1660 L Street, NW, Suite 1100, Washington DC 20036. 202/457-0911. **Fax:** 202/331-1388. **World Wide Web address:** http://www.icac.com. **Description:** The nonprofit national association of companies that supply air pollution monitoring and control systems, equipment, and services for stationary sources.

NATIONAL SOLID WASTES MANAGEMENT ASSOCIATION
4301 Connecticut Avenue, NW, Suite 300, Washington DC 20008-2304. 202/244-4700. **Fax:** 202/364-3792. **Toll-free phone:** 800/424-2869. **World Wide Web address:** http://www.nswma.org. **Description:** A non-profit, trade association that represents the interests of the North American waste services industry.

WATER ENVIRONMENT FEDERATION
601 Wythe Street, Alexandria VA 22314-1994. 703/684-2452. **Fax:** 703/684-2492. **Toll-free phone:** 800/666-0206. **World Wide Web address:** http://www.wef.org. **Description:** A not-for-profit technical and educational organization, founded in 1928, with members from varied disciplines. The federation's mission is to preserve and enhance the global water environment. The WEF network includes water quality professionals from 79 Member Associations in over 30 countries.

FABRICATED METAL PRODUCTS AND PRIMARY METALS

ASM INTERNATIONAL: THE MATERIALS INFORMATION SOCIETY
9639 Kinsman Road, Materials Park OH 44073-0002. 440/338-5151. **Fax:** 440/338-4634. **Toll-free phone:** 800/336-5152. **E-mail address:** cust-srv@asminternational.org. **World Wide Web address:** http://www.asm-intl.org. **Description:** An organization for materials engineers and scientists, dedicated to advancing industry, technology and applications of metals and materials.

AMERICAN FOUNDRYMEN'S SOCIETY
1695 Penny Lane, Schaumburg IL 60173-4555. 847/824-0181. **Fax:** 847/824-7848. **Toll-free phone:** 800/537-4237. **World Wide Web address:** http://www.afsinc.org. **Description:** An international organization dedicated to provide and promote knowledge and services that strengthen the metalcasting industry. AFS was founded in 1896 and has approximately 10,000 members in 47 countries.

AMERICAN WELDING SOCIETY
550 NW LeJeune Road, Miami FL 33126. 305/443-9353. **Toll-free phone:** 800/443-9353. **E-mail address:** info@aws.org. **World Wide Web address:** http://www.aws.org. **Description:** Founded in 1919 as a multifaceted, nonprofit organization with a goal to advance the science, technology and application of welding and related joining disciplines.

FINANCIAL SERVICES

THE BOND MARKET ASSOCIATION
360 Madison Avenue, New York NY 10017-7111. 646/637-9200. **Fax:** 646/637-9126. **World Wide Web address:** http://www.bondmarkets.com. **Description:** The trade association representing the largest securities markets in the world. The Association speaks for the bond industry, advocating its positions and representing its interests in New York; Washington, D.C.; London; Frankfurt; Brussels and Tokyo; and with issuer and investor groups worldwide. The Association represents a diverse mix of securities firms and banks, whether they are large, multi-product firms or companies with special market niches.

FINANCIAL EXECUTIVES INSTITUTE
200 Campus Drive, PO Box 674, Florham Park NJ 07932-0674. 973/765-1000. **Fax:** 973/765-1018. **E-mail address:** conf@fei.org. **World Wide Web address:** http://www.fei.org. **Description:** An association for financial executives working to alert members to emerging issues, develop the professional and management skills of members, provide forums for peer networking, advocate the views of financial executives, and promote ethical conduct.

NATIONAL ASSOCIATION FOR BUSINESS ECONOMICS
1233 20th Street, NW, #505, Washington DC 20036. 202/463-6223. **Fax:** 202/463-6239. **E-mail address:** nabe@nabe.com. **World Wide Web address:** http://www.nabe.com. **Description:** An association of professionals who have an interest in business economics and who want to use the latest economic data and trends to enhance their ability to make sound business decisions. Founded in 1959.

NATIONAL ASSOCIATION OF CREDIT MANAGEMENT
8840 Columbia 100 Parkway, Columbia MD 21045. 410/740-5560. **Fax:** 410/740-5574. **E-mail address:** nacm_info@nacm.org. **World Wide Web address:** http://www.nacm.org. **Description:** Founded in 1896 to promote good laws for sound credit, protect businesses against fraudulent debtors, improve the interchange of credit information, develop better credit practices and methods, and establish a code of ethics.

NATIONAL ASSOCIATION OF REAL ESTATE INVESTMENT TRUSTS
1875 Eye Street, NW, Washington DC 20006. 202/739-9400. **Fax:** 202/739-9401. **E-mail address:** info@nareit.org. **World Wide Web address:** http://www.nareit.com. **Description:** NAREIT is the national trade association for REITs and publicly traded real estate companies. Members are real estate investment trusts (REITs) and other businesses that own, operate and finance income-producing real estate, as well as those firms and individuals who advise, study and service these businesses.

SECURITIES INDUSTRY ASSOCIATION
120 Broadway, 35th Floor, New York NY 10271-0080. 212/608-1500. **Fax:** 212/968-0703. **E-mail address:** info@sia.com. **World Wide Web address:** http://www.sia.com. **Description:** The Securities Industry Association (SIA) was established in 1972 through the merger of the Association of Stock Exchange Firms (1913) and the Investment Banker's Association (1912). The Securities Industry Association brings together the shared interests of more than 600 securities firms to accomplish common goals. SIA member-firms (including

investment banks, broker-dealers, and mutual fund companies) are active in all U.S. and foreign markets and in all phases of corporate and public finance.

WOMEN'S INSTITUTE OF FINANCIAL EDUCATION
PO Box 910014, San Diego CA 92191. 760/736-1660. **E-mail address:** info@wife.org. **World Wide Web address:** http://www.wife.org. **Description:** A non-profit organization dedicated to providing financial education to women in their quest for financial independence.

FOOD AND BEVERAGES/AGRICULTURE

AMERICAN ASSOCIATION OF CEREAL CHEMISTS (AACC)
3340 Pilot Knob Road, St. Paul MN 55121-2097. 651/454-7250. **Fax:** 651/454-0766. **World Wide Web address:** http://www.aaccnet.org. **Description:** A non-profit international organization of nearly 4,000 members who are specialists in the use of cereal grains in foods. The association gathers and disseminates scientific and technical information to professionals in the grain-based foods industry worldwide for over 85 years.

AMERICAN BEVERAGE ASSOCIATION
1101 16th Street, NW, Washington DC 20036. 202/463-6732. **Fax:** 202/659-5349. **World Wide Web address:** http://www.ameribev.org. **Description:** An association for America's non-alcoholic beverage industry, serving the public and its members for more than 75 years.

AMERICAN FROZEN FOOD INSTITUTE
2000 Corporate Ridge, Suite 1000, McLean VA 22102. 703/821-0770. **Fax:** 703/821-1350. **E-mail address:** info@affi.com. **World Wide Web address:** http://www.affi.com. **Description:** A national trade association representing all aspects of the frozen food industry supply chain, from manufacturers to distributors to suppliers to packagers; the Institute is industry's voice on issues crucial to future growth and progress.

AMERICAN SOCIETY OF AGRICULTURAL ENGINEERS
2950 Niles Road, St. Joseph MI 49085. 269/429-0300. **Fax:** 269/429-3852. **World Wide Web address:** http://www.asae.org. **Description:** An educational and scientific organization dedicated to the advancement of engineering applicable to agricultural, food, and biological systems.

AMERICAN SOCIETY OF BREWING CHEMISTS
3340 Pilot Knob Road, St. Paul MN 55121-2097. 651/454-7250. **Fax:** 651/454-0766. **World Wide Web address:** http://www.asbcnet.org. **Description:** Founded in 1934 to improve and bring uniformity to the brewing industry on a technical level.

CIES – THE FOOD BUSINESS FORUM
8455 Colesville Road, Suite 705, Silver Spring MD 20910. 301/563-3383. **Fax:** 301/563-3386. **E-mail address:** us.office@ciesnet.com. **World Wide Web address:** http://www.ciesnet.com. **Description:** An independent global food business network. Membership in CIES is on a company basis and includes more than two thirds of the world's largest food retailers and their suppliers.

CROPLIFE AMERICA
1156 15th Street, NW, Suite 400, Washington DC 20005. 202/296-1585. **Fax:** 202/463-0474. **World Wide Web address:** http://www.croplifeamerica.org. **Description:** Fosters the interests of the general public and member companies by promoting innovation and the environmentally sound manufacture, distribution, and use of crop protection and production technologies for safe, high-quality, affordable and abundant food, fiber and other crops.

INTERNATIONAL DAIRY FOODS ASSOCIATION
1250 H Street, NW, Suite 900, Washington DC 20005. 202/737-4332. **Fax:** 202/331-7820. **E-mail address:** membership@idfa.org. **World Wide Web**

address: http://www.idfa.org. **Description:** IDFA represents more than 500 dairy food manufacturers, marketers, distributors and industry suppliers in the U.S. and 20 other countries, and encourages the formation of favorable domestic and international dairy policies.

NATIONAL BEER WHOLESALERS' ASSOCIATION
1101 King Street, Suite 600, Alexandria VA 22314-2944. 703/683-4300. **Fax:** 703/683-8965. **E-mail address:** info@nbwa.org. **World Wide Web address:** http://www.nbwa.org. **Description:** Founded in 1938 as a trade association for the nations' beer wholesalers. NBWA provides leadership which enhances the independent malt beverage wholesale industry; advocates before government and the public on behalf of its members; encourages the responsible consumption of beer; and provides programs and services that will enhance members' efficiency and effectiveness.

NATIONAL FOOD PROCESSORS ASSOCIATION
1350 I Street, NW, Suite 300, Washington DC 20005. 202/639.5900. **E-mail address:** nfpa@nfpa-food.org. **World Wide Web address:** http://www.nfpa-food.org. **Description:** NFPA is the voice of the $500 billion food processing industry on scientific and public policy issues involving food safety, nutrition, technical and regulatory matters and consumer affairs.

HEALTH CARE SERVICES, EQUIPMENT, AND PRODUCTS

ACCREDITING COMMISSION ON EDUCATION FOR HEALTH SERVICES ADMINISTRATION
2000 14th Street North, Arlington VA 22201. 703/894-0960. **Fax:** 703/894-0941. **World Wide Web address:** http://www.acehsa.org. **Description:** An association of educational, professional, clinical, and commercial organizations devoted to accountability and quality improvement in the education of health care management and administration professionals.

AMERICAN ACADEMY OF ALLERGY, ASTHMA, AND IMMUNOLOGY
555 East Wells Street, Suite 1100, Milwaukee WI 53202-3823. 414/272-6071. **E-mail address:** info@aaaai.org. **World Wide Web address:** http://www.aaaai.org. **Description:** A professional medical specialty organization representing allergists, asthma specialists, clinical immunologists, allied health professionals, and other physicians with a special interest in allergy. Established in 1943.

AMERICAN ACADEMY OF FAMILY PHYSICIANS
11400 Tomahawk Creek Parkway, Leawood KS 66211-2672. 913/906-6000. **Toll-free phone:** 800/274-2237. **E-mail address:** fp@aafp.org. **World Wide Web address:** http://www.aafp.org. **Description:** Founded in 1947, the Academy represents family physicians, family practice residents and medical students nationwide. AAFP's mission is to preserve and promote the science and art of family medicine and to ensure high quality, cost-effective health care for patients of all ages.

AMERICAN ACADEMY OF PEDIATRIC DENTISTRY
211 East Chicago Avenue, Suite 700, Chicago IL 60611-2663. 312/337-2169. **Fax:** 312/337-6329. **World Wide Web address:** http://www.aapd.org. **Description:** A membership organization representing the specialty of pediatric dentistry.

AMERICAN ACADEMY OF PERIODONTOLOGY
737 North Michigan Avenue, Suite 800, Chicago IL 60611-2690. 312/787-5518. **Fax:** 312/787-3670. **World Wide Web address:** http://www.perio.org. **Description:** A 7,900-member association of dental professionals specializing in the prevention, diagnosis and treatment of diseases affecting the gums and supporting structures of the teeth and in the placement and maintenance of dental implants. The Academy's purpose is to advocate, educate, and set standards for advancing the periodontal and general health of the public and promoting excellence in the practice of periodontics.

AMERICAN ACADEMY OF PHYSICIANS ASSISTANTS
950 North Washington Street, Alexandria VA 22314-1552. 703/836-2272. **Fax:** 703/684-1924. **E-mail address:** aapa@aapa.org. **World Wide Web address:** http://www.aapa.org. **Description:** Promotes quality, cost-effective, accessible health care, and the professional and personal development of physician assistants.

AMERICAN ASSOCIATION FOR CLINICAL CHEMISTRY
2101 L Street, NW, Suite 202, Washington DC 20037-1558. 202/857-0717. **Fax:** 202/887-5093. **Toll-free phone:** 800/892-1400. **World Wide Web address:**

http://www.aacc.org. **Description:** Founded in 1948 as an international scientific/medical society of clinical laboratory professionals, physicians, research scientists and other individuals involved with clinical chemistry and other clinical laboratory science-related disciplines. The society has 10,000 members.

AMERICAN ASSOCIATION FOR ORAL AND MAXILLOFACIAL SURGEONS
9700 West Bryn Mawr Avenue, Rosemont IL 60018-5701. 847/678-6200. **E-mail address:** inquiries@aaoms.org. **World Wide Web address:** http://www.aaoms.org. **Description:** The American Association of Oral and Maxillofacial Surgeons (AAOMS), is a not-for-profit professional association serving the professional and public needs of the specialty of oral and maxillofacial surgery.

AMERICAN ASSOCIATION FOR RESPIRATORY CARE
9425 North MacArthur Boulevard, Suite 100, Irving TX 75063-4706. 972/243-2272. **Fax:** 972/484-2720. **E-mail address:** info@aarc.org. **World Wide Web address:** http://www.aarc.org. **Description:** Advances the science, technology, ethics, and art of respiratory care through research and education for its members and teaches the general public about pulmonary health and disease prevention.

AMERICAN ASSOCIATION OF COLLEGES OF OSTEOPATHIC MEDICINE
5550 Friendship Boulevard, Suite 310, Chevy Chase MD 20815-7231. 301/968-4100. **Fax:** 301/968-4101. **World Wide Web address:** http://www.aacom.org. **Description:** Promotes excellence in osteopathic medical education throughout the educational continuum, in research and in service; to enhance the strength and quality of the member colleges; and to improve the health of the American public.

AMERICAN ASSOCIATION OF COLLEGES OF PODIATRIC MEDICINE
15850 Crabbs Branch Way, Suite 320, Rockville MD 20855. **Fax:** 301/948-1928. **Toll-free phone:** 800/922-9266. **E-mail address:** aacpmas@aacpm.org. **World Wide Web address:** http://www.aacpm.org. **Description:** An organization advancing podiatric medicine and its education system.

AMERICAN ASSOCIATION OF HEALTHCARE CONSULTANTS
5938 North Drake Avenue, Chicago IL 60659. **Fax:** 773/463-3552. **Toll-free phone:** 888/350-2242. **E-mail address:** info@aahc.net. **World Wide Web address:** http://www.aahc.net. **Description:** Founded in 1949 as the professional membership society for leading healthcare consultants and consulting firms.

AMERICAN ASSOCIATION OF HOMES AND SERVICES FOR THE AGING
2519 Connecticut Avenue, NW, Washington DC 20008. 202/783.2242. **Fax:** 202/783-2255. **World Wide Web address:** http://www.aahsa.org. **Description:** The American Association of Homes and Services for the Aging (AAHSA) is committed to advancing the vision of healthy, affordable, ethical aging services for America. The association represents 5,600 not-for-profit nursing homes, continuing care retirement communities, assisted living and senior housing facilities, and home and community-based service providers.

AMERICAN ASSOCIATION OF MEDICAL ASSISTANTS
20 North Wacker Drive, Suite 1575, Chicago IL 60606. 312/899-1500. **World Wide Web address:** http://www.aama-ntl.org. **Description:** The mission of the American Association of Medical Assistants is to enable medical assisting professionals to enhance and demonstrate the knowledge, skills and

professionalism required by employers and patients; protect medical assistants' right to practice; and promote effective, efficient health care delivery through optimal use of multiskilled Certified Medical Assistants (CMAs).

AMERICAN ASSOCIATION OF NURSE ANESTHETISTS
222 South Prospect Avenue, Park Ridge IL 60068. 847/692-7050. **World Wide Web address:** http://www.aana.com. **Description:** Founded in 1931 as the professional association representing more than 30,000 Certified Registered Nurse Anesthetists (CRNAs) nationwide. The AANA promulgates education, and practice standards and guidelines, and affords consultation to both private and governmental entities regarding nurse anesthetists and their practice.

AMERICAN CHIROPRACTIC ASSOCIATION
1701 Clarendon Boulevard, Arlington VA 22209. **Fax:** 703/243-2593. **Toll-free phone:** 800/986-4636. **E-mail address:** memberinfo@amerchiro.org. **World Wide Web address:** http://www.americhiro.org. **Description:** A professional association representing doctors of chiropractic that provides lobbying, public relations, professional and educational opportunities for doctors of chiropractic, funds research regarding chiropractic and health issues, and offers leadership for the advancement of the profession.

AMERICAN COLLEGE OF HEALTH CARE ADMINISTRATORS
300 North Lee Street, Suite 301, Alexandria VA 22314. 703/739-7900. **Fax:** 703/739-7901. **Toll-free phone:** 888/882-2422. **E-mail address:** membership@achca.org. **World Wide Web address:** http://www.achca.org. **Description:** A non-profit membership organization that provides educational programming, certification in a variety of positions, and career development for its members. Founded in 1962.

AMERICAN COLLEGE OF HEALTHCARE EXECUTIVES
One North Franklin Street, Suite 1700, Chicago IL 60606-4425. 312/424-2800. **Fax:** 312/424-0023. **World Wide Web address:** http://www.ache.org. **Description:** An international professional society of nearly 30,000 healthcare executives who lead our nation's hospitals, healthcare systems, and other healthcare organizations.

AMERICAN COLLEGE OF MEDICAL PRACTICE EXECUTIVES
104 Inverness Terrace East, Englewood CO 80112-5306. 303/799-1111. **Fax:** 303/643-4439. **Toll-free phone:** 877/275-6462. **E-mail address:** acmpe@mgma.com. **World Wide Web address:** http://www.mgma.com/acmpe. **Description:** Established in 1956, the ACMPE offers board certification, self-assessment and leadership development for medical practice executives.

AMERICAN COLLEGE OF OBSTETRICIANS AND GYNECOLOGISTS
409 12th Street, SW, PO Box 96920, Washington DC 20090-6920. **World Wide Web address:** http://www.acog.org. **Description:** Founded in 1951, the 46,000-member organization is the nation's leading group of professionals providing health care for women.

AMERICAN COLLEGE OF PHYSICIAN EXECUTIVES
4890 West Kennedy Boulevard, Suite 200, Tampa FL 33609. 813/287-2000. **Fax:** 813/287-8993. **Toll-free phone:** 800/562-8088. **E-mail address:** acpe@acpe.org. **World Wide Web address:** http://www.acpe.org. **Description:** A specialty society representing physicians in health care leadership. Provides educational and career development programs.

AMERICAN DENTAL ASSOCIATION
211 East Chicago Avenue, Chicago IL 60611-2678. 312/440-2500. **World Wide Web address:** http://www.ada.org. **Description:** A dental association serving both public and private physicians. Founded in 1859.

AMERICAN DENTAL EDUCATION ASSOCIATION
1400 K Street, NW Suite 1100, Washington DC 20005. 202/289-7201. **Fax:** 202/289-7204. **World Wide Web address:** http://www.adea.org. **Description:** A national organization for dental education. Members include all U.S. and Canadian dental schools, advanced dental education programs, hospital dental education programs, allied dental education programs, corporations, faculty, and students.

AMERICAN DENTAL HYGIENISTS ASSOCIATION
444 North Michigan Avenue, Suite 3400, Chicago IL 60611. 312/440-8900. **E-mail address:** mail@adha.net. **World Wide Web address:** http://www.adha.org. **Description:** Founded in 1923, the association develops communication and mutual cooperation among dental hygienists and represents the professional interests of the more than 120,000 registered dental hygienists (RDHs) in the United States.

AMERICAN HEALTH INFORMATION MANAGEMENT ASSOCIATION
233 North Michigan Avenue, Suite 2150, Chicago IL 60601-5800. 312/233-1100. **Fax:** 312/233-1090. **E-mail address:** info@ahima.org. **World Wide Web address:** http://www.ahima.org. **Description:** Represents more than 46,000 specially educated health information management professionals who work throughout the healthcare industry. Health information management professionals serve the healthcare industry and the public by managing, analyzing, and utilizing data vital for patient care -- and making it accessible to healthcare providers when it is needed most.

AMERICAN HOSPITAL ASSOCIATION
One North Franklin, Chicago IL 60606-3421. 312/422-3000. **Fax:** 312/422-4796. **World Wide Web address:** http://www.aha.org. **Description:** A national organization that represents and serves all types of hospitals, health care networks, and their patients and communities. Approximately 5,000 institutional, 600 associate, and 27,000 personal members belong to the AHA.

AMERICAN MEDICAL ASSOCIATION
515 North State Street, Chicago IL 60610. **Toll-free phone:** 800/621-8335. **World Wide Web address:** http://www.ama-assn.org. **Description:** American Medical Association speaks out on issues important to patients and the nation's health. AMA policy on such issues is decided through its democratic policy-making process, in the AMA House of Delegates, which meets twice a year.

AMERICAN MEDICAL INFORMATICS ASSOCIATION
4915 St. Elmo Avenue, Suite 401, Bethesda MD 20814. 301/657-1291. **Fax:** 301/657-1296. **World Wide Web address:** http://www.amia.org. **Description:** The American Medical Informatics Association is a nonprofit membership organization of individuals, institutions, and corporations dedicated to developing and using information technologies to improve health care. Founded in 1990.

AMERICAN MEDICAL TECHNOLOGISTS
710 Higgins Road, Park Ridge IL 60068. 847/823-5169. **Fax:** 847/823-0458. **Toll-free phone:** 800/275-1268. **World Wide Web address:** http://www.amt1.com. **Description:** A nonprofit certification agency and

professional membership association representing nearly 27,000 individuals in allied health care. Provides allied health professionals with professional certification services and membership programs to enhance their professional and personal growth.

AMERICAN MEDICAL WOMEN'S ASSOCIATION
801 North Fairfax Street, Suite 400, Alexandria VA 22314. 703/838-0500. **Fax:** 703/549-3864. **E-mail address:** info@amwa-doc.org. **World Wide Web address:** http://www.amwa-doc.org. **Description:** An organization of 10,000 women physicians and medical students dedicated to serving as the unique voice for women's health and the advancement of women in medicine.

AMERICAN NURSES ASSOCIATION
8515 Georgia Avenue, Suite 400 West, Silver Spring MD 20910. 301/628-5000. **Fax:** 301//628-5001. **Toll-free phone:** 800/274-4ANA. **World Wide Web address:** http://www.nursingworld.org. **Description:** A professional organization representing the nation's 2.6 million Registered Nurses through its 54 constituent state associations and 13 organizational affiliate members. Fosters high standards of nursing practice, promotes the economic and general welfare of nurses in the workplace, projects a positive and realistic view of nursing, and by lobbies Congress and regulatory agencies on health care issues affecting nurses and the public.

AMERICAN OCCUPATIONAL THERAPY ASSOCIATION
4720 Montgomery Lane, PO Box 31220, Bethesda MD 20824-1220. 301/652-2682. **Fax:** 301/652-7711. **Toll-free phone:** 800/377- 8555. **World Wide Web address:** http://www.aota.org. **Description:** A professional association of approximately 40,000 occupational therapists, occupational therapy assistants, and students of occupational therapy.

AMERICAN OPTOMETRIC ASSOCIATION
243 North Lindbergh Boulevard, St. Louis MO 63141. 314/991-4100. **Fax:** 314/991-4101. **World Wide Web address:** http://www.aoanet.org. **Description:** The American Optometric Association is the acknowledged leader and recognized authority for primary eye and vision care in the world.

AMERICAN ORGANIZATION OF NURSE EXECUTIVES
325 Seventh Street, NW, Washington DC 20004. 202/626-2240. **Fax:** 202/638-5499. **E-mail address:** aone@aha.org. **World Wide Web address:** http://www.aone.org. **Description:** Founded in 1967, the American Organization of Nurse Executives (AONE), a subsidiary of the American Hospital Association, is a national organization of nearly 4,000 nurses who design, facilitate, and manage care. Its mission is to represent nurse leaders who improve healthcare.

AMERICAN ORTHOPAEDIC ASSOCIATION
6300 North River Road, Suite 505, Rosemont IL 60018-4263. 847/318-7330. **Fax:** 847/318-7339. **E-mail address:** info@aoassn.org **World Wide Web address:** http://www.aoassn.org. **Description:** Founded in 1887, The American Orthopaedic Association is the oldest orthopaedic association in the world.

AMERICAN PHYSICAL THERAPY ASSOCIATION
1111 North Fairfax Street, Alexandria VA 22314-1488. 703/684-2782. **Fax:** 703/684-7343. **Toll-free phone:** 800/999-2782. **World Wide Web address:** http://www.apta.org. **Description:** The American Physical Therapy Association (APTA) is a national professional organization representing more than 63,000

214 /The Colorado JobBank

members. Its goal is to foster advancements in physical therapy practice, research, and education.

AMERICAN PODIATRIC MEDICAL ASSOCIATION
9312 Old Georgetown Road, Bethesda MD 20814. 301/571-9200. **Fax:** 301/530-2752. **Toll-free phone:** 800/FOOTCARE. **World Wide Web address:** http://www.apma.org. **Description:** The American Podiatric Medical Association is the premier professional organization representing the nation's Doctors of Podiatric Medicine (podiatrists). The APMA represents approximately 80 percent of the podiatrists in the country. APMA includes 53 component societies in states and other jurisdictions, as well as 22 affiliated and related societies.

AMERICAN PSYCHIATRIC ASSOCIATION
1000 Wilson Boulevard, Suite 1825, Arlington VA.22209-3901. 703/907-7300. **E-mail address:** apa@psych.org **World Wide Web address:** http://www.psych.org. **Description:** With 35,000 members, the American Psychiatric Association is a medical specialty society recognized worldwide.

AMERICAN PUBLIC HEALTH ASSOCIATION
800 I Street, NW, Washington DC 20001. 202/777-2742. **Fax:** 202/777-2534. **E-mail address:** comments@apha.org. **World Wide Web address:** http://www.apha.org. **Description:** The American Public Health Association (APHA) is the oldest and largest organization of public health professionals in the world, representing more than 50,000 members from over 50 occupations of public health.

AMERICAN SOCIETY OF ANESTHESIOLOGISTS
520 N. Northwest Highway, Park Ridge IL 60068-2573. 847/825-5586. **Fax:** 847/825-1692. **E-mail address:** mail@asahq.org. **World Wide Web address:** http://www.asahq.org. **Description:** An educational, research and scientific association of physicians organized to raise and maintain the standards of the medical practice of anesthesiology and improve the care of the patient. Founded in 1905.

AMERICAN SPEECH-LANGUAGE-HEARING ASSOCIATION
10801 Rockville Pike, Rockville MD 20852-3226. **Toll-free phone:** 800/638-8255. **E-mail address:** actioncenter@asha.org. **World Wide Web address:** http://www.asha.org. **Description:** The professional, scientific, and credentialing association for more than 110,000 audiologists, speech-language pathologists, and speech, language, and hearing scientists with a mission to ensure that all people with speech, language, and hearing disorders have access to quality services to help them communicate more effectively.

AMERICAN VETERINARY MEDICAL ASSOCIATION
1931 North Meacham Road, Suite 100, Schaumburg IL 60173. 847/925-8070. **Fax:** 847/925-1329. **E-mail address:** avmainfo@avma.org. **World Wide Web address:** http://www.avma.org. **Description:** A not-for-profit association founded in 1863 representing more than 69,000 veterinarians working in private and corporate practice, government, industry, academia, and uniformed services.

ASSOCIATION OF AMERICAN MEDICAL COLLEGES
2450 N Street, NW, Washington DC 20037-1126. 202/828-0400. **Fax:** 202/828-1125. **World Wide Web address:** http://www.aamc.org. **Description:** A non-profit association founded in 1876 to work for reform in medical education. The association represents the nation's 126 accredited medical schools, nearly 400

major teaching hospitals, more than 105,000 faculty in 96 academic and scientific societies, and the nation's 66,000 medical students and 97,000 residents.

ASSOCIATION OF UNIVERSITY PROGRAMS IN HEALTH ADMINISTRATION
2000 North 14th Street, Suite 780, Arlington VA 22201. 703/894-0940. **Fax:** 703/894-0941. **E-mail address:** aupha@aupha.org. **World Wide Web address:** http://www.aupha.org. **Description:** A not-for-profit association of university-based educational programs, faculty, practitioners, and provider organizations. Its members are dedicated to continuously improving the field of health management and practice. It is the only non-profit entity of its kind that works to improve the delivery of health services throughout the world - and thus the health of citizens - by educating professional managers.

HEALTH INFORMATION AND MANAGEMENT SYSTEMS SOCIETY
230 East Ohio Street, Suite 500, Chicago IL 60611-3269. 312/664-4467. **Fax:** 312/664-6143. **World Wide Web address:** http://www.himss.org. **Description:** Founded in 1961 and provides leadership for the optimal use of healthcare information technology and management systems for the betterment of human health.

HEALTHCARE FINANCIAL MANAGEMENT ASSOCIATION
2 Westbrook Corporate Center, Suite 700, Westchester IL 60154-5700. 708/531-9600. **Fax:** 708/531-0032. **Toll-free phone:** 800/252-4362. **World Wide Web address:** http://www.hfma.org. **Description:** A membership organization for healthcare financial management professionals with 32,000 members.

NATIONAL ASSOCIATION FOR CHIROPRACTIC MEDICINE
15427 Baybrook Drive, Houston TX 77062. 281/280-8262. **Fax:** 281/280-8262. **World Wide Web address:** http://www.chiromed.org. **Description:** A consumer advocacy association of chiropractors striving to make legitimate the utilization of professional manipulative procedures in mainstream health care delivery.

NATIONAL MEDICAL ASSOCIATION
1012 Tenth Street, NW, Washington DC 20001. 202/347-1895. **Fax:** 202/898-2510. **World Wide Web address:** http://www.nmanet.org. **Description:** Promotes the collective interests of physicians and patients of African descent with a mission to serve as the collective voice of physicians of African descent and a leading force for parity in medicine, elimination of health disparities and promotion of optimal health.

HOTELS AND RESTAURANTS

AMERICAN HOTEL AND LODGING ASSOCIATION
1201 New York Avenue, NW, #600, Washington DC 20005-3931. 202/289-3100.
Fax: 202/289-3199. **World Wide Web address:** http://www.ahla.com.
Description: Provides its members with assistance in operations, education, and communications, and lobbies on Capitol Hill to provide a business climate in which the industry can continue to prosper. Individual state associations provide representation at the state level and offer many additional cost-saving benefits.

THE EDUCATIONAL FOUNDATION OF THE NATIONAL RESTAURANT ASSOCIATION
175 West Jackson Boulevard, Suite 1500, Chicago IL 60604-2702. 312/715-1010. **Toll-free phone:** 800/765-2122. **E-mail address:** info@nraef.org. **World Wide Web address:** http://www.nraef.org. **Description:** A not-for-profit organization dedicated to fulfilling the educational mission of the National Restaurant Association. Focusing on three key strategies of risk management, recruitment, and retention, the NRAEF is the premier provider of educational resources, materials, and programs, which address attracting, developing and retaining the industry's workforce.

NATIONAL RESTAURANT ASSOCIATION
1200 17th Street, NW, Washington DC 20036. 202/331-5900. 202/331-5900.
Fax: 202/331-2429. **Toll-free phone:** 800/424-5156. **World Wide Web address:** http://www.restaurant.org. **Description:** Founded in 1919 as a business association for the restaurant industry with a mission to represent, educate and promote a rapidly growing industry that is comprised of 878,000 restaurant and foodservice outlets employing 12 million people.

INSURANCE

AMERICA'S HEALTH INSURANCE PLANS
601 Pennsylvania Avenue, NW, S0uth Building, Suite 500, Washington DC 20004. 202/778-3200. **Fax:** 202/331-7487. **World Wide Web address:** http://www.ahip.org. **Description:** A national association representing nearly 1,300 member companies providing health insurance coverage to more than 200 million Americans.

INSURANCE INFORMATION INSTITUTE
110 William Street, New York NY 10038. 212/346-5500. **World Wide Web address:** http://www.iii.org. **Description:** Provides definitive insurance information. Recognized by the media, governments, regulatory organizations, universities and the public as a primary source of information, analysis and referral concerning insurance.

NATIONAL ASSOCIATION OF PROFESSIONAL INSURANCE AGENTS
400 North Washington Street, Alexandria VA 22314. 703/836-9340. **Fax:** 703/836-1279. **E-mail address:** piaweb@pianet.org. **World Wide Web address:** http://www.pianet.com. **Description:** Represents independent agents in all 50 states, Puerto Rico and the District of Columbia. Founded in 1931.

PROPERTY CASUALTY INSURERS ASSOCIATION OF AMERICA
2600 South River Road, Des Plaines IL 60018-3286. 847/297-7800. **Fax:** 847/297-5064. **World Wide Web address:** http://www.pciaa.net. **Description:** A property/casualty trade association representing more than 1,000 member companies, PCI advocates its members' public policy positions at the federal and state levels and to the public.

LEGAL SERVICES

AMERICAN BAR ASSOCIATION
321 North Clark Street, Chicago IL 60610. 312/988-5000. **E-mail address:** askaba@abanet.org. **World Wide Web address:** http://www.abanet.org. **Description:** A voluntary professional association with more than 400,000 members, the ABA provides law school accreditation, continuing legal education, information about the law, programs to assist lawyers and judges in their work, and initiatives to improve the legal system for the public.

FEDERAL BAR ASSOCIATION
2215 M Street, NW, Washington DC 20037. 202/785-1614. **Fax:** 202/785-1568. **E-mail address:** fba@fedbar.org. **World Wide Web address:** http://www.fedbar.org. **Description:** The professional organization for private and government lawyers and judges involved in federal practice.

NATIONAL ASSOCIATION OF LEGAL ASSISTANTS
1516 South Boston, #200, Tulsa OK 74119. 918/587-6828. **World Wide Web address:** http://www.nala.org. **Description:** A professional association for legal assistants and paralegals, providing continuing education and professional development programs. Founded in 1975.

NATIONAL FEDERATION OF PARALEGAL ASSOCIATIONS
2517 Eastlake Avenue East, Suite 200, Seattle WA 98102. 206/652-4120. **Fax:** 206/652-4122. **E-mail address:** info@paralegals.org. **World Wide Web address:** http://www.paralegals.org. **Description:** A non-profit professional organization representing more than 15,000 paralegals in the United States and Canada. NFPA is the national voice and the standard for excellence for the paralegal profession through its work on the issues of regulation, ethics and education.

MANUFACTURING: MISCELLANEOUS CONSUMER

ASSOCIATION FOR MANUFACTURING EXCELLENCE
380 Palantine Road West, Wheeling IL 60090-5863. 847/520-3282. **Fax:** 847/520-0163. **World Wide Web address:** http://www.ame.org. **Description:** A not-for-profit organization founded in 1985 consisting of 6000 executives, senior and middle managers who wish to improve the competitiveness of their organizations.

ASSOCIATION FOR MANUFACTURING TECHNOLOGY
7901 Westpark Drive, McLean VA 22102-4206. 703/893-2900. **Fax:** 703/893-1151. **Toll-free phone:** 703/893-2900. **World Wide Web address:** http://www.amtonline.org. **Description:** Supports and promotes American manufacturers of machine tools and manufacturing technology. Provides members with industry expertise and assistance on critical industry concerns.

ASSOCIATION OF HOME APPLIANCE MANUFACTURERS
1111 19th Street, NW, Suite 402, Washington DC 20036. 202/872-5955. **Fax:** 202/872-9354. **World Wide Web address:** http://www.aham.org. **Description:** Represents the manufacturers of household appliances and products/services associated with household appliances.

SOCIETY OF MANUFACTURING ENGINEERS
One SME Drive, Dearborn MI 48121. 313/271-1500. **Fax:** 313/425-3401. **Toll-free phone:** 800/733-4763. **World Wide Web address:** http://www.sme.org. **Description:** Promotes an increased awareness of manufacturing engineering and helps keep manufacturing professionals up to date on leading trends and technologies. Founded in 1932.

MANUFACTURING: MISCELLANEOUS INDUSTRIAL

ASSOCIATION FOR MANUFACTURING EXCELLENCE
380 Palantine Road West, Wheeling IL 60090-5863. 847/520-3282. **Fax:** 847/520-0163. **World Wide Web address:** http://www.ame.org. **Description:** A not-for-profit organization founded in 1985 consisting of 6000 executives, senior and middle managers who wish to improve the competitiveness of their organizations.

INSTITUTE OF INDUSTRIAL ENGINEERS
3577 Parkway Lane, Suite 200, Norcross GA 30092. 770/449-0460. **Fax:** 770/441-3295. **Toll-free phone:** 800/494-0460. **World Wide Web address:** http://www.iienet.org. **Description:** A non-profit professional society dedicated to the support of the industrial engineering profession and individuals involved with improving quality and productivity. Founded in 1948.

NATIONAL ASSOCIATION OF MANUFACTURERS
1331 Pennsylvania Avenue, NW, Washington DC 20004-1790. 202/637-3000. **Fax:** 202/637-3182. **E-mail address:** manufacturing@nam.org. **World Wide Web address:** http://www.nam.org. **Description:** With 14,000 members, NAM's mission is to enhance the competitiveness of manufacturers and to improve American living standards by shaping a legislative and regulatory environment conducive to U.S. economic growth, and to increase understanding among policymakers, the media and the public about the importance of manufacturing to America's economic strength.

NATIONAL TOOLING AND MACHINING ASSOCIATION
9300 Livingston Road, Fort Washington MD 20744-4998. 800/248-6862. **Fax:** 301/248-7104. **World Wide Web address:** http://www.ntma.org. **Description:** A trade organization representing the precision custom manufacturing industry throughout the United States.

SOCIETY OF MANUFACTURING ENGINEERS
One SME Drive, Dearborn MI 48121. 313/271-1500. **Fax:** 313/425-3401. **Toll-free phone:** 800/733-4763. **World Wide Web address:** http://www.sme.org. **Description:** Promotes an increased awareness of manufacturing engineering and helps keep manufacturing professionals up to date on leading trends and technologies. Founded in 1932.

MINING, GAS, PETROLEUM, ENERGY RELATED

AMERICAN ASSOCIATION OF PETROLEUM GEOLOGISTS
P.O. Box 979, Tulsa OK 74101-0979. 918/584-2555. **Physical address:** 1444 South Boulder, Tulsa OK 74119. **Fax:** 918/560-2665. **Toll-free phone:** 800/364-2274. **E-mail address:** postmaster@aapg.org. **World Wide Web address:** http://www.aapg.org. **Description:** Founded in 1917, the AAPG's purpose is to foster scientific research, advance the science of geology, promote technology, and inspire high professional conduct. The AAPG has over 30,000 members.

AMERICAN GEOLOGICAL INSTITUTE
4220 King Street, Alexandria VA 22302-1502. 703/379-2480. **Fax:** 703/379-7563. **World Wide Web address:** http://www.agiweb.org. **Description:** A nonprofit federation of 42 geoscientific and professional associations that represents more than 100,000 geologists, geophysicists, and other earth scientists. Provides information services to geoscientists, serves as a voice of shared interests in the profession, plays a major role in strengthening geoscience education, and strives to increase public awareness of the vital role the geosciences play in society's use of resources and interaction with the environment.

AMERICAN NUCLEAR SOCIETY
555 North Kensington Avenue, La Grange Park IL 60526. 708/352-6611. **Fax:** 708/352-0499. **World Wide Web address:** http://www.ans.org. **Description:** A not-for-profit, international, scientific and educational organization with a membership of 10,500 engineers, scientists, administrators, and educators representing 1,600 corporations, educational institutions, and government agencies.

AMERICAN PETROLEUM INSTITUTE
1220 L Street, NW, Washington DC 20005-4070. 202/682-8000. **World Wide Web address:** http://www.api.org. **Description:** Functions to insure a strong, viable U.S. oil and natural gas industry capable of meeting the energy needs of our Nation in an efficient and environmentally responsible manner.

GEOLOGICAL SOCIETY OF AMERICA
3300 Penrose Place, P.O. Box 9140, Boulder CO 80301. 303/447-2020. **Fax:** 303/357-1070. **Toll-free phone:** 888/443-4472. **E-mail address:** gsaservice@geosociety.org. **World Wide Web address:** http://www.geosociety.org. **Description:** The mission of GSA is to advance the geosciences, to enhance the professional growth of its members, and to promote the geosciences in the service of humankind.

SOCIETY FOR MINING, METALLURGY, AND EXPLORATION
8307 Shaffer Parkway, Littleton CO 80127-4102. 303/973-9550. **Fax:** 303/973-3845. **Toll-free phone:** 800/763-3132. **E-mail address:** sme@smenet.org. **World Wide Web address:** http://www.smenet.org. **Description:** An international society of professionals in the mining and minerals industry.

SOCIETY OF PETROLEUM ENGINEERS
P.O. Box 833836, Richardson TX 75083-3836. 972/952-9393. **Physical address:** 222 palisades Creek Drive, Richardson TX 75080. **Fax:** 972/952-9435. **E-mail address:** spedal@spe.org. **World Wide Web address:** http://www.spe.org. **Description:** SPE is a professional association whose

60,000-plus members worldwide are engaged in energy resources development and production. SPE is a key resource for technical information related to oil and gas exploration and production and provides services through its publications, meetings, and online.

PAPER AND WOOD PRODUCTS

AMERICAN FOREST AND PAPER ASSOCIATION
1111 Nineteenth Street, NW, Suite 800, Washington DC 20036. **Toll-free phone:** 800/878-8878. **E-mail address:** info@afandpa.org. **World Wide Web address:** http://www.afandpa.org. **Description:** The national trade association of the forest, pulp, paper, paperboard and wood products industry.

FOREST PRODUCTS SOCIETY
2801 Marshall Court, Madison WI 53705-2295. 608/231-1361. **Fax:** 608/231-2152. **E-mail address:** info@forestprod.org. **World Wide Web address:** http://www.forestprod.org. **Description:** An international not-for-profit technical association founded in 1947 to provide an information network for all segments of the forest products industry.

NPTA ALLIANCE
500 Bi-County Boulevard, Suite 200E, Farmingdale NY 11735. 631/777-2223. **Fax:** 631/777-2224. **Toll-free phone:** 800/355-NPTA. **World Wide Web address:** http://www.gonpta.com. **Description:** An association for the $60 billion paper, packaging, and supplies distribution industry.

PAPERBOARD PACKAGING COUNCIL
201 North Union Street, Suite 220, Alexandria VA 22314. 703/836-3300. **Fax:** 703/836-3290. **E-mail address:** http://www.ppcnet.org. **World Wide Web address:** http://www.ppcnet.org. **Description:** A trade association representing the manufacturers of paperboard packaging in the United States.

TECHNICAL ASSOCIATION OF THE PULP AND PAPER INDUSTRY
15 Technology Parkway South, Norcross GA 30092. 770/446-1400. **Fax:** 770/446-6947. **Toll-free phone:** 800/332-8686. **World Wide Web address:** http://www.tappi.org. **Description:** The leading technical association for the worldwide pulp, paper, and converting industry.

PRINTING AND PUBLISHING

AMERICAN BOOKSELLERS ASSOCIATION
828 South Broadway, Tarrytown NY 10591. 914/591-2665. **Fax:** 914/591-2720. **Toll-free phone:** 800/637-0037. **E-mail address:** info@bookweb.org. **World Wide Web address:** http://www.bookweb.org. **Description:** A not-for-profit organization founded in 1900 devoted to meeting the needs of its core members of independently owned bookstores with retail storefront locations through advocacy, education, research, and information dissemination.

AMERICAN INSTITUTE OF GRAPHIC ARTS
164 Fifth Avenue, New York NY 10010. 212/807-1990. **Fax:** 212/807-1799. **E-mail address:** comments@aiga.org. **World Wide Web address:** http://www.aiga.org. **Description:** Furthers excellence in communication design as a broadly defined discipline, strategic tool for business and cultural force. AIGA is the place design professionals turn to first to exchange ideas and information, participate in critical analysis and research and advance education and ethical practice. Founded in 1914.

AMERICAN SOCIETY OF NEWSPAPER EDITORS
11690B Sunrise Valley Drive, Reston VA 20191-1409. 703/453-1122. **Fax:** 703/453-1133. **E-mail address:** asne@asne.org. **World Wide Web address:** http://www.asne.org. **Description:** A membership organization for daily newspaper editors, people who serve the editorial needs of daily newspapers and certain distinguished individuals who have worked on behalf of editors through the years.

ASSOCIATION OF AMERICAN PUBLISHERS, INC.
71 Fifth Avenue, 2nd Floor, New York NY 10003. 212/255-0200. **Fax:** 212/255-7007. **World Wide Web address:** http://www.publishers.org. **Description:** Representing publishers of all sizes and types located throughout the U.S., the AAP is the principal trade association of the book publishing industry.

ASSOCIATION OF GRAPHIC COMMUNICATIONS
330 Seventh Avenue, 9th Floor, New York NY 10001-5010. 212/279-2100. **Fax:** 212/279-5381. **E-mail address:** info@agcomm.org. **World Wide Web address:** http://www.agcomm.org. **Description:** The AGC serves as a network for industry information and idea exchange, provides graphic arts education and training, promotes and markets the industry, and advocates legislative and environmental issues.

BINDING INDUSTRIES OF AMERICA
100 Daingerfield Road, Alexandria VA 22314. 703/519-8137. **Fax:** 703/548-3227. **World Wide Web address:** http://www.bindingindustries.org. **Description:** A trade association representing Graphic Finishers, Loose-Leaf Manufacturers, and suppliers to these industries throughout the United States, Canada, and Europe.

THE DOW JONES NEWSPAPER FUND
P.O. Box 300, Princeton NJ 08543-0300. 609/452-2820. **Fax:** 609/520-5804. **E-mail address:** newsfund@wsj.dowjones.com. **World Wide Web address:** http://djnewspaperfund.dowjones.com. **Description:** Founded in 1958 by editors of The Wall Street Journal to improve the quality of journalism education and the pool of applicants for jobs in the newspaper business. It provides internships and scholarships to college students, career literature, fellowships for high school

journalism teachers and publications' advisers and training for college journalism instructors. The Fund is a nonprofit foundation supported by the Dow Jones Foundation, Dow Jones & Company, Inc. and other newspaper companies.

GRAPHIC ARTISTS GUILD

90 John Street, Suite 403, New York NY 10038-3202. 212/791-3400. **World Wide Web address:** http://www.gag.org. **Description:** A national union of illustrators, designers, web creators, production artists, surface designers and other creatives who have come together to pursue common goals, share their experience, raise industry standards, and improve the ability of visual creators to achieve satisfying and rewarding careers.

INTERNATIONAL GRAPHIC ARTS EDUCATION ASSOCIATION

1899 Preston White Drive, Reston VA 20191-4367. 703/758-0595. **World Wide Web address:** http://www.igaea.org. **Description:** An association of educators in partnership with industry, dedicated to sharing theories, principles, techniques and processes relating to graphic communications and imaging technology.

MAGAZINE PUBLISHERS OF AMERICA

810 Seventh Avenue, 24th Floor, New York NY 10019. 212/872-3746. **E-mail address:** infocenter@magazine.org. **World Wide Web address:** http://www.magazine.org. **Description:** An industry association for consumer magazines representing more than 240 domestic publishing companies with approximately 1,400 titles, more than 80 international companies and more than 100 associate members.

NATIONAL ASSOCIATION FOR PRINTING LEADERSHIP

75 West Century Road, Paramus NJ 07652-1408. 201/634-9600. **Fax:** 201/986-2976. **E-mail address:** information@napl.org. **World Wide Web address:** http://www.napl.org. **Description:** A not-for-profit trade association founded in 1933 for commercial printers and related members of the Graphic Arts Industry.

NATIONAL NEWSPAPER ASSOCIATION

P.O. Box 7540,, Columbia MO 65205-7540. 573/882-5800. **Fax:** 573/884-5490. **Toll-free phone:** 800/829-4662. **World Wide Web address:** http://www.nna.org. **Description:** A non-profit association promoting the common interests of newspapers.

NATIONAL PRESS CLUB

529 14th Street, NW, Washington DC 20045. 202/662-7500. **Fax:** 202/662-7512. **World Wide Web address:** http://npc.press.org. **Description:** Provides people who gather and disseminate news a center for the advancement of their professional standards and skills, the promotion of free expression, mutual support and social fellowship. Founded in 1908.

NEWSPAPER ASSOCIATION OF AMERICA

1921 Gallows Road, Suite 600, Vienna VA 22182-3900. 703/902-1600. **Fax:** 703/917-0636. **World Wide Web address:** http://www.naa.org. **Description:** A nonprofit organization representing the $55 billion newspaper industry.

THE NEWSPAPER GUILD

501 Third Street, NW, Suite 250, Washington DC 20001. 202/434-7177. **Fax:** 202/434-1472. **E-mail address:** guild@cwa-union.org. **World Wide Web address:** http://www.newsguild.org. **Description:** Founded as a print journalists' union, the Guild today is primarily a media union whose members are diverse in their occupations, but who share the view that the best working conditions are achieved by people who have a say in their workplace.

TECHNICAL ASSOCIATION OF THE GRAPHIC ARTS
200 Deer Run Road, Sewickley PA 15213. 412/259-1813. **Fax:** 412/741-2311. **E-mail address:** jallen@piagatf.org. **World Wide Web address:** http://www.taga.org. **Description:** A professional technical association founded in 1948 for the graphic arts industries.

WRITERS GUILD OF AMERICA WEST
7000 West Third Street, Los Angeles CA 90048. 323/951-4000. **Fax:** 323/782-4800. **Toll-free phone:** 800/548-4532. **E-mail address: World Wide Web address:** http://www.wga.org. **Description:** Represents writers in the motion picture, broadcast, cable and new technologies industries.

REAL ESTATE

INSTITUTE OF REAL ESTATE MANAGEMENT
430 North Michigan Avenue, Chicago IL 60611-4090. 312/329-6000. **Fax:** 800/338-4736. **Toll-free phone:** 800/837-0706. **E-mail address:** custserv@irem.org. **World Wide Web address:** http://www.irem.org. **Description:** IREM, an affiliate of the National Association of Realtors, is an association of professional property and asset managers who have met strict criteria in the areas of education, experience, and a commitment to a code of ethics.

INTERNATIONAL REAL ESTATE INSTITUTE
1224 North Nokomis, NE, Alexandria MN 56308. 320/763-4648. **Fax:** 320/763-9290. **E-mail address:** irei@iami.org. **World Wide Web address:** http://www.iami.org/irei. **Description:** A real estate association with members in more than 100 countries, providing media to communicate on an international basis.

NATIONAL ASSOCIATION OF REALTORS
30700 Russell Ranch Road, Westlake Village CA 91362. 805/557-2300. **Fax:** 805/557-2680. **World Wide Web address:** http://www.realtor.com. **Description:** An industry advocate of the right to own, use, and transfer real property; the acknowledged leader in developing standards for efficient, effective, and ethical real estate business practices; and valued by highly skilled real estate professionals and viewed by them as crucial to their success.

RETAIL

INTERNATIONAL COUNCIL OF SHOPPING CENTERS
1221 Avenue of the Americas, 41st floor, New York NY 10020-1099. 646/728-3800. **Fax:** 732/694-1755. **E-mail address:** icsc@icsc.org. **World Wide Web address:** http://www.icsc.org. **Description:** A trade association of the shopping center industry founded in 1957.

NATIONAL ASSOCIATION OF CHAIN DRUG STORES
413 North Lee Street, PO Box 1417-D49, Alexandria VA 22313-1480. 703/549-3001. **Fax:** 703/836-4869. **World Wide Web address:** http://www.nacds.org. **Description:** Represents the views and policy positions of member chain drug companies accomplished through the programs and services provided by the association.

NATIONAL RETAIL FEDERATION
325 7th Street, NW, Suite 1100, Washington DC 20004. 202/783-7971. **Fax:** 202/737-2849. **Toll-free phone:** 800/NRF-HOW2. **World Wide Web address:** http://www.nrf.com. **Description:** A retail trade association, with membership that comprises all retail formats and channels of distribution including department, specialty, discount, catalog, Internet and independent stores as well as the industry's key trading partners of retail goods and services. NRF represents an industry with more than 1.4 million U.S. retail establishments, more than 20 million employees - about one in five American workers - and 2003 sales of $3.8 trillion.

STONE, CLAY, GLASS, AND CONCRETE PRODUCTS

THE AMERICAN CERAMIC SOCIETY
PO Box 6136, Westerville OH 43086-6136. 614/890-4700. **Fax:** 614/899-6109. **E-mail address:** info@ceramics.org. **World Wide Web address:** http://www.acers.org. **Description:** An organization dedicated to the advancement of ceramics.

NATIONAL GLASS ASSOCIATION
8200 Greensboro Drive, Suite 302, McLean VA 22102-3881. 866/342-5642. **Fax:** 703/442-0630. **World Wide Web address:** http://www.glass.org. **Description:** A trade association founded in 1948 representing the flat (architectural and automotive) glass industry. The association represents nearly 5,000 member companies and locations, and produces the industry events and publications.

TRANSPORTATION AND TRAVEL

AIR TRANSPORT ASSOCIATION OF AMERICA
1301 Pennsylvania Avenue, NW, Suite 1100, Washington DC 20004-1707. 202/626-4000. **Fax:** 301/206-9789. **Toll-free phone:** 800/497-3326. **E-mail address:** ata@airlines.org. **World Wide Web address:** http://www.air-transport.org. **Description:** A trade organization for the principal U.S. airlines.

AMERICAN SOCIETY OF TRAVEL AGENTS
1101 King Street, Suite 200, Alexandria VA 22314. 703/739-2782. **Fax:** 703/684-8319. **World Wide Web address:** http://www.astanet.com. **Description:** An association of travel professionals whose members include travel agents and the companies whose products they sell such as tours, cruises, hotels, car rentals, etc.

AMERICAN TRUCKING ASSOCIATIONS
2200 Mill Road, Alexandria VA 22314. 703/838-1700. **Toll-free phone:** 888/333-1759. **World Wide Web address:** http://www.trucking.org. **Description:** Serves and represents the interests of the trucking industry with one united voice; positively influences Federal and State governmental actions; advances the trucking industry's image, efficiency, competitiveness, and profitability; provides educational programs and industry research; promotes highway and driver safety; and strives for a healthy business environment.

ASSOCIATION OF AMERICAN RAILROADS
50 F Street, NW, Washington DC 20001-1564. 202/639-2100. **World Wide Web address:** http://www.aar.org. **Description:** A trade associations representing the major freight railroads of the United States, Canada and Mexico.

INSTITUTE OF TRANSPORTATION ENGINEERS
1099 14th Street, NW, Suite 300 West, Washington DC 20005-3438. 202/289-0222. **Fax:** 202/289-7722. **E-mail address:** ite_staff@ite.org. **World Wide Web address:** http://www.ite.org. **Description:** An international individual member educational and scientific association whose members are traffic engineers, transportation planners and other professionals who are responsible for meeting society's needs for safe and efficient surface transportation through planning, designing, implementing, operating and maintaining surface transportation systems worldwide.

MARINE TECHNOLOGY SOCIETY
5565 Sterrett Place, Suite 108, Columbia MD 21044. 410/884-5330. **Fax:** 410/884-9060. **E-mail address:** mtsmbrship@erols.com. **World Wide Web address:** http://www.mtsociety.org. **Description:** A member-based society supporting all the components of the ocean community: marine sciences, engineering, academia, industry and government. The society is dedicated to the development, sharing and education of information and ideas.

NATIONAL TANK TRUCK CARRIERS
2200 Mill Road, Alexandria VA 22314. 703/838-1960. **Fax:** 703/684-5753. **E-mail address:** inquiries@tanktruck.org. **World Wide Web address:** http://www.tanktruck.net. **Description:** A trade association founded in 1945 and composed of approximately 180 trucking companies, which specialize in the nationwide distribution of bulk liquids, industrial gases and dry products in cargo tank motor vehicles.

UTILITIES: ELECTRIC, GAS, AND WATER

AMERICAN PUBLIC GAS ASSOCIATION

201 Massachusetts Avenue, NE, Suite C-4 Washington DC 20002. 202/464-2742. **Fax:** 202/464-0246. **E-mail address:** website@apga.org. **World Wide Web address:** http://www.apga.org. **Description:** A nonprofit trade organization representing publicly owned natural gas local distribution companies (LDCs). APGA represents the interests of public gas before Congress, federal agencies and other energy-related stakeholders by developing regulatory and legislative policies that further the goals of our members. In addition, APGA organizes meetings, seminars, and workshops with a specific goal to improve the reliability, operational efficiency, and regulatory environment in which public gas systems operate.

AMERICAN PUBLIC POWER ASSOCIATION (APPA)

2301 M Street, NW, Washington DC 20037-1484. 202/467-2900. **Fax:** 202/467-2910. **World Wide Web address:** http://www.appanet.org. **Description:** The service organization for the nation's more than 2,000 community-owned electric utilities that serve more than 40 million Americans. Its purpose is to advance the public policy interests of its members and their consumers, and provide member services to ensure adequate, reliable electricity at a reasonable price with the proper protection of the environment.

AMERICAN WATER WORKS ASSOCIATION

6666 West Quincy Avenue, Denver CO 80235. 303/794-7711. **Fax:** 303/347-0804. **Toll-free phone:** 800/926-7337. **World Wide Web address:** http://www.awwa.org. **Description:** A resource for knowledge, information, and advocacy to improve the quality and supply of drinking water in North America. The association advances public health, safety and welfare by uniting the efforts of the full spectrum of the drinking water community.

NATIONAL RURAL ELECTRIC COOPERATIVE ASSOCIATION

4301 Wilson Boulevard, Arlington VA 22203. 703/907-5500. **E-mail address:** nreca@nreca.coop. **World Wide Web address:** http://www.nreca.org. **Description:** A national organization representing the national interests of cooperative electric utilities and the consumers they serve. Founded in 1942.

MISCELLANEOUS WHOLESALING

NATIONAL ASSOCIATION OF WHOLESALER-DISTRIBUTORS (NAW)
1725 K Street, NW, Washington DC 20006-1419. 202/872-0885. **Fax:** 202/785-0586. **World Wide Web address:** http://www.naw.org. **Description:** A trade association that represents the wholesale distribution industry active in government relations and political action; research and education; and group purchasing.

INDEX OF PRIMARY EMPLOYERS